IMAGES
of America

CORDOVA

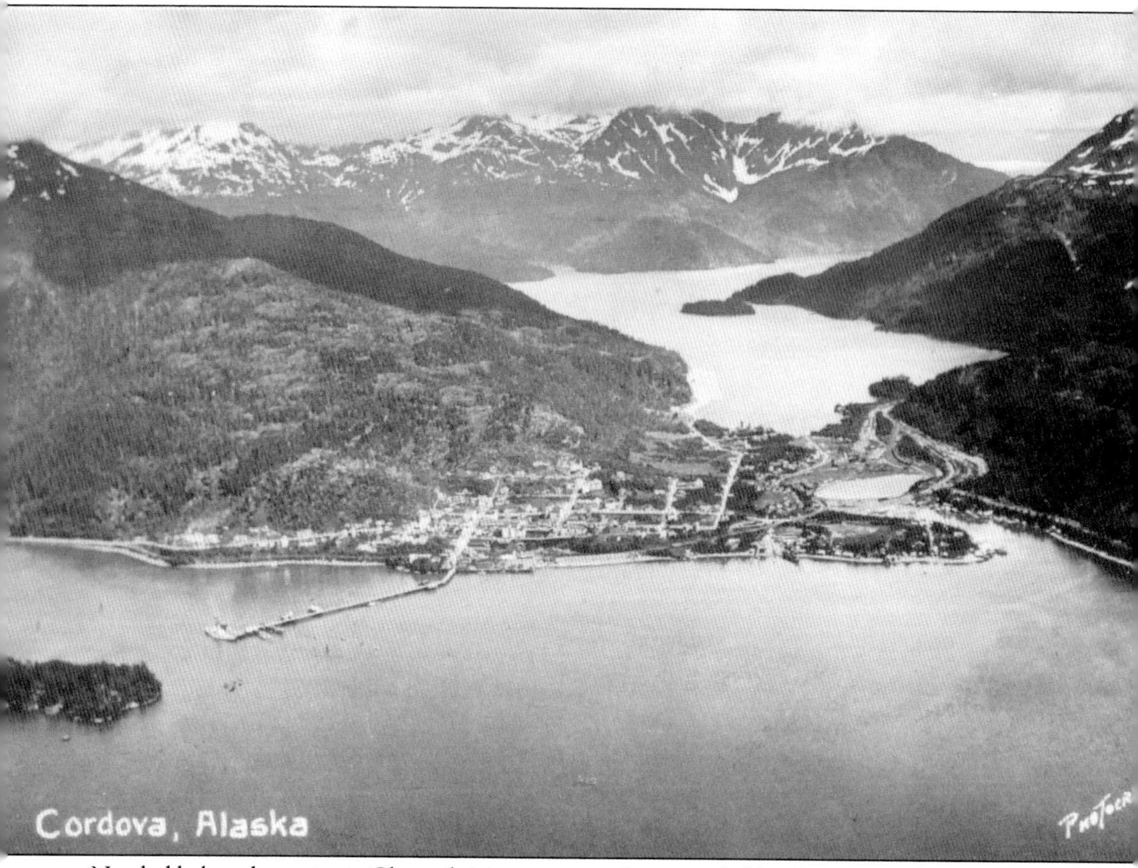

Nestled below the majestic Chugach Mountains and surrounded by the waters of Orca Inlet and Eyak Lake, Cordova remains an authentic Alaskan fishing village. It is home to the famous Copper River salmon and a couple thousand sturdy individuals, who have survived economic booms and busts, fires, earthquakes, oil spills, and close to 200 inches of rain a year. Cordova still proudly embraces its moniker of "the Friendly City." (Cordova Historical Society.)

On the Cover: Cordovans enjoy a day at the Million Dollar Bridge around 1915, after riding the excursion train of the Copper River & Northwest Railway. Completed in 1911, the Copper River & Northwest (CR&NW) Railway was 196 miles long and delivered copper ore from the Bonanza Mine to the wharfs of Cordova. (Cordova Historical Society.)

IMAGES
of America

CORDOVA

Cathy R. Sherman with photographs
from the Cordova Historical Society

ARCADIA
PUBLISHING

ISBN 978-0-7385-8169-9

Published by Arcadia Publishing
Charleston, South Carolina

Printed in the United States of America

Library of Congress Control Number: 2010932074

For all general information, please contact Arcadia Publishing:
Telephone 843-853-2070
Fax 843-853-0044
E-mail sales@arcadiapublishing.com
For customer service and orders:
Toll-Free 1-888-313-2665

Visit us on the Internet at www.arcadiapublishing.com

To the Cordova Historical Society, thank you for
preserving the past for Cordova's future.
To my friend Susan who has read more books than one can
imagine and who provided encouragement in the dark of winter
To Rach, for the use of "Speedo," the fabulous pink eraser
To my husband, Dixon, for having such patience and faith in me

Contents

Acknowledgments

What a pleasure to work with the Cordova Historical Society to compile a story on this unique and very special community of Cordova! Thankfully, those founding members back in 1966 recognized the importance of preserving the memories of the past, which has now enabled us to share this tale. The Cordova Historical Society and Museum have preserved thousands of historic photographs of the community of Cordova, and thanks go to the many active and past members of the society—200 strong. A special note of thanks goes to Lavon Branshaw, Judy Fulton, Sharon Ermold, Mimi Briggs, and Frances Mallory who worked over the past 40 years to strengthen the archival records of the society. Also thanks go to Aurora Lang, the current curator of collections and exhibits at the Cordova Historical Museum, who assisted in the collecting of the perfect photographs for this work. Thanks go to Dave and Clay for the last-minute help with photographs, and unless otherwise noted, all images appearing in this book are from the collection of the Cordova Historical Society.

Additional thanks go to the folks at Arcadia, who showed extreme patience with a multitasking author. Finally, thanks go to my mom and dad for all those history vacations you took us on when we were kids; guess I was really paying attention after all.

Introduction

Nestled between the Chugach Mountains and Orca Inlet, Cordova is built upon a rich and diverse foundation of bounties from both the sea and land. The Copper River delta and Prince William Sound regions have been a melting pot for native cultures and those to follow later. Add together the traditions of a myriad of many cultures of people and you have a novel Alaskan community with a rich and fascinating story to tell.

Eyak and Chugach natives lived near the shores of Eyak Lake and lined the coastal areas of Prince William Sound. The constant and expected return of salmon each season guaranteed a winter's larder to these area natives. Their traditions led them to respect the gifts the land and sea provided and to appreciate the value of the seasons. The Eyak occupied the Copper River delta and west to what is present-day Cordova. The Chugach Aleut inhabited the coastal areas and islands of Prince William Sound. These two groups were hunters and gatherers, and each had distinct subsistence practices. Interactions between the Eyak; the Chugach; a third group, the Ahtna, who occupied the upriver regions of the Copper River; and the Tlingit, who came as far north as Katalla, did exist before European contact.

The Chugach comprised eight geographic groups within Prince William Sound, and while all spoke Alutiiq and shared the same culture, each was politically independent, with its own leader and village. Russian fur traders brought native hunters from the Kodiak Archipelago and the Aleutian Islands to Prince William Sound to hunt sea otters in the early historic period. Although there was friction between them, the groups intermarried, and many local natives share Russian descent.

Although small in population, the Eyak played a pivotal role in trade between coastal and interior areas. In 1868, after a measles epidemic resulted in a feud between the Chugach and Ahtna, the Eyak acted as middlemen in the exchange of goods between the other two, trading copper, furs, and other goods. Each group used oral tradition to pass on its cultural values from generation to generation. Early European and American visitors were interested primarily in trade and resource extraction, not local culture. By the 20th century, anthropologists found native cultures had undergone significant change due to interaction with explorers, traders, and prospectors.

The date of first contact between the Eyak and Europeans is unknown. Europeans often confused the Eyaks with other groups, especially the Chugach, even though the Eyak spoke a unique language more closely related to Athabascan.

Exploration of this region began in July 1741 when Vitus Bering, commanding the vessel *St. Peter*, made the first recorded Russian landing in Alaska, arriving on Kayak Island southeast of Prince William Sound. Thirty-seven years later, Capt. James Cook, commanding the English vessel *Resolution*, entered Prince William Sound on a voyage seeking the Northwest Passage.

Cook gave the sound and many of its geographic features their present names and christened the entire body of water as "Sandwich Sound" after his benefactor John Montagu, the Earl of Sandwich. Map editors in England, however, renamed the sound after George III's son who later became William IV.

French explorers arrived in 1786, followed by Spanish explorer navy lieutenant Salvador Fidalgo, who sailed the *San Carlos* in 1790 into Prince William Sound. Fidalgo not only named a bay of water after himself but also named the bay of water in front of present-day Cordova in honor of his patron, Don Luis Cordoba de Cordoba. The United States' purchase of Russian America in 1867 opened Alaska to American traders and military expeditions. In 1885, Lt. Henry S. Allen led a successful American expedition up the Copper River valley and was the first to make note of the extensive use of copper tools by the natives in the upriver region. The American-led Harriman Alaska Expedition in 1889 sailed extensively through Prince William Sound and named many of the glaciers and bays after American colleges, like Columbia, Harvard, and Yale.

Salmon continued to be the draw, and after the United States purchased Alaska, profiteers and adventurers began discovering the bountiful resources of the area. By 1887, two canneries were operating in the Odiak Slough area adjacent to Eyak Lake. And by the mid-1920s, the Copper River delta and Prince William Sound region was dotted with over 50 canneries. By then, Cordova had also become known as the "Razor Clam Capital of the World," and at the canneries' peak, they produced over half of the United States' clam products. Salmon has for the most part formed the bulk of the catch, but halibut, black cod, shrimp, crab, and other seafood have also been harvested. Today, the Copper River salmon are world-renowned and regaled in restaurants and fish markets from coast to coast.

While fish were already being harvested from the Copper River region, the land-based natural resources were being discovered, and in an era of rapid development in the United States, the new lands of Alaska were considered fair game and ripe for picking. Gold-seekers who were not having any luck found their way to the region to search for a new ore, copper. This discovery turned out to be the highest-grade commercial copper deposit ever found and the single most valuable mineral deposit discovered in Alaska. The Kennecott Mine became the source, but the copper needed a railroad to get to Cordova.

The construction of the Copper River & Northwest Railway, backed by wealthy East Coast financiers, took place between 1906 and 1911, with some of the most difficult engineering challenges known to man. Mike Heney had experience in the north building the White Pass & Yukon Railroad, but this route would challenge him more and would be the world's first example of arctic engineering. The 196-mile railway was completed on March 29, 1911, with a copper spike driven before the first load of nearly pure copper ore worth $250,000 made its way to the steamship docks. The railroad and fishing industries led to an era of prosperity and growth for the now booming town of Cordova.

As the population grew, along came a school, hospital, dairy, and residences. Cordova was the first year-round port of call for steamship lines west of the Gulf of Alaska. The first airplane landed in Cordova in 1929, and a small city strip was created in 1934. Cordova has since survived the loss of the railroad, devastating fires, nature's earthquakes, and man's oil spills. Read on to learn how this tough Alaskan town has stayed strong, thriving for over 100 years.

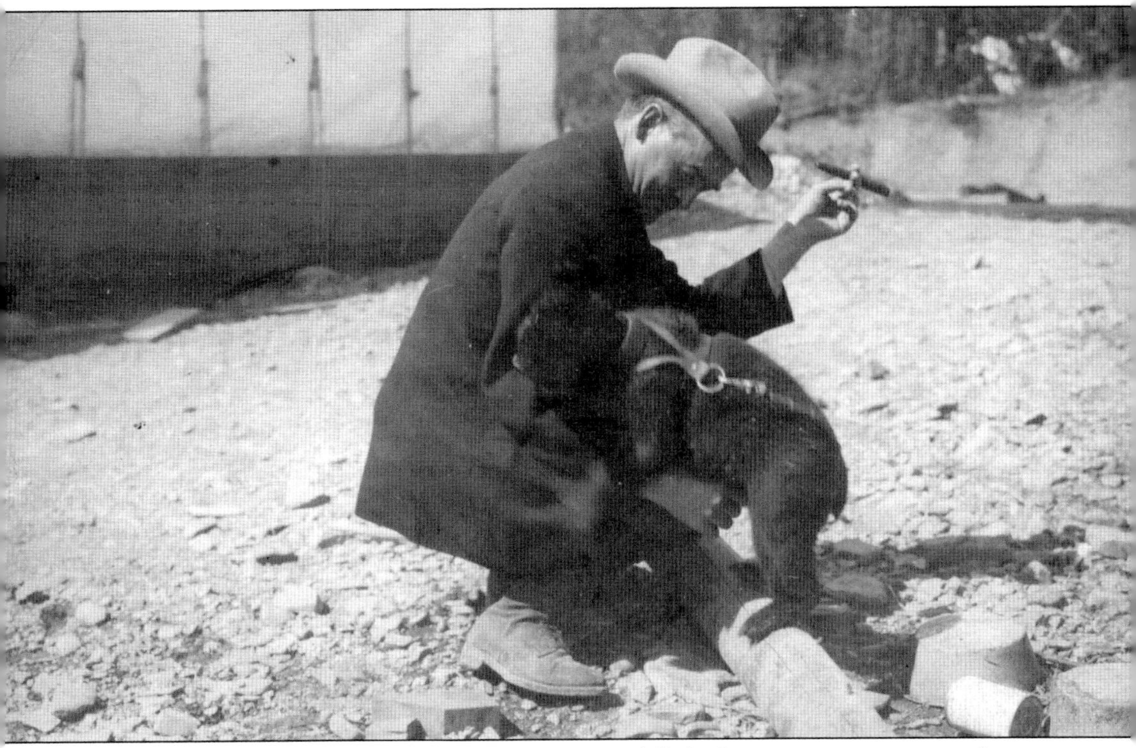

Michael J. Heney, nicknamed the "Irish Prince," successfully built two arctic engineering feats in the most difficult of conditions—the White Pass Yukon Railroad and Cordova's Copper River & Northwest Railway. The men who worked for him revered Heney. He is seen here with his trademark hat and cigar as well as the camp watchdog.

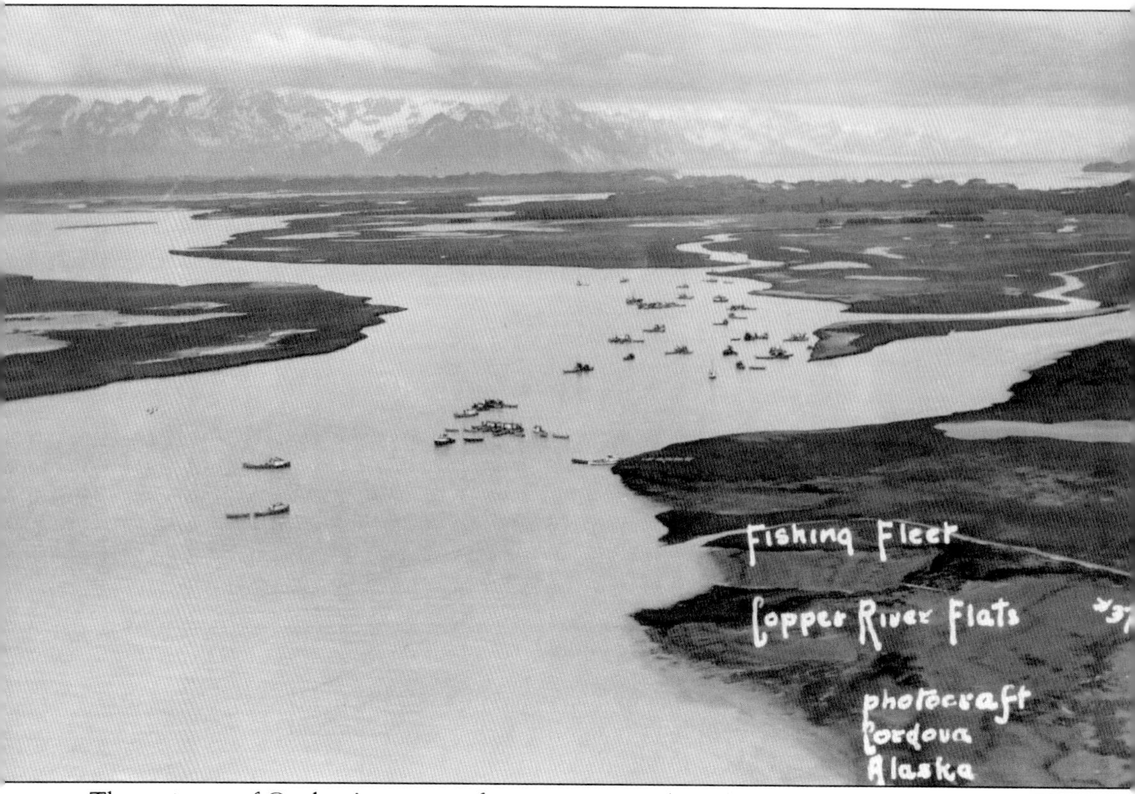

The mainstay of Cordova's economy for over 100 years have been the salmon that return year after year to spawn in the streams they were born in. The Copper River Flats comprise a unique sanctuary of glacial rivers perfect for salmon habitat. While techniques, equipment, and production methods have changed, the fish continue to be the one constant providing sustenance for the local residents and, thanks to air transportation, the world over.

One

The Foundation 1741–1867

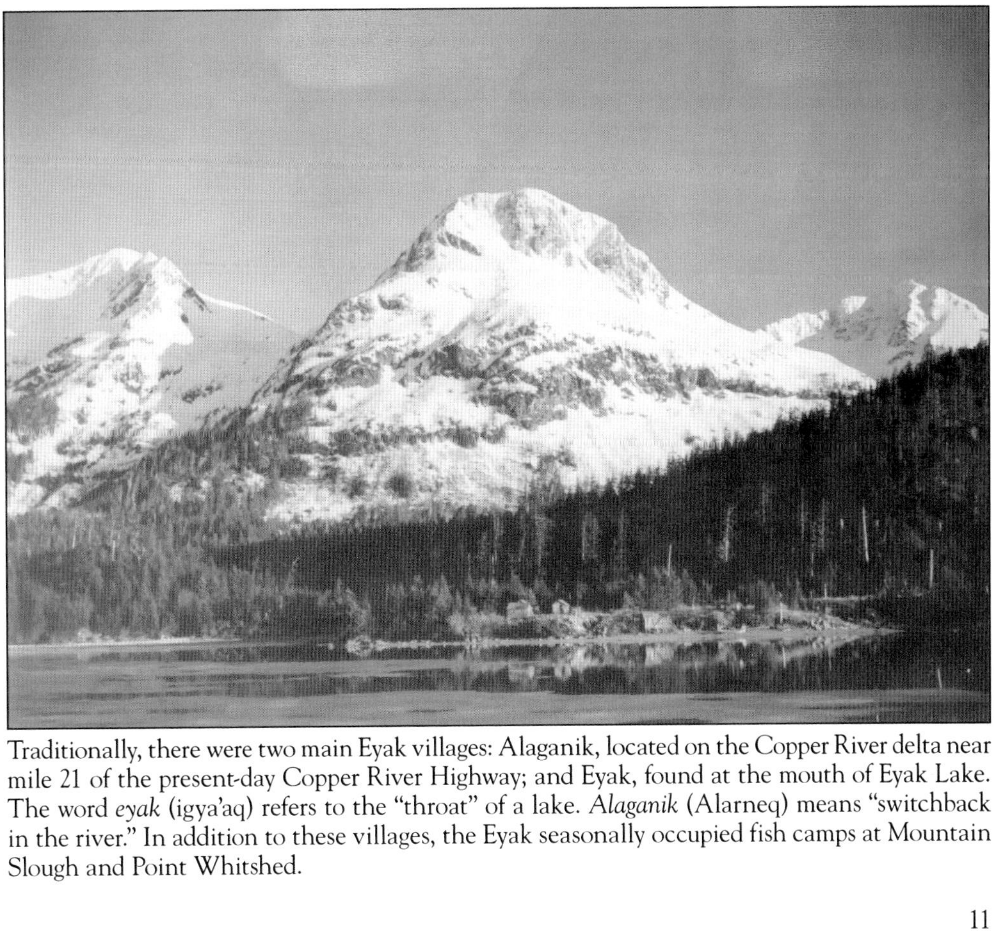

Traditionally, there were two main Eyak villages: Alaganik, located on the Copper River delta near mile 21 of the present-day Copper River Highway; and Eyak, found at the mouth of Eyak Lake. The word *eyak* (igya'aq) refers to the "throat" of a lake. *Alaganik* (Alarneq) means "switchback in the river." In addition to these villages, the Eyak seasonally occupied fish camps at Mountain Slough and Point Whitshed.

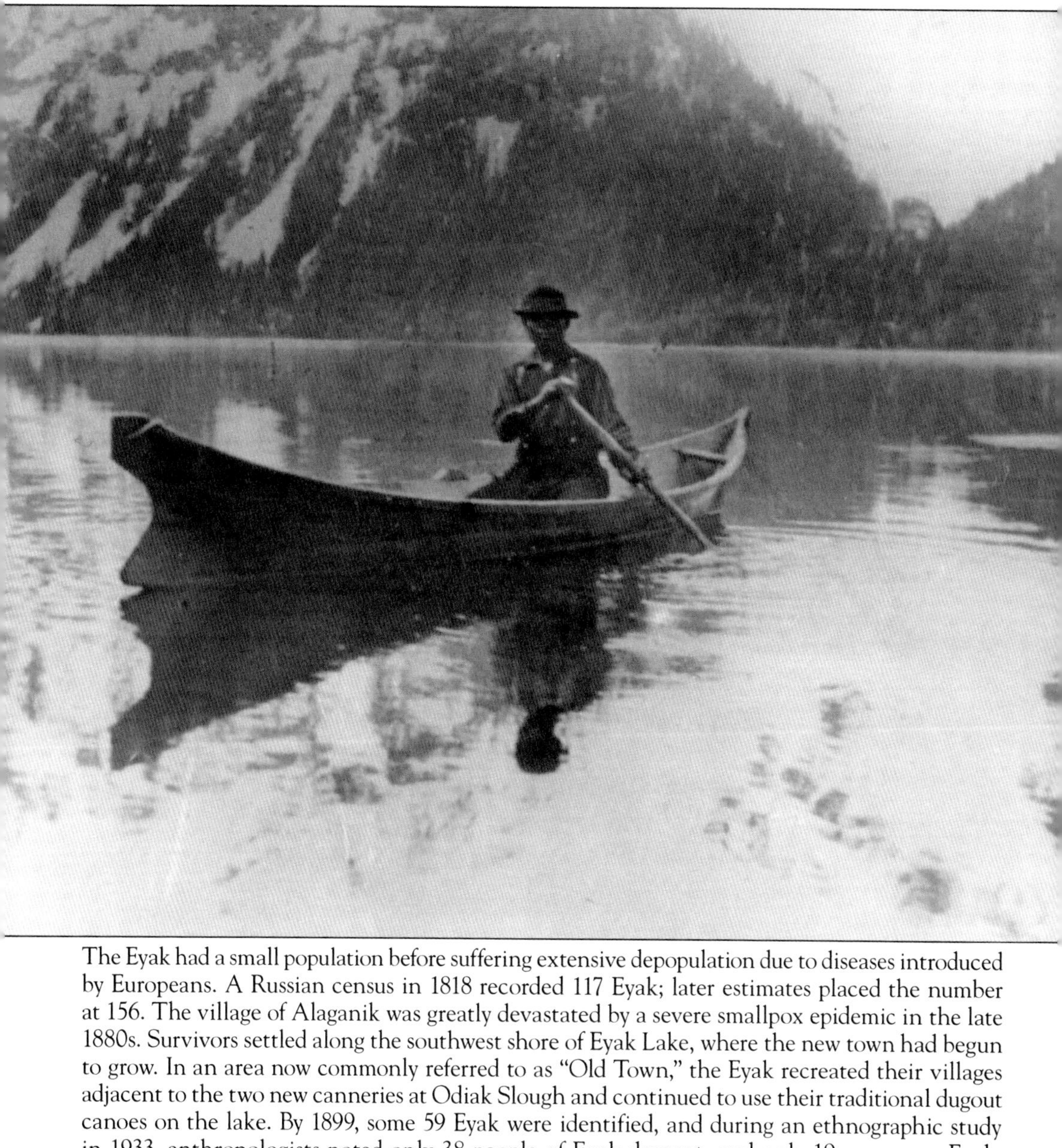

The Eyak had a small population before suffering extensive depopulation due to diseases introduced by Europeans. A Russian census in 1818 recorded 117 Eyak; later estimates placed the number at 156. The village of Alaganik was greatly devastated by a severe smallpox epidemic in the late 1880s. Survivors settled along the southwest shore of Eyak Lake, where the new town had begun to grow. In an area now commonly referred to as "Old Town," the Eyak recreated their villages adjacent to the two new canneries at Odiak Slough and continued to use their traditional dugout canoes on the lake. By 1899, some 59 Eyak were identified, and during an ethnographic study in 1933, anthropologists noted only 38 people of Eyak descent, and only 19 were pure Eyak. (Courtesy of F. DeLaguna.)

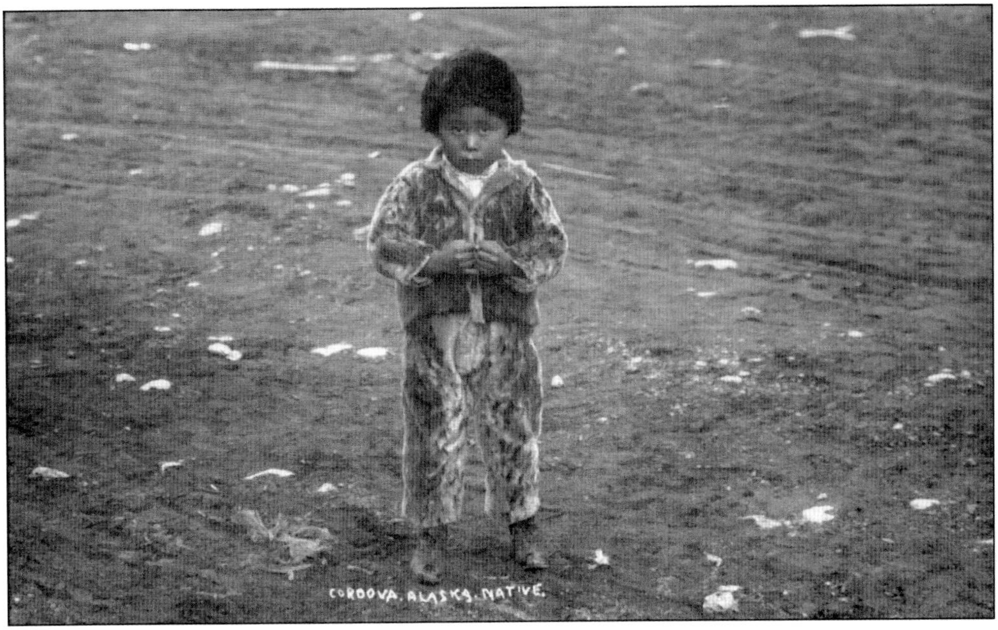

The Eyak wore clothing made of furs, gut, and skin, often using seal skin for leggings or pants and bear or seal intestine sewn together horizontally for shirts and jackets. They lived in wooden plank houses and relied upon salmon, bear, and small seals for food. Eyak was spoken in the 19th century from Yakutat along the north gulf coast to Eyak at the Copper River delta, but by 1900, only at Eyak. There are currently no surviving fluent speakers, but work at the Department of Language of the University of Alaska is striving to preserve this unique language to keep it from being lost forever.

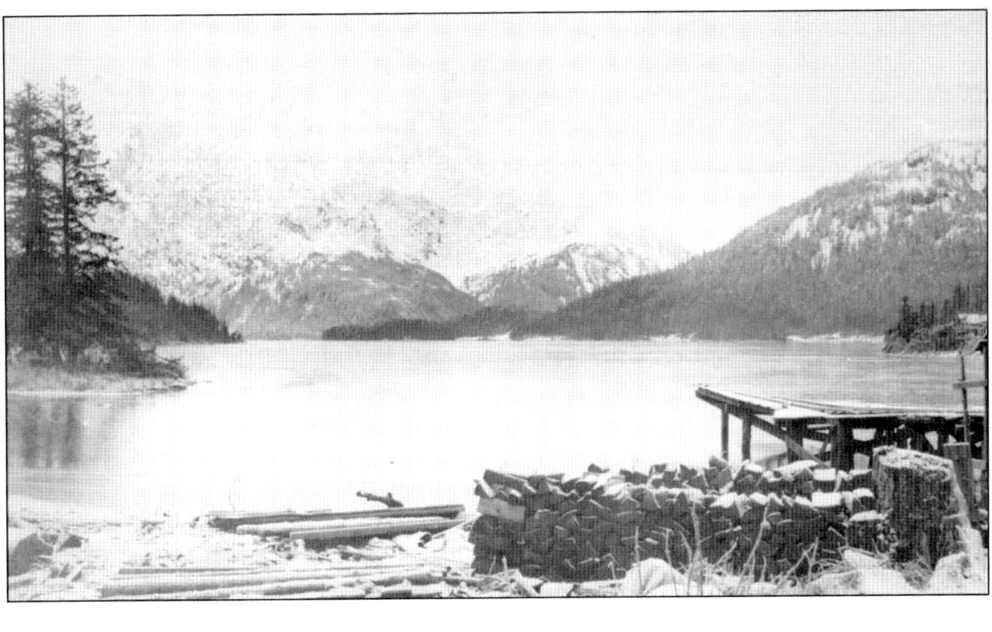

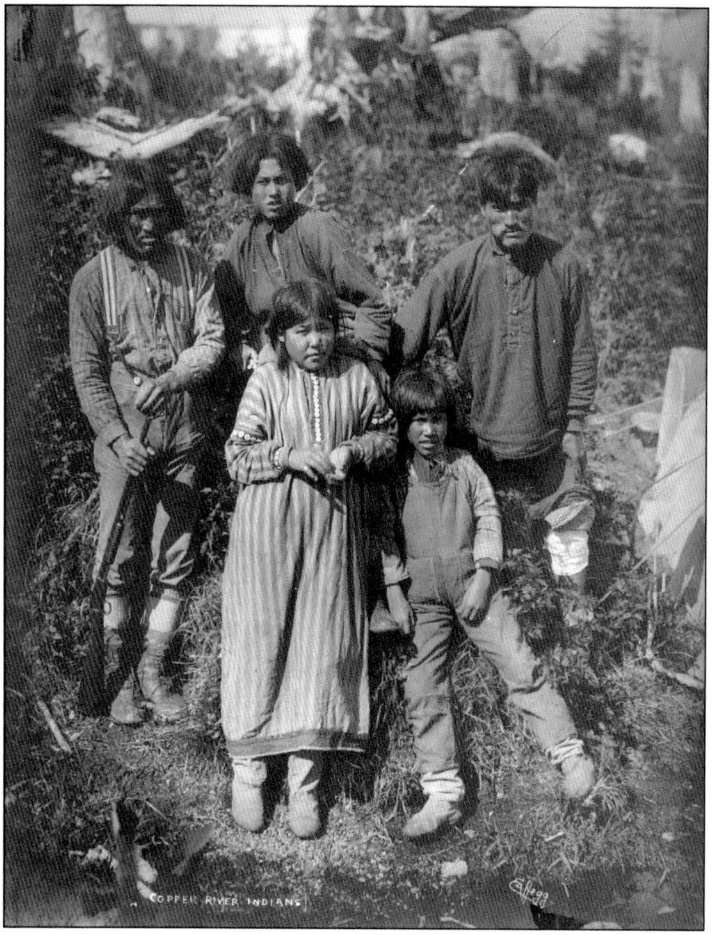

During the 19th century, Ahtna territory included the Copper River valley except for the Copper River delta, which was occupied by the Eyak. Ahtna settlements consisted of permanent winter villages and seasonal hunting and fishing camps with each settlement under a local chief. One of the most prominent leaders was Chief Nicolai of Taral, who held a monopoly on the trade of copper down the river to the Eyak and Tlingit. After 1868, Ahtna traders descended the Copper River in March, while the river was frozen, and in May and September, when the water was low, traveled to Alaganik where they traded with the Eyak.

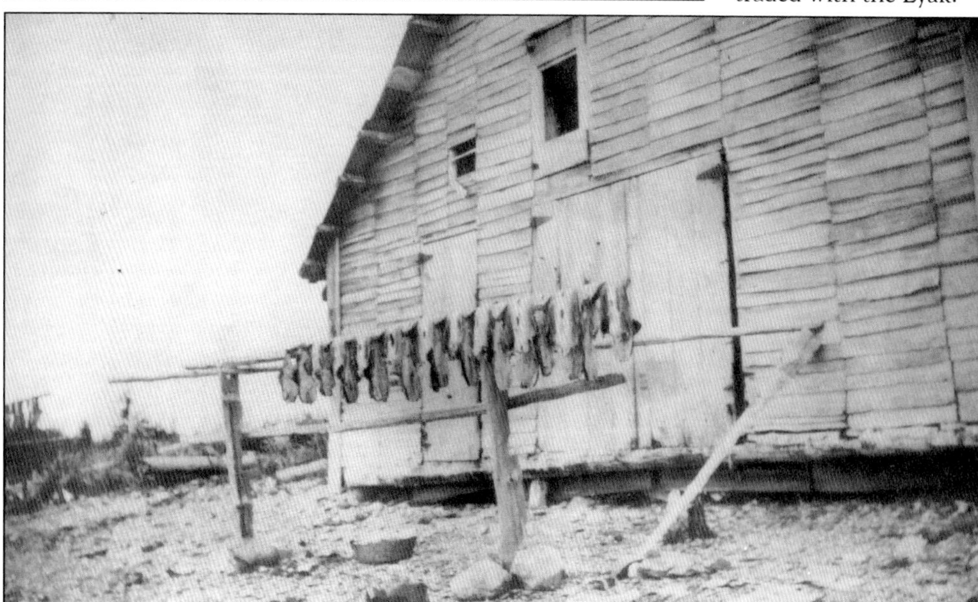

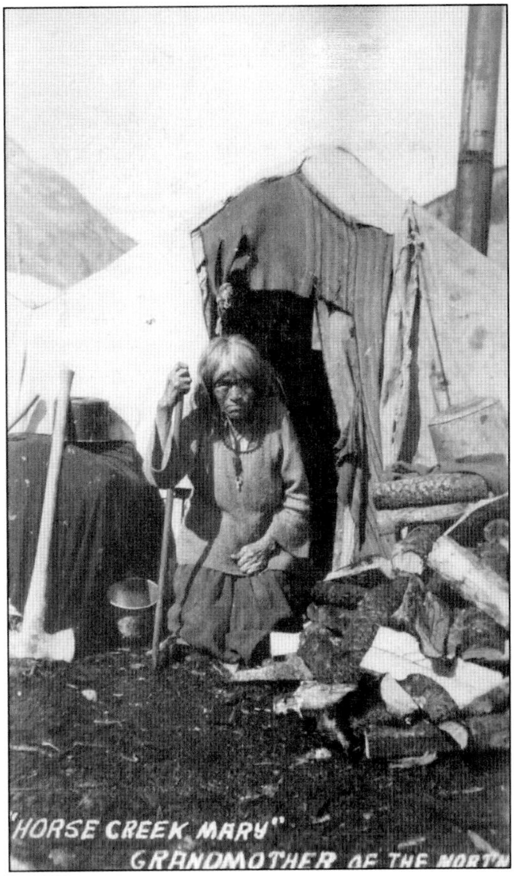

Horse Creek Mary was born of an Ahtna native mother and a Russian father and was originally from the village of Taral. She had two husbands and four children who all unfortunately preceded her in death; afterwards, she kept to herself and lived alone beside the Chitina Trail. Before the advent of the railroad, Mary mushed for her supplies from her home on Horse Creek, traveling only with her dog and pulling the sled herself to either Valdez or Cordova. Proud and independent, she was often the subject of artists and photographers in the region, including Eustace Ziegler, E.A. Hegg, and Jules Dahlager.

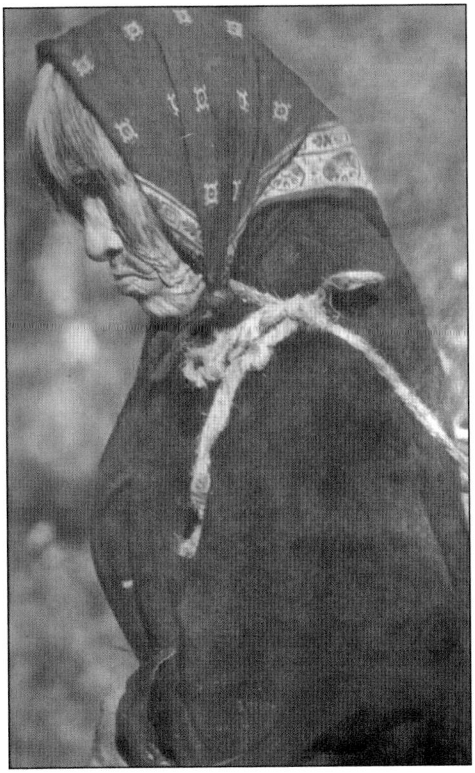

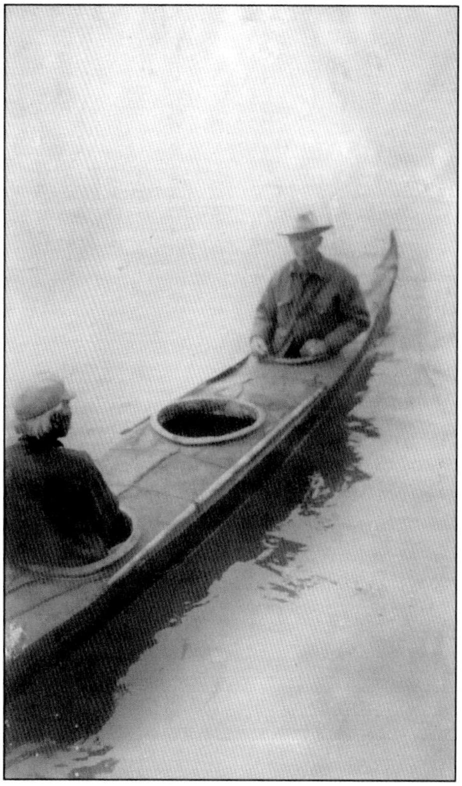

The Chugach traditionally occupied Prince William Sound in the area west of present-day Cordova, primarily subsisting on fish and sea mammals. Seals and sea lions were taken throughout the year; although, spring was the most favored time. Whales and sea otters were taken whenever possible. The Chugach harvested halibut, cod, and herring in the spring and salmon and shellfish during the summer. From the land, the Chugach hunted mountain goats and bear and collected plants and berries. The Chugach lived in wood-plank, semisubterranean houses and utilized their skin kayaks for almost every aspect of their lives, which were so closely associated with the water. The Chugach obtained European trade goods, such as glass beads and iron, from other native groups before they had direct contact with Europeans. Once direct contact was established, the Chugach were eager to trade for more of these items.

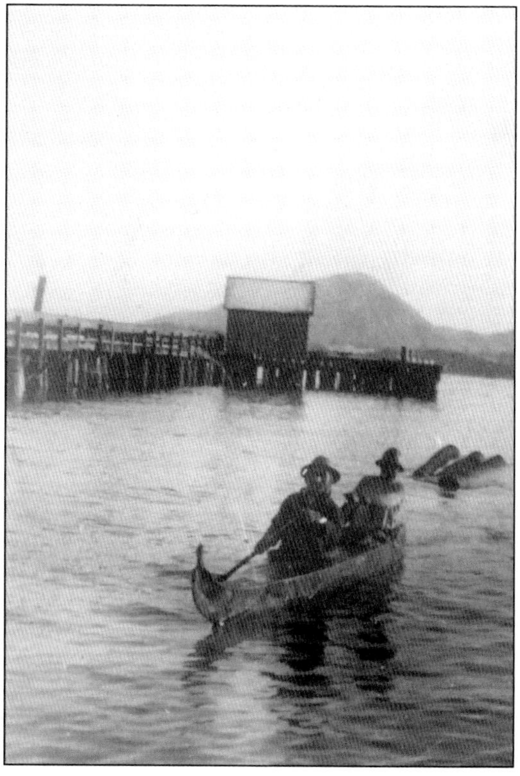

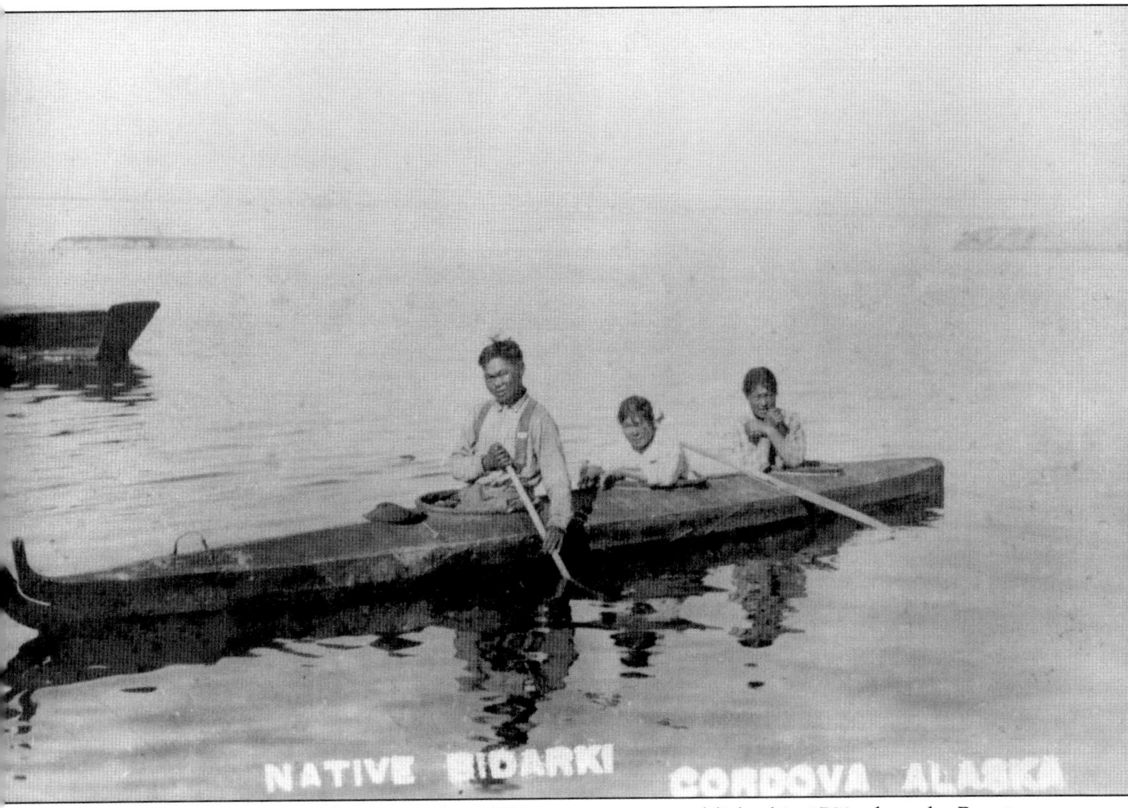

Regular contact between the Chugach and Europeans was established in 1791 when the Russians set up a permanent Russian trading post, called Fort Constantine, near the Chugach native village of Nuchek on Hinchinbrook Island. The primary motivation for the Russian presence was the acquisition of furs, especially sea otter, for the thriving markets in Asia and Europe. Nuchek became the focus for this trade, not only with the Chugach but also with the Tlingit to the southeast and the Ahtna and Eyak of the Copper River area. The Russians forced local inhabitants of the sound and elsewhere to work as hunters. Native males between the ages of 18 and 50 were required to work for the Russian American Company for three years. Women were required to dry fish and gather materials needed by the company. After the sale of Alaska to the United States in 1867, the trading company at Nuchek was taken over by the Alaska Commercial Company.

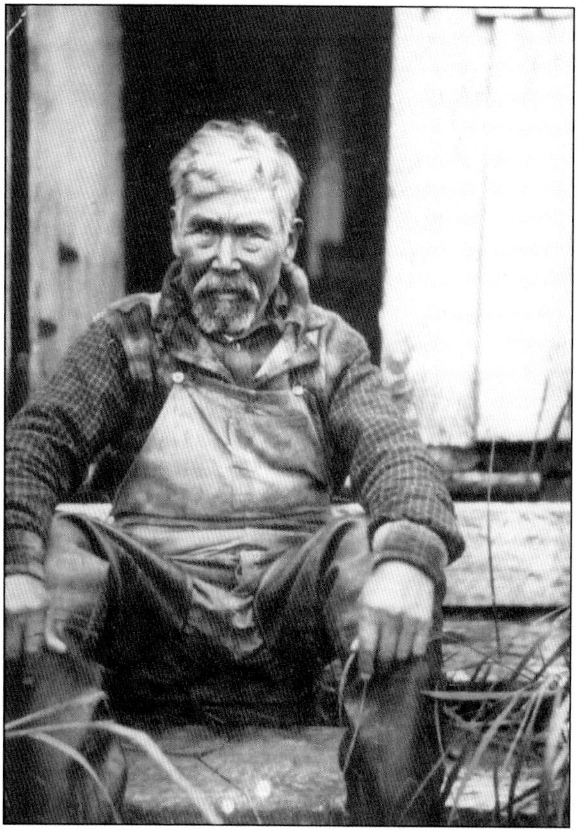

Chief Makari "Makaka" Chimovitski was born in the village of Nuchek on Hinchinbrook Island. His ancestry reflects the cultural diversity of the Prince William Sound region—with a grandmother from Kodiak Island, a great-grandfather from Yakutat, and a great-grandmother who was the daughter of a Chugach chief from Mummy Island near Cordova. In 1933, the first Danish-American Alaska Expedition, led by Dr. Kai Birket Smith of the National Museum of Denmark and Dr. Frederica De Laguna of the University of Pennsylvania, came to the area and began recording Chugach legends. Chief Chimovitski's daughter Matrona, shown here cooking crabs on the beach, served as an interpreter for the stories. (Both, courtesy of F. DeLaguna.)

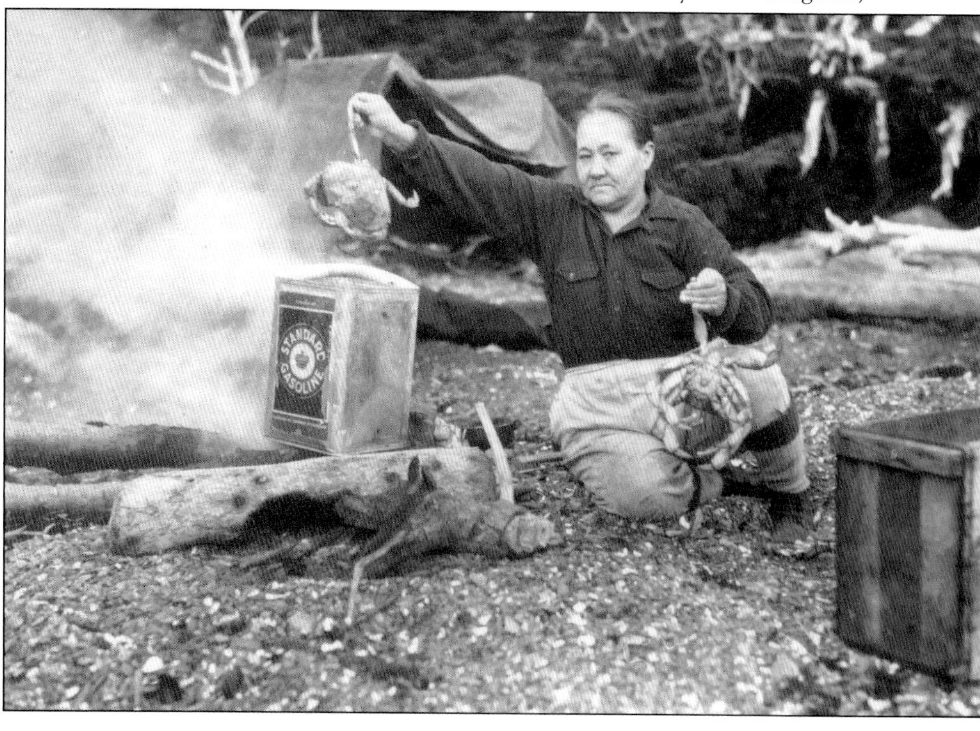

Two

Cordova Discovered 1867–1915

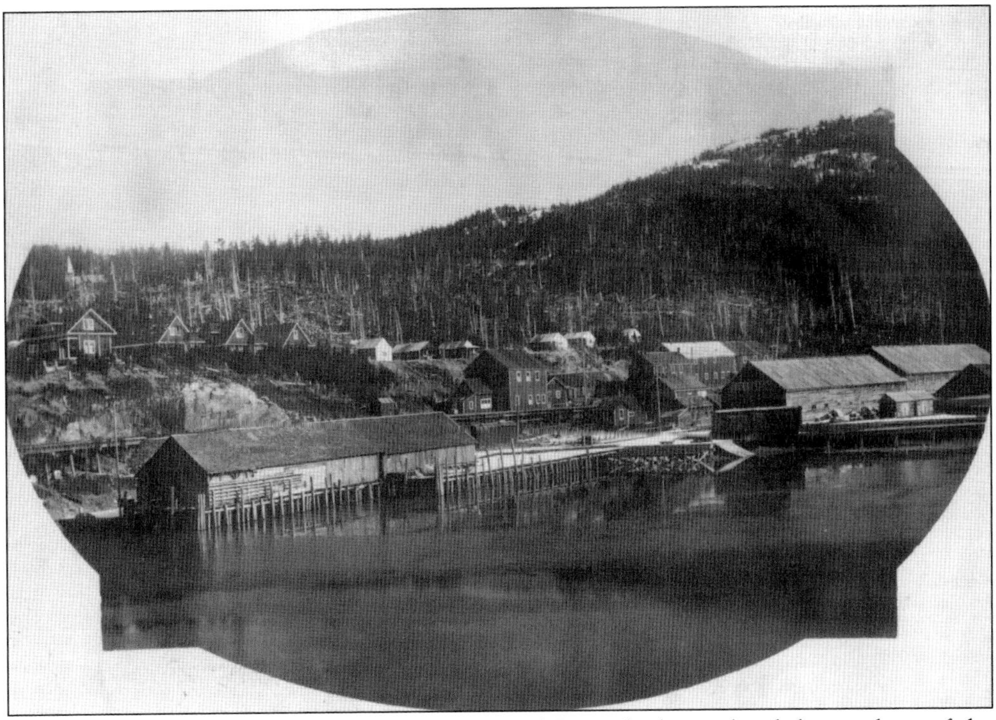

As the 19th century wound to a close, the United States had completed the purchase of the territory, and the natural resources of the region were being discovered. The first successful ascent of the Copper River was undertaken in 1885 by US Army lieutenant Henry S. Allen in one of America's epic journeys of exploration. By 1887, the first cannery, financed by Pacific Packing Company of San Francisco, was built along Odiak Slough with tidal access to Orca Inlet.

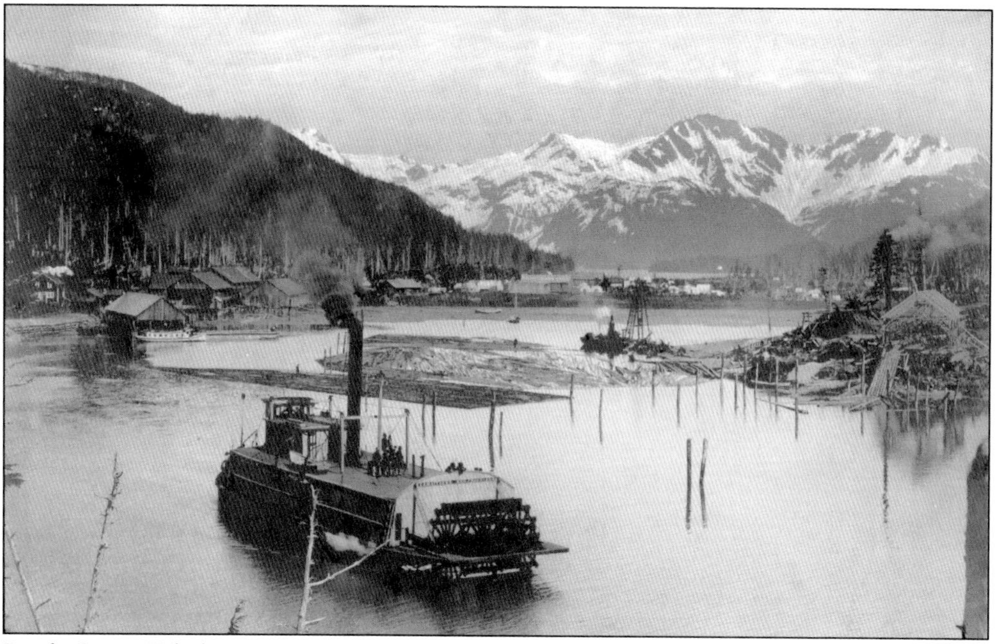

Pacific Steam Whaling Company built a second cannery at Odiak in 1888, but after a fire, it was rebuilt at nearby Orca and was visited in 1898 by the American-led Harriman Alaska Expedition. Harriman's journal details their visit as follows: "The idea of stretching their legs on solid ground appealed to most of the expeditioners [*sic*] and several boats were soon splashing through the water toward town. Dominated by the Pacific Steam Whaling Company's salmon cannery, Orca boasted three buildings and the foul odor of rotting fish. For miles along the coastline, discarded salmon heads and fins littered the ocean lending the water an oily look. About two hundred Chinese laborers worked long hours in the cannery and [naturalist John] Muir sadly shook his head at the sight of the men brought up from San Francisco to work for low wages. 'Men in this business,' he wrote, 'are themselves canned.' "

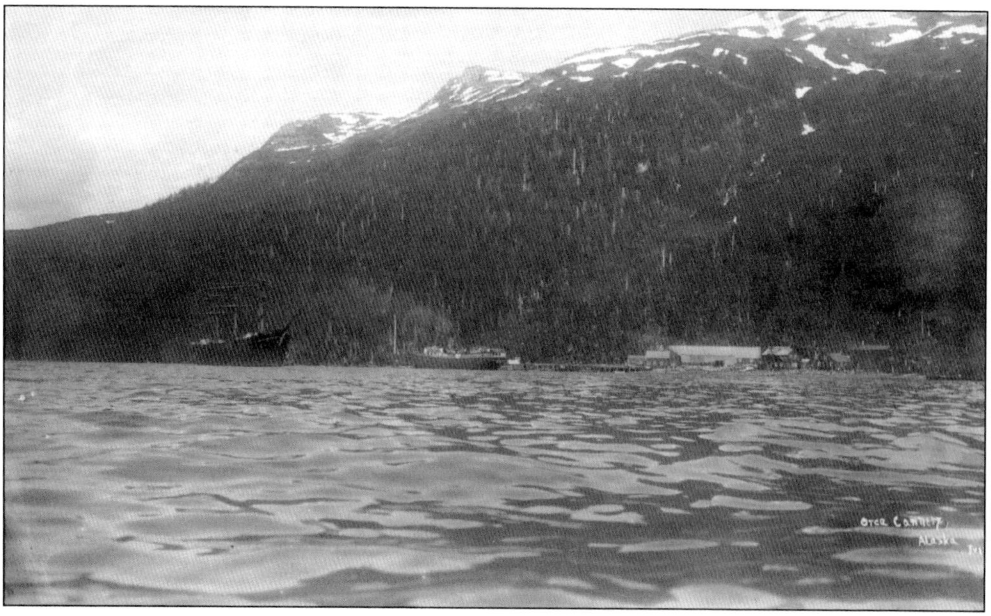

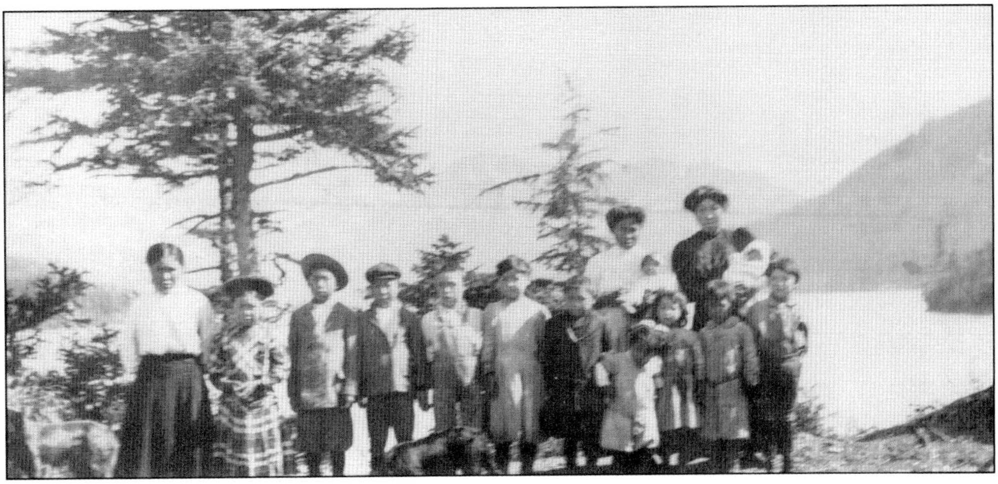

Natives at the nearby traditional village of Eyak began relocating to the new town to be near the canneries, and by 1890, Odiak was a thriving town of 200 people. In 1892, the village of Alaganik was abandoned following a major epidemic, and around this same time, the name changed from Odiak to Eyak. When gold was discovered on the Klondike in 1896, mining and transportation became important in the development region. The influx of prospectors up the Copper River began to change the Eyak and Ahtna's way of life. During the Alaskan expedition of US Army lieutenant Henry S. Allen, it is notable that Allen and his men not only recorded information about the people they found but also became trusted enough that on one occasion the Taral chief Nicolai led him to the secret outcropping of nearly pure copper ore.

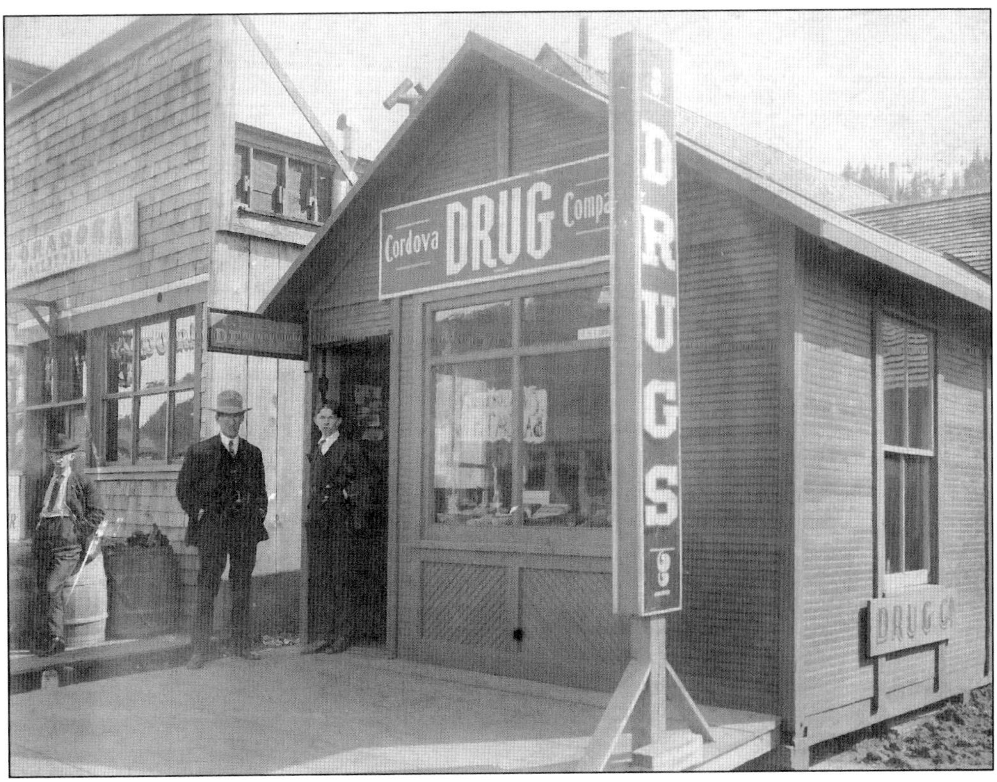

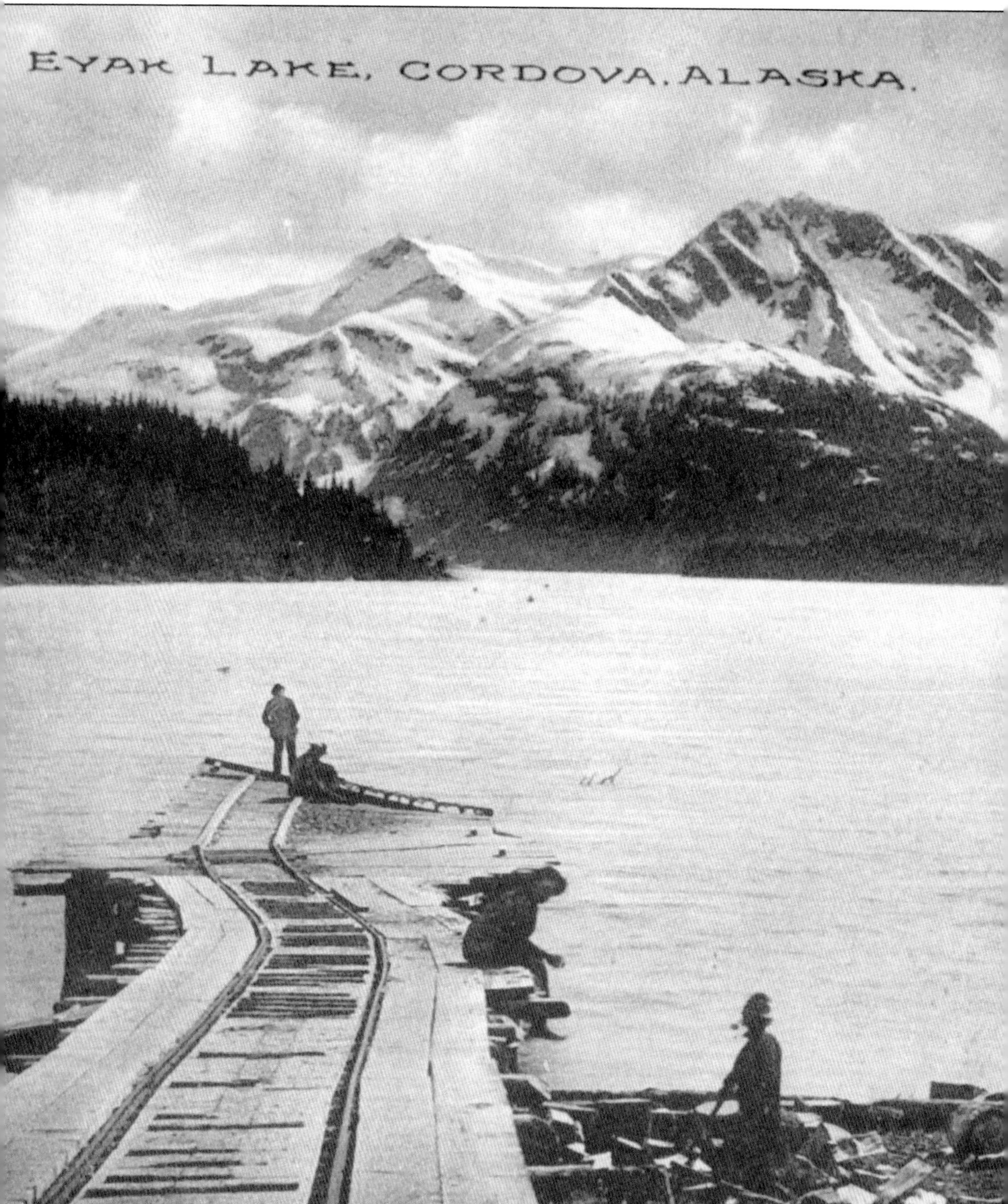

The new town of Eyak was located at the west end of the lake, and salmon were harvested from the freshwaters of the lake and Eyak River and brought to the shore. Then a tram system hauled the fish to the canneries a half mile away. Once caught, salmon spoiled quickly, so canneries were built near river mouths where the salmon schooled before ascending the stream to spawn. Salmon were caught in barricades placed across the mouths of streams. Incredibly efficient, barricades

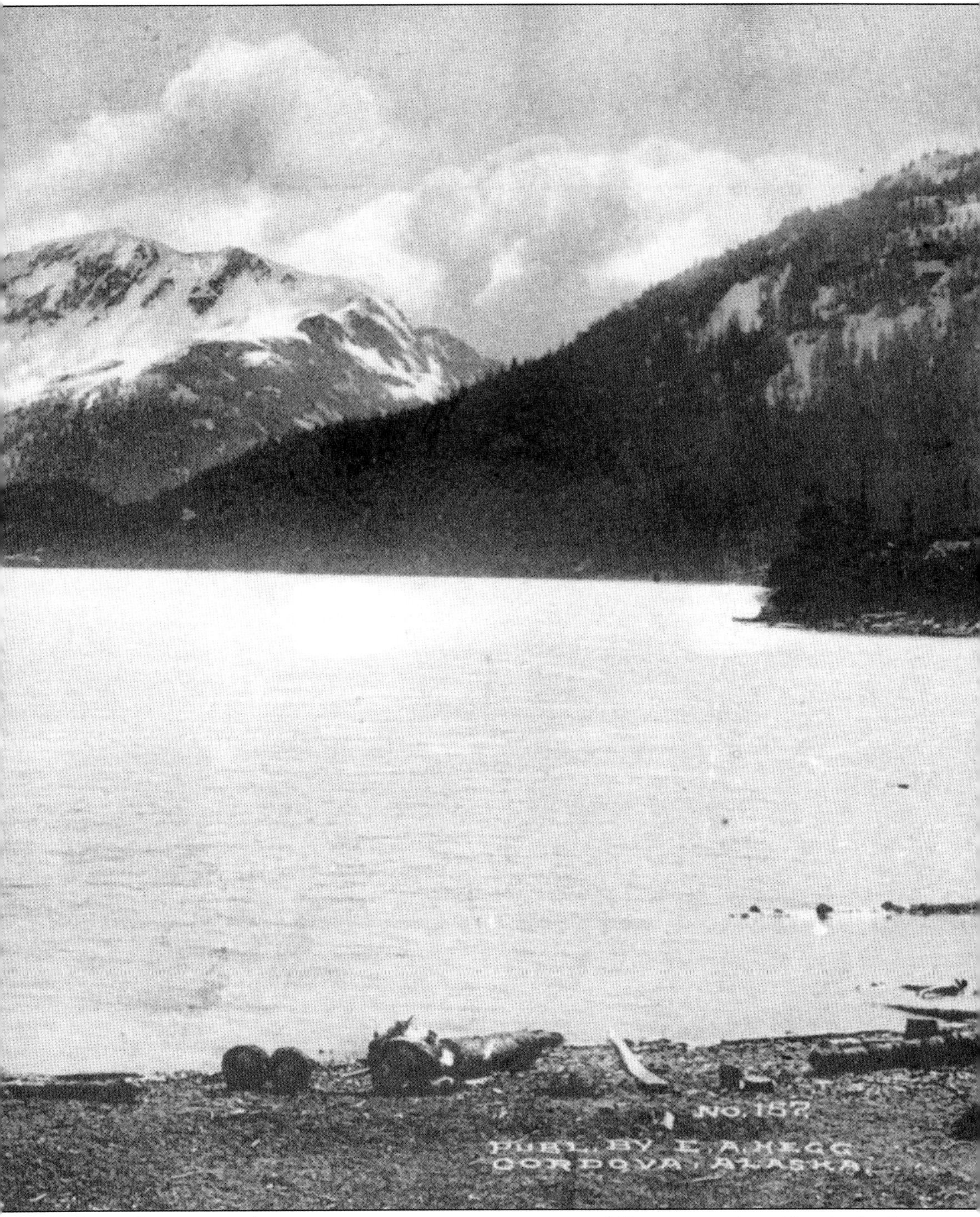

did not allow many salmon to escape upstream to spawn, and Congress outlawed barricades in 1889. In these first few years of commercial fishing, 25,000 cases of salmon were taken from the new Copper River canneries. By 1900, some 42 salmon canneries were operating in Alaska, and 1.5 million cases of product were packed that same year.

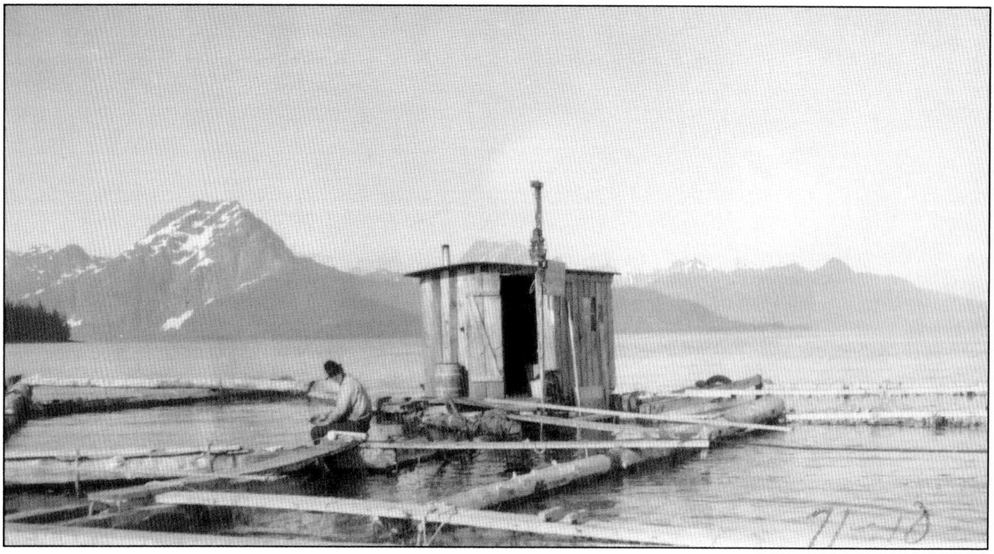

At the turn of the century, the Alaska Packers Association and Alaska Syndicate were powerful entities that owned nearly all the canneries in Alaska and canned 85 percent of the statewide salmon pack. These operations, which were dominated by nonresidents, fished Alaskan waters with shortsighted aggressiveness. They consolidated to keep prices paid to fisherman low and lease prices of the boats, the fish traps, and canneries high and controlled the shipping of salmon to the West Coast markets. In short, the two groups monopolized the fisheries. The use of traps, pile, and floating traps brought much debate. The monopolies loved traps; they could be maintained by one trap watchman, with just a few more hands to brail fish. Traps were operated six days per week, 24 hours a day, during the fishing season.

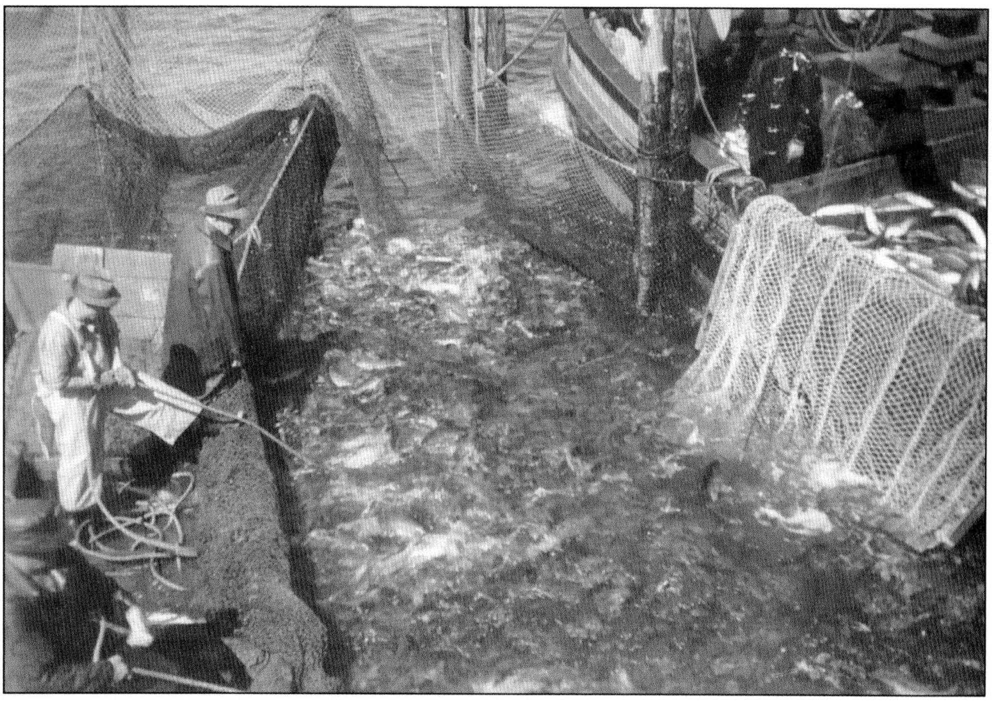

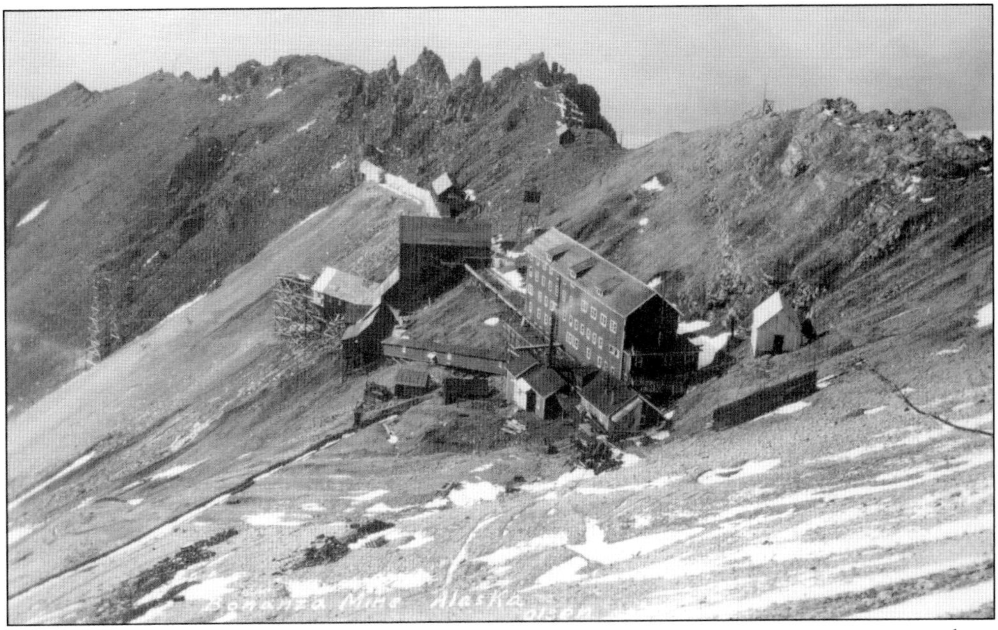

Allen's expedition opened up the interior of the Copper River region to prospectors such as Clarence Warner and "Tarantula" Jack Smith, who discovered the rich copper deposits of legendary Nicolai's Mine. Young entrepreneur Stephen Birch acquired options on the claims and, backed by J.P. Morgan and Daniel Guggenheim, reorganized to form the Alaska Syndicate. To get the ore out of the remote interior, the syndicate built a railroad from the Kennecott mill site to tidewater at Prince William Sound. Railroad promoters had considered Valdez or Katalla as headquarters for routes into the interior. Another player in the development of a railroad was Michael J. Heney. Having just completed the White Pass & Yukon Railroad, Heney was ready for a new challenge and knew Eyak was the right choice for a port.

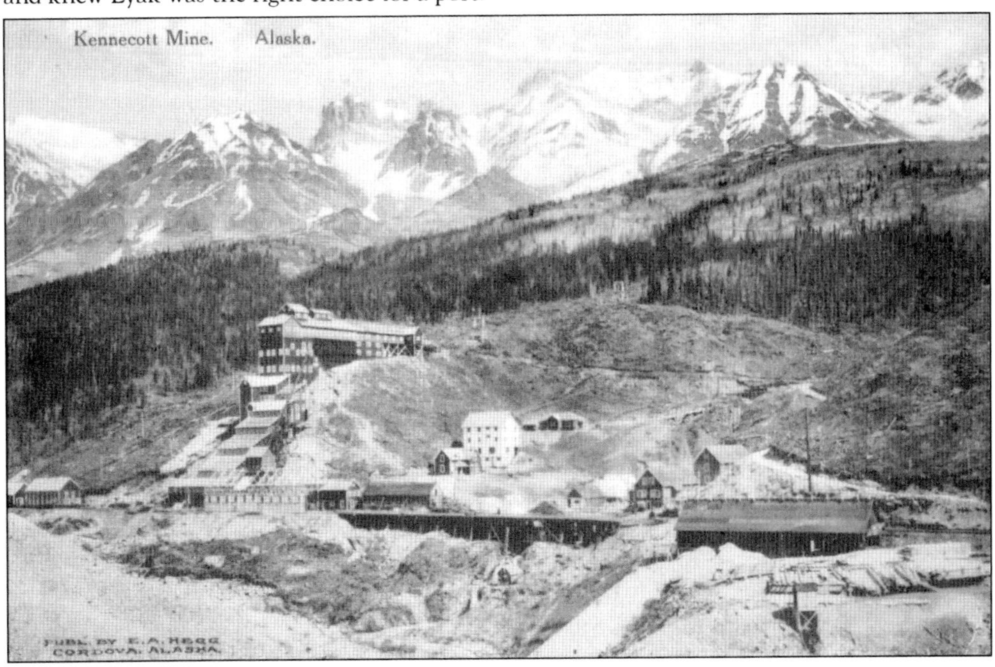

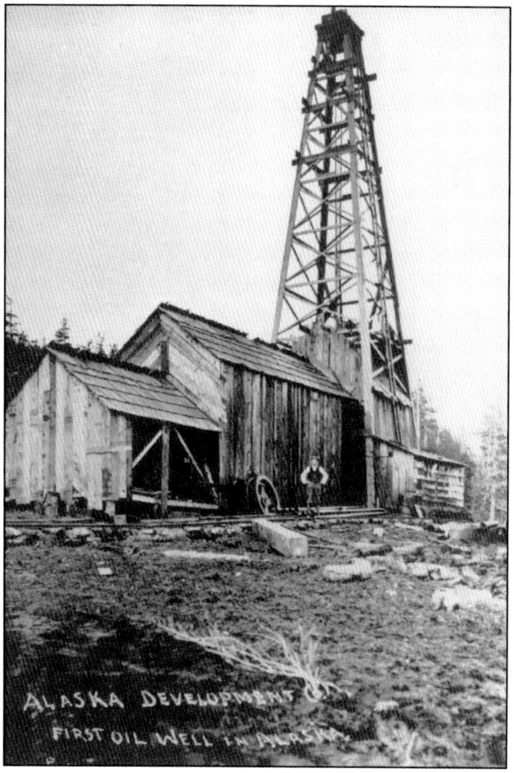

Katalla, located southeast of Eyak, was quick to take on the challenge of being the gateway to the region's abundance of natural resources. In the late 1800s, Katalla was a trading post of sorts for the Eyak and Tlingit natives with settlements in the area. Oil seeps had been spotted for years, and by 1897, most of the promising locations, found on a 25-mile stretch of territory, had been staked out. In 1902, the Alaska Development Co. struck oil after drilling 550 feet, and over its lifetime, it would produce 154,000 barrels of oil (1904–1933). An extensive coalfield also lay underground near the copper mine. Determined to be the terminus and perfect shipping port, Katalla began construction of a railroad and a breakwater at the water's edge.

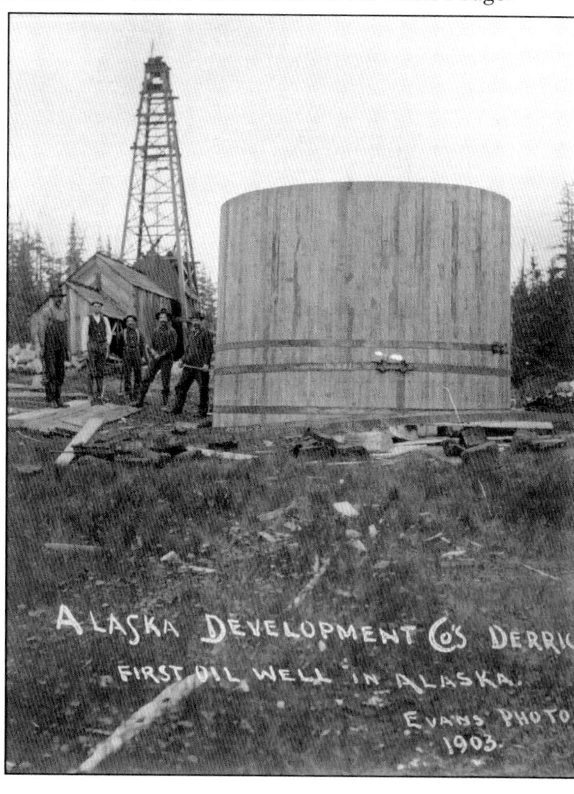

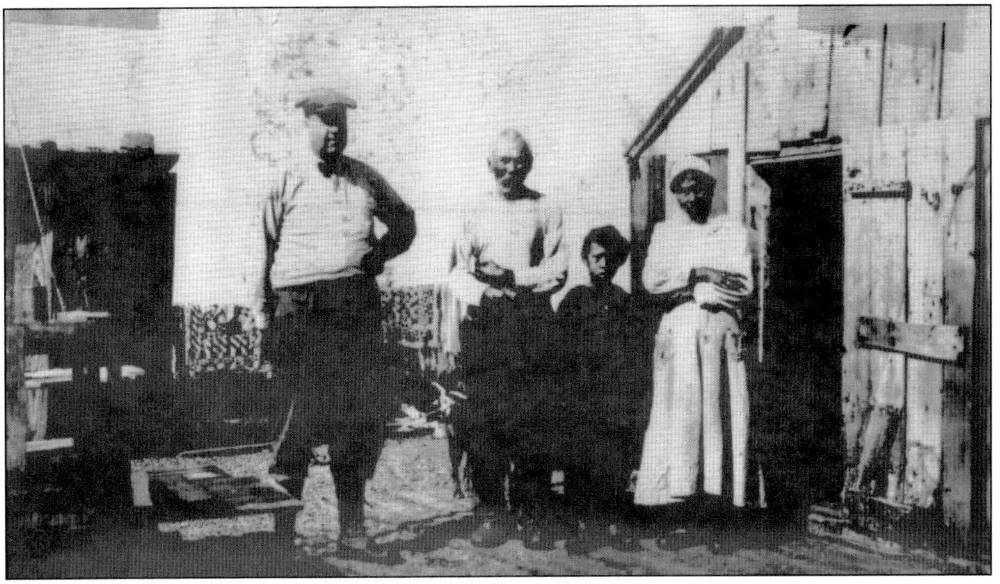

Established in 1907 to secure those natural resources, the Chugach National Forest brought more Euro-American contact to the Chugach natives in Prince William Sound. Forest supervisor Lehi Pratt regularly traveled to the islands in the sound and is shown here visiting the Chimovitski family. After a smallpox epidemic struck Nuchek in the early 1920s, Chief Chimovitski moved the village with many orphan children to Makaka Point.

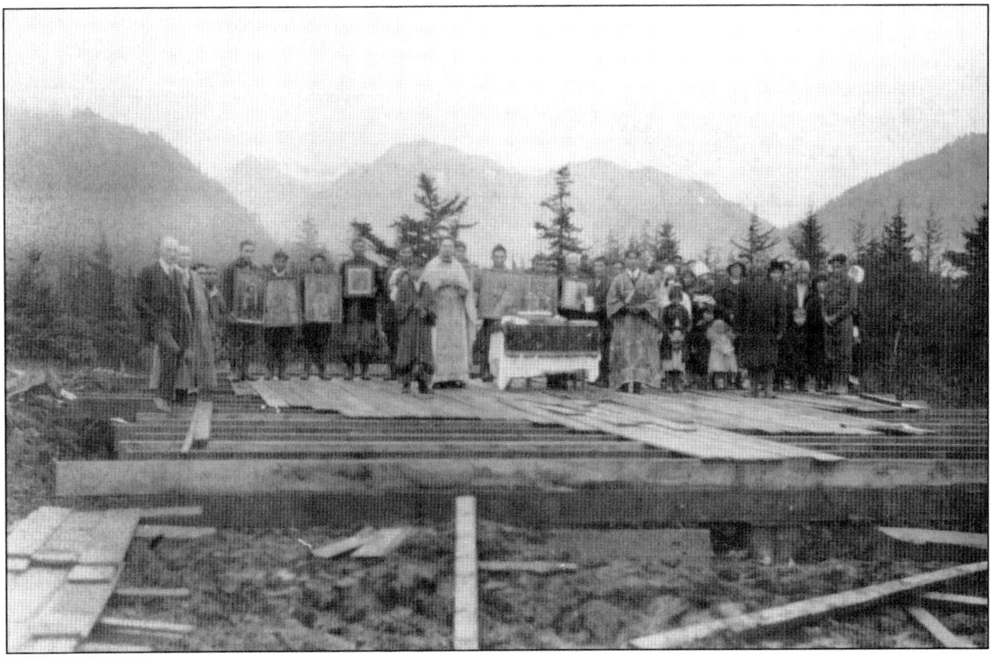

In 1794, St. Herman from Siberia Russia established a religious presence in Nuchek and baptized hundreds of new Chugach believers. The village moved from Nuchek to Makaka Point, and the relics and icons of the church traveled with the natives, eventually arriving safely at Cordova where St. Michael's Orthodox Church was built in 1925. The 2009 St. Michael's Church contains the very same relics and icons from Nuchek.

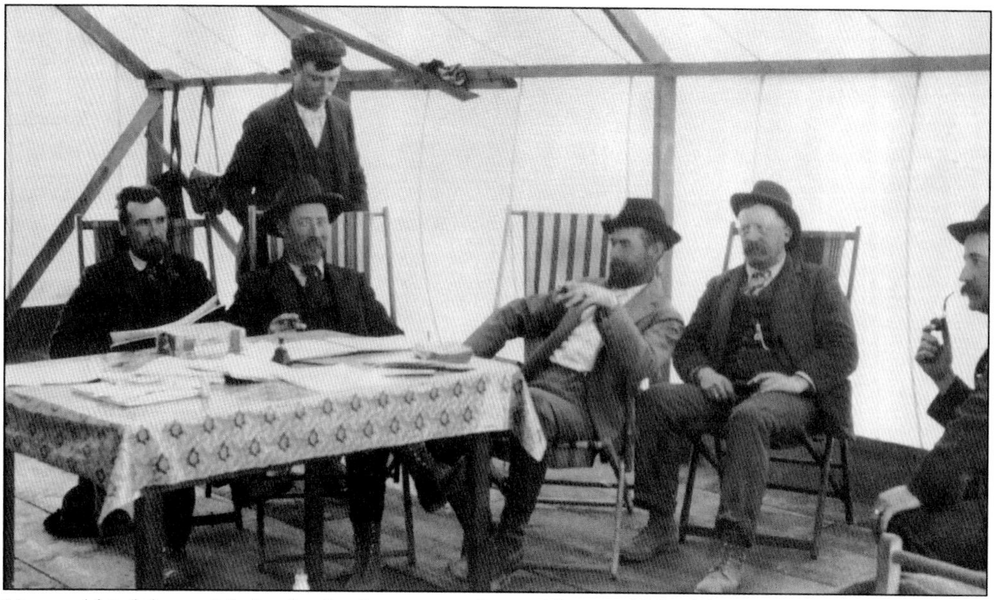

Heney (third from right), who had once proclaimed he could build any railroad with enough "dynamite and snoose," began to scout out a location. Knowing other competitors were looking at Valdez and Katalla, Heney selected Eyak because he was convinced that the more protected inside waters of Orca Inlet would prove perfect for a steamship dock. He purchased the abandoned cannery buildings along Odiak and decided to use them for his railroad headquarters. (Courtesy of Alaska State Library.)

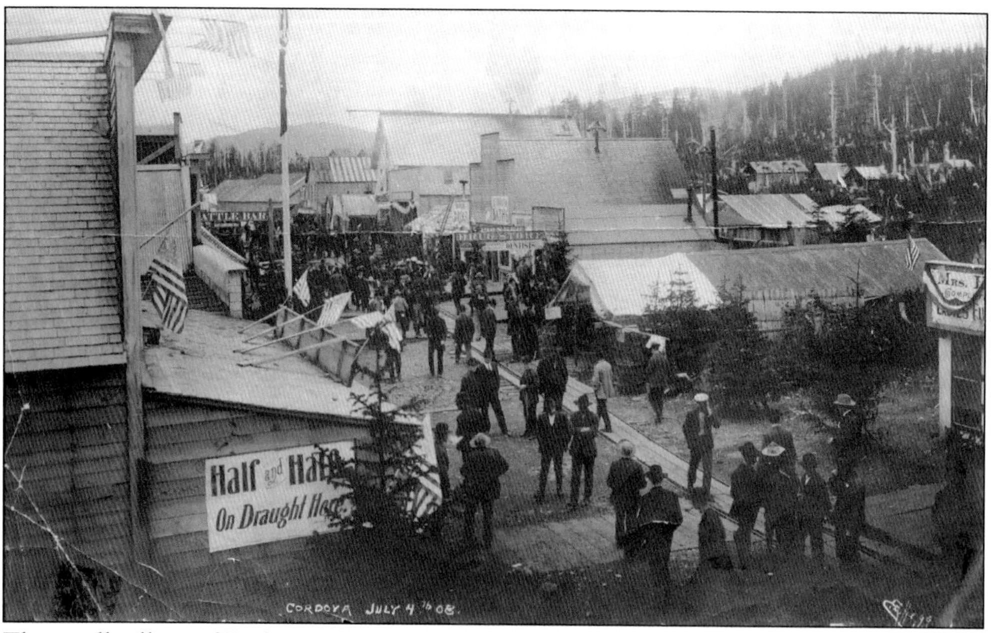

The small village of Eyak was now being transformed into a boomtown. The *Seattle Times* reported Eyak was having the wildest real estate rush that any northern city had experienced. Just before Christmas in 1907, land north of Eyak was surveyed, and on May 19, 1908, lots in the new townsite were placed on sale. Businesses in Eyak, now described as "Old Town," relocated to the Heney-christened Cordova.

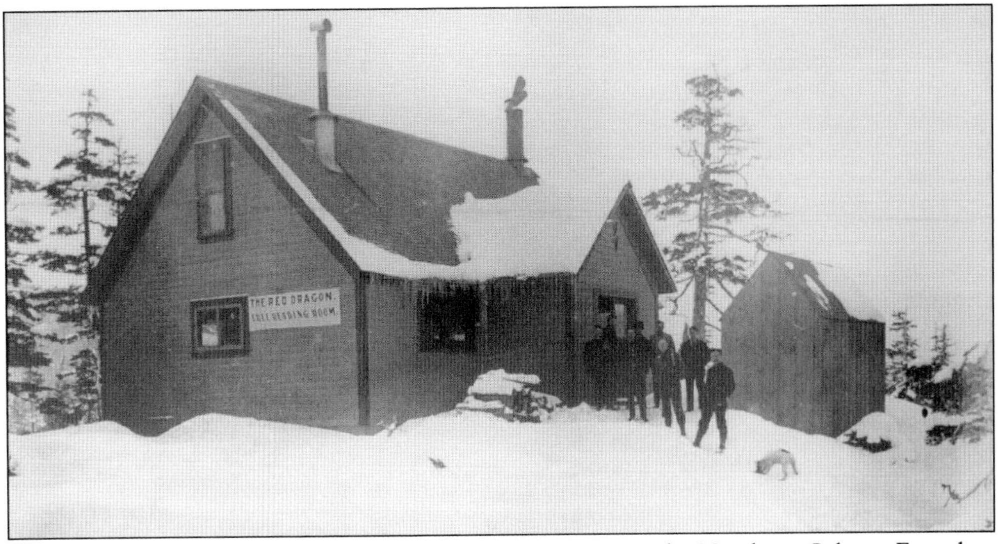

The first structure to be completed in the new townsite was the Northern Saloon. Four days later, on July 14, 1908, the Red Dragon opened. Outbid for the one scarce pile of lumber by the saloon, Rev. E.P. Newton designed the building as a clubhouse to be open day and night, seven days a week. Described as a plain, well-built frame building, it had one room, and its center of life was an open fireplace. Easy chairs, couches with pillows, a table stocked with magazines, writing materials and Cordova's very first lending library, chess and other games, and a piano and pool table all provided comfort. On Sundays, an altar was lowered from a landing above the rafters, and the Red Dragon was ready for church services.

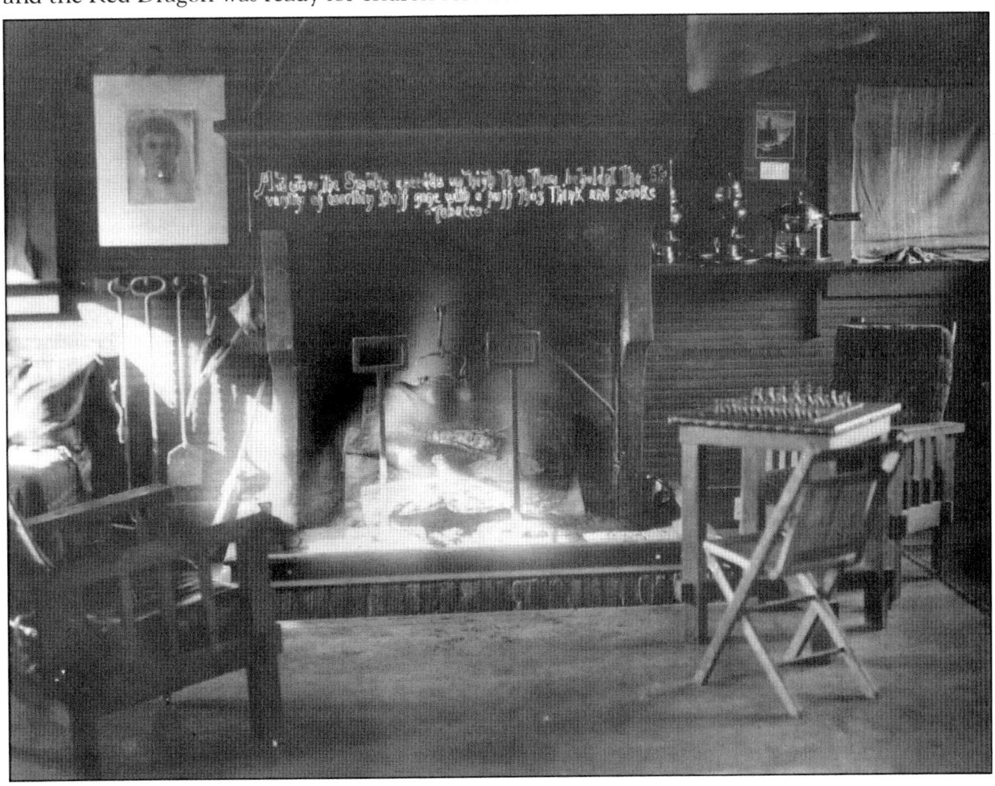

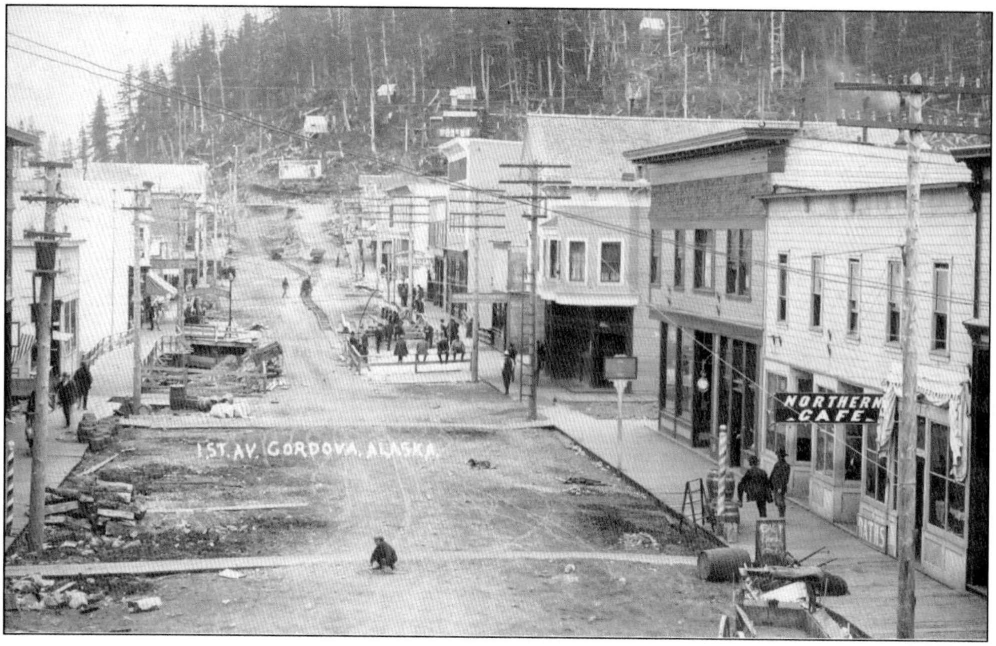

Mike Heney chose the name *Cordova* for the new townsite after learning of Spanish explorer Salvador Fidalgo's naming of Cordoba Bay. The incorporation of the city took place on July 8, 1909, and during that same month, the first section of the Copper River & Northwest Railway opened to traffic. Mike Heney was not an individual to let moss grow under his feet; he had immediately begun construction of the railroad.

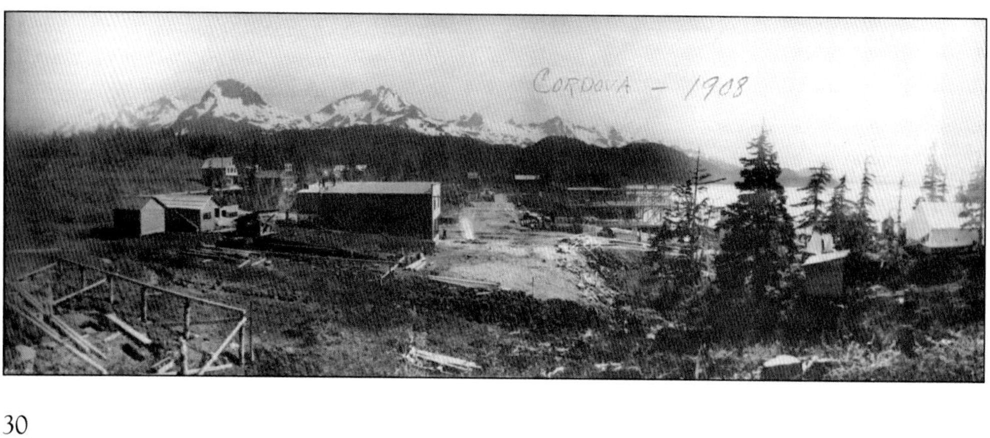

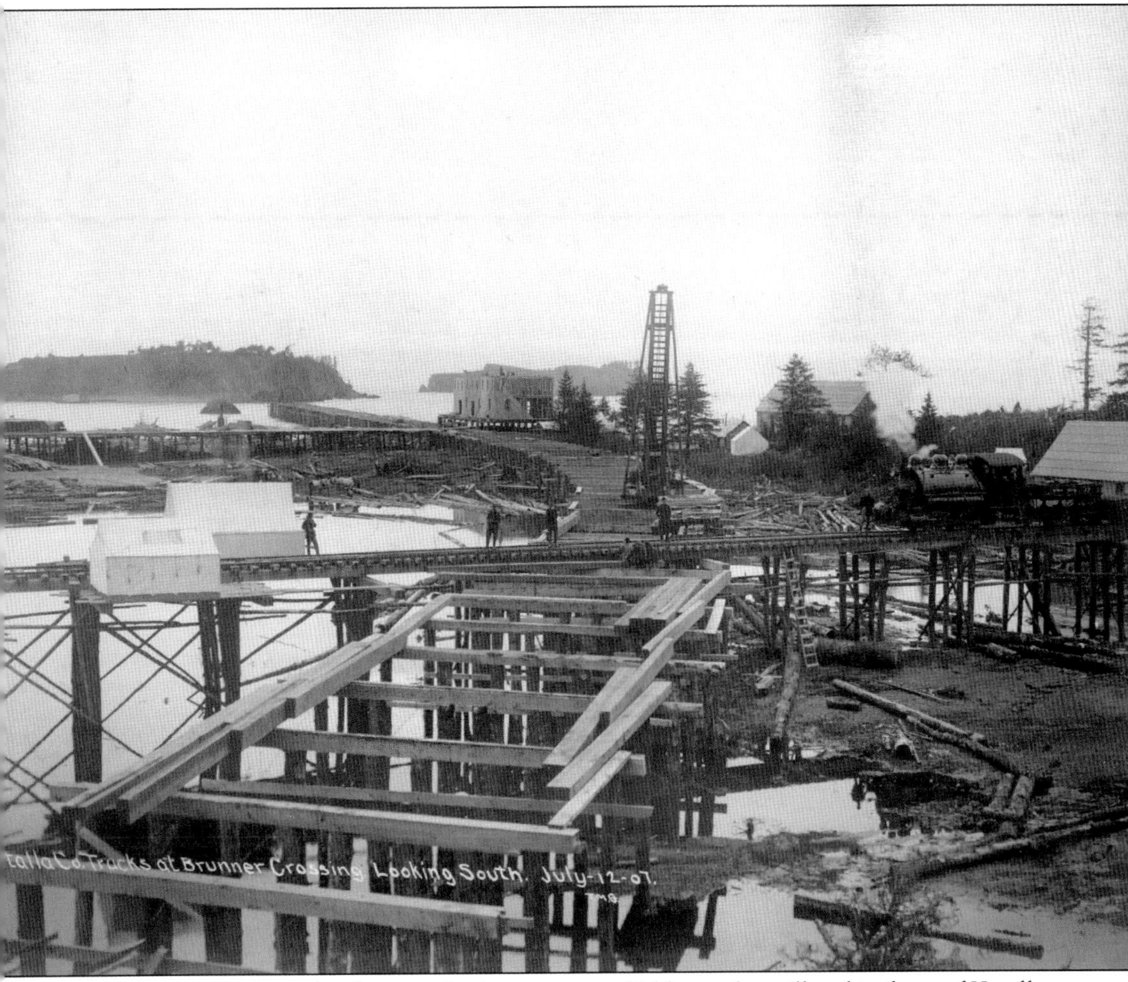

The Alaskan Syndicate by this time had given up on Valdez as the railhead in favor of Katalla, which was closer to the Bering River coal. The syndicate even began rail construction prior to securing the right-of-way to the copper deposits. It did not file for access up the Copper River, believing that the Childs and Miles Glaciers were impassable. Mike Heney believed otherwise and quickly filed for right-of-way with the land office in Juneau. To use the Katalla route to access Kennecott via the Copper River, the syndicate was forced to buy Heney's right-of-way and ended up paying Heney $250,000 for the Abercrombie Canyon access. After that purchase, the syndicate resumed construction from Katalla.

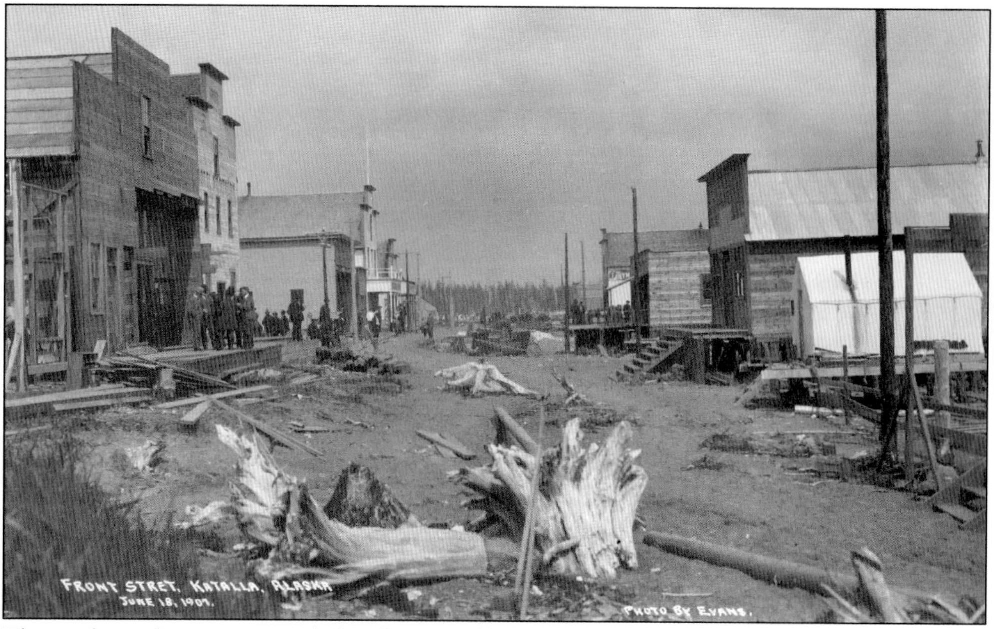

The syndicate, however, struggled with its Katalla route. Open to the Gulf of Alaska and its fierce weather, the docks and breakwaters that the crews constructed were continually breached and broken by heavy, relentless fall storms. A political storm hurt its efforts as well when, in November 1906, Pres. Theodore Roosevelt closed the Bering River coalfields from development, eliminating another source of revenue the syndicate had counted on. Finally, a huge winter storm destroyed the Katalla seawall, which doomed the site as a safe and reliable port. In early 1907, the powerful East Coast–based Alaskan Syndicate abandoned the Katalla terminus and hired Heney as general contractor for constructing the railroad.

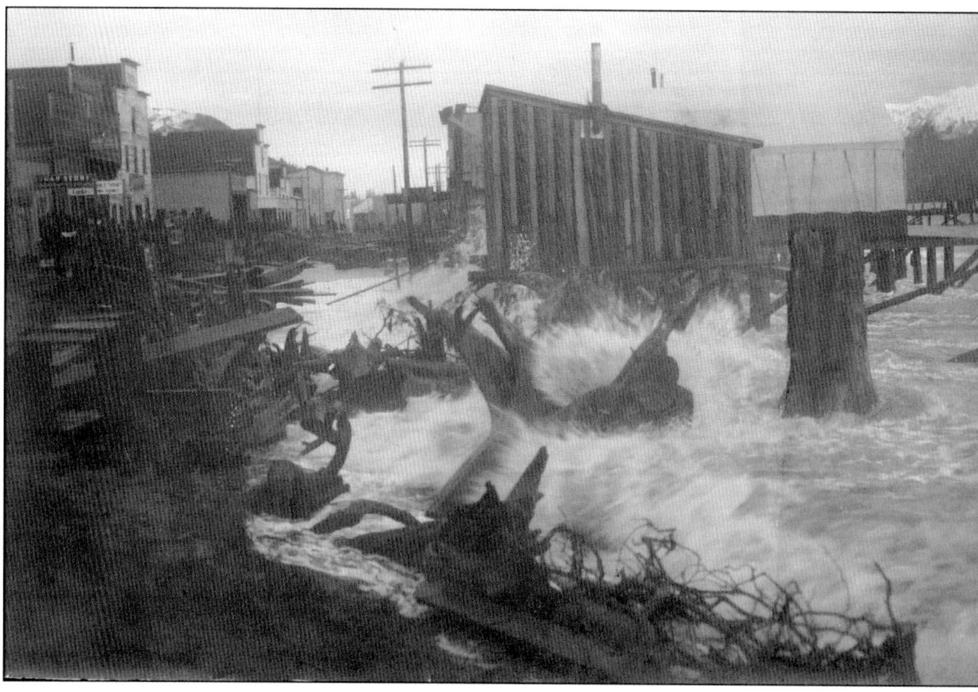

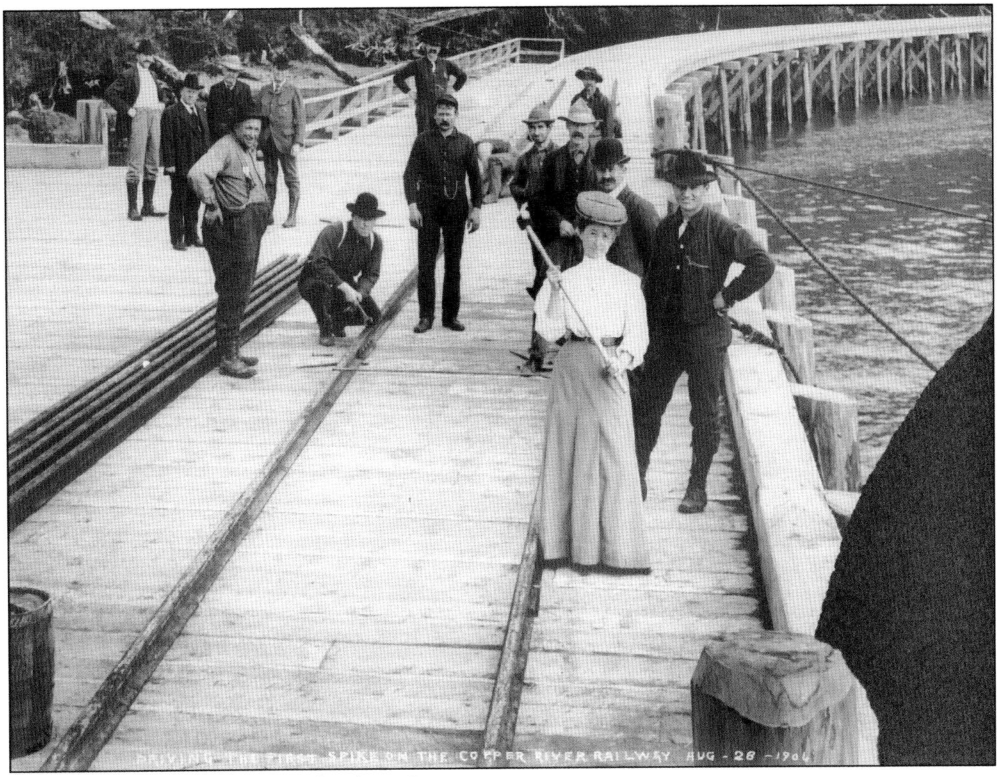

At the start of construction, the first objective was to get track to mile 49 as rapidly as possible so that materials for the Miles Glacier Bridge could be delivered by rail. Engineers began designing, specifying, and ordering materials, as logistics were challenging to say the least. Much of the steel for the bridges came from eastern states, and deliveries to the port of Cordova frequently required six months. The company's terminal at Cordova was the first component to be completed. It included a substantial pile and 700-by-80-foot wharf, located about a mile north of the newly laid-out townsite. Three service spurs ran onto the wharf from the start of the main track. The main track followed the bluff and shoreline southward to the trestles near the headquarters facility.

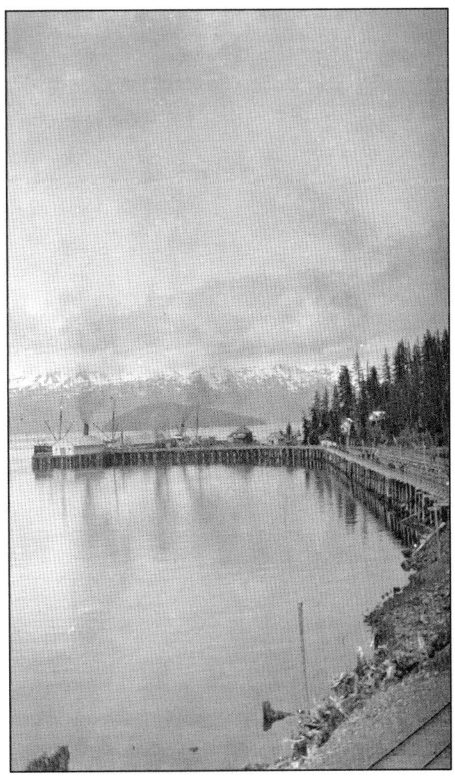

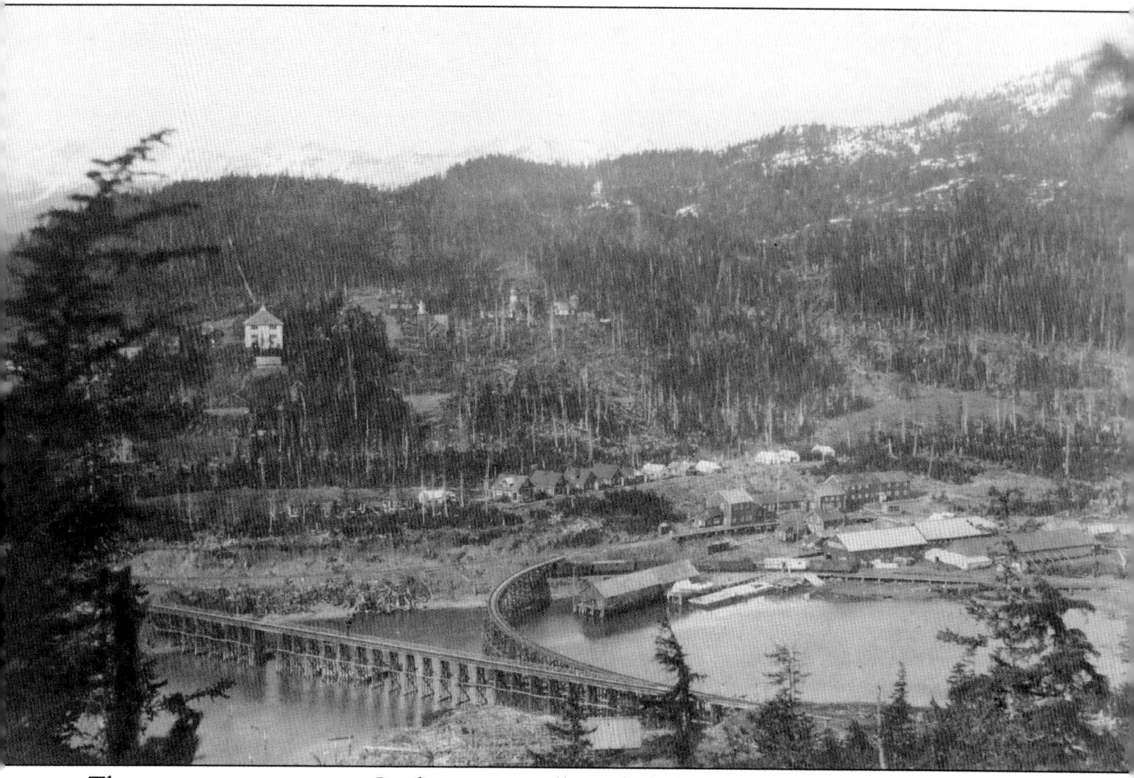

The company property in Cordova eventually included two office buildings, a hospital, two storehouses, one 11-stall roundhouse, one cinder-pit barn, one galvanized iron warehouse, and a general shop building, which included a machine shop, paint shop, car shops, and power plant. The equipment in the shops was adequate enough to service all the rolling stock used in the railroad operations, and the large wharf adjoining the shop allowed for deliveries directly from barges to railroad cars. The company also provided housing by building a number of cabins along a street that became known as Railroad Row. These cabins were used by the superintendents and were all connected by a series of boardwalks to help avoid the muddy streets. The unmarried workmen were housed in large bunkhouses near the old cannery/headquarters site. Heney established a hospital in the old cannery buildings to serve the railroad crews.

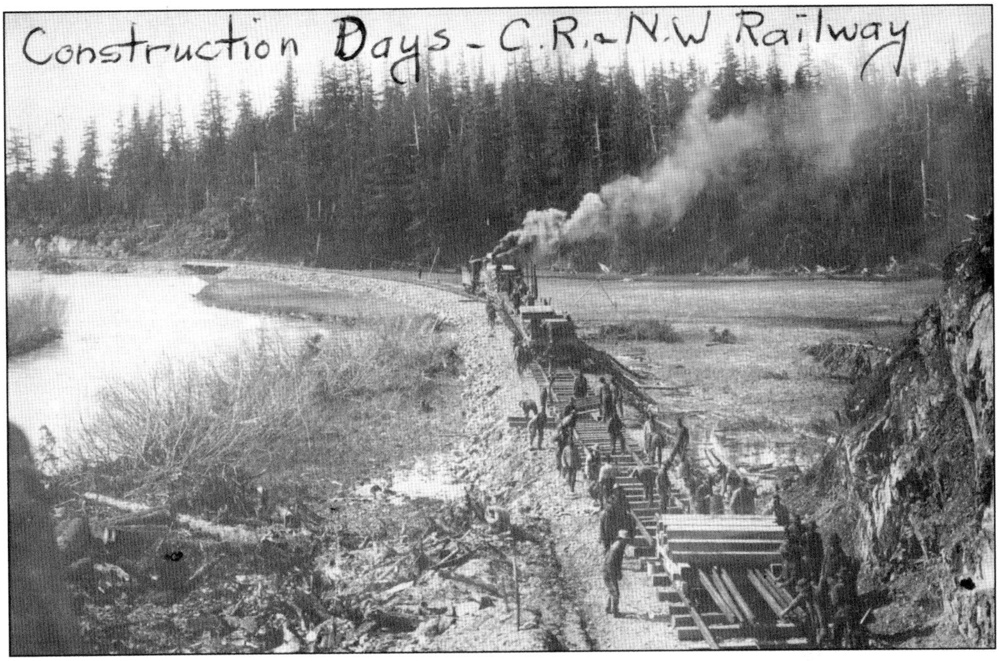

For the first 20 miles, the route followed old Eyak trails from the lake to Alaganik. Plenty of gravel was available from all the outwash in the glacial streams, and the route was fairly flat so construction was relatively easy, and the crews made good progress. The first 49 miles of the line, which crossed over the delta of the Copper River, contained more than 100 wooden trestles, some of considerable length. The longest was the Gilahina trestle that was wooden and 880 feet long and 90 feet above the river. Built during 1911, it required almost a half a million board feet of lumber. When the railroad was completed in 1911, with a distance of 196 miles, about 15 percent of the track was on bridges or trestles.

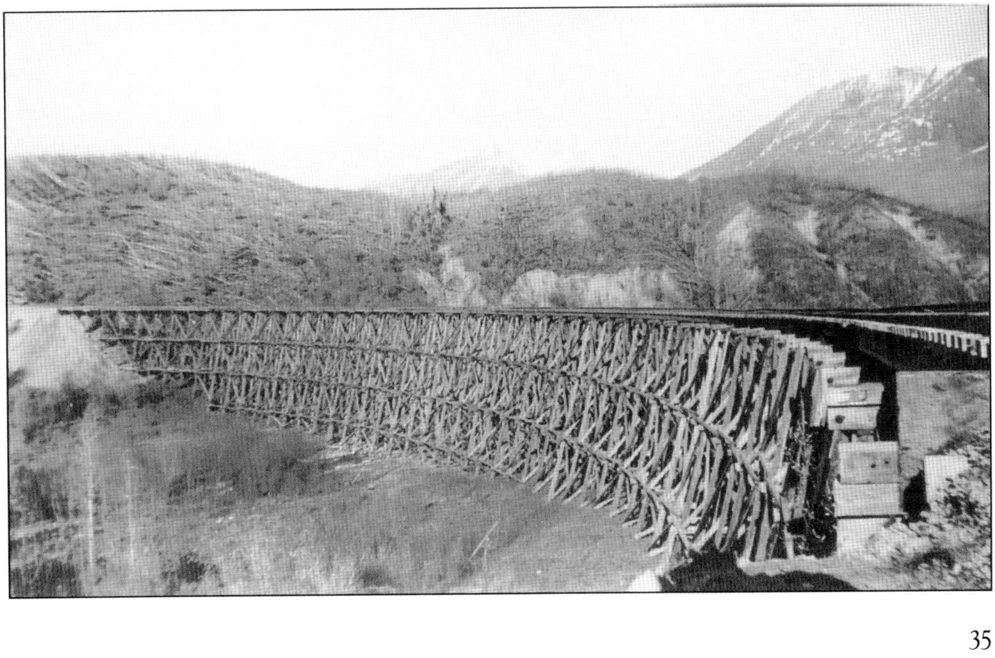

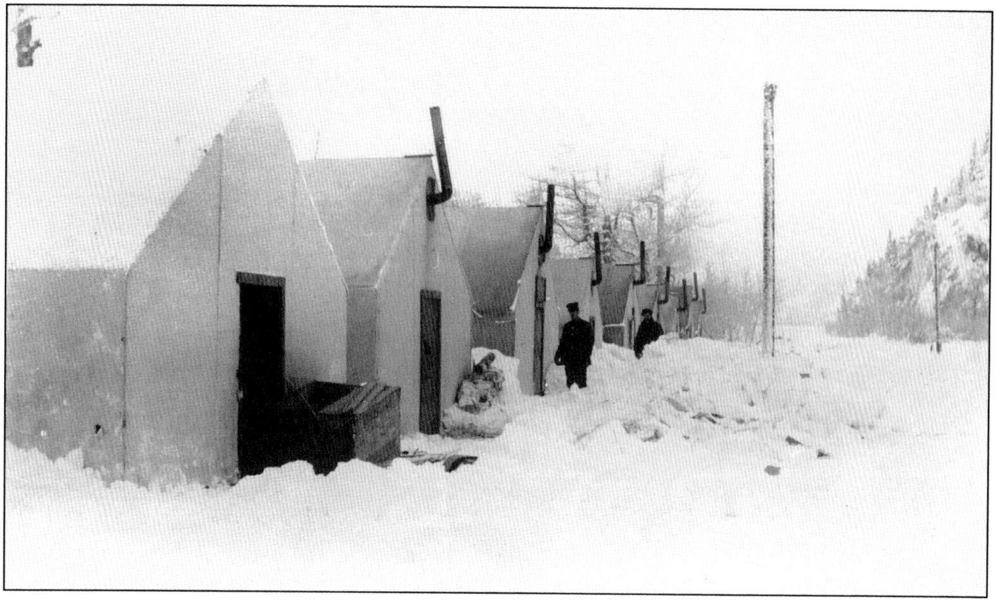

Camps were set up along the route and moved once a section was complete. Rex Beach, a popular author of Alaskan stories, was lured by his desire to visit his old friend Mike Heney and dropped in on Heney's headquarters, staying for a summer of fishing and hunting. Beach was intrigued by the drama being portrayed in the building of the railroad. During this time, he collected a vast amount of information about the railroad, the workers, and the Copper River. He made numerous visits to the Million Dollar Bridge during its construction. Beach's book *The Iron Trail* became a classic tale about the building of a railroad, which he called the Salmon River & Northwestern. His friend Mike Heney took on the pseudonym of Murray O'Neil in the book. First published in 1912, it has been reprinted many times. (Both, courtesy of Geoff Bleakly.)

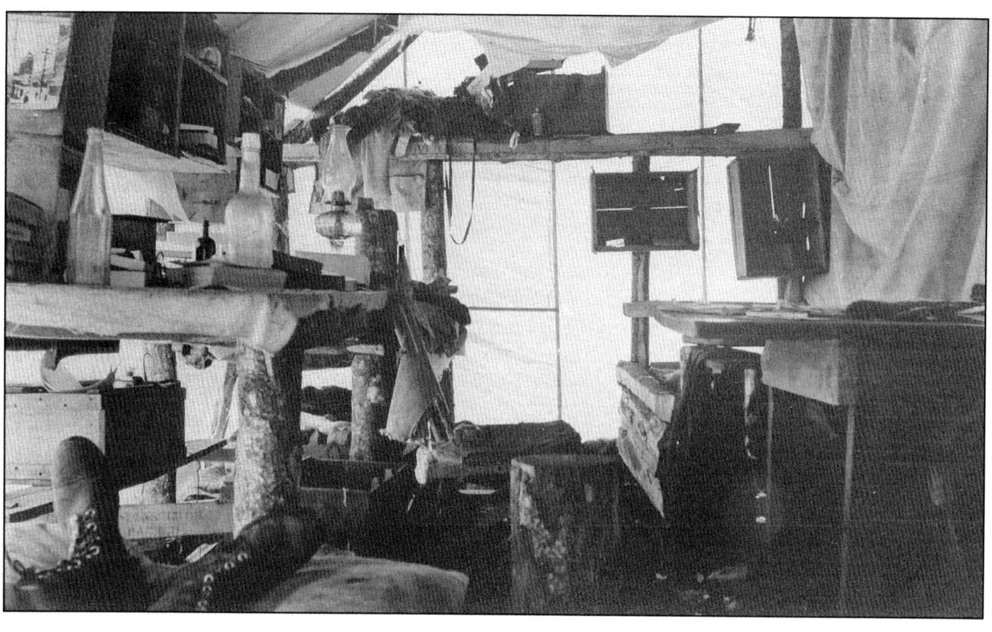

The bridge at mile 27 was the first crossing of the Copper River and required nine steel spans supported on concrete piers. Wherever possible, engineers used existing sandbars to save construction time and money; five major steel bridges had to be built, requiring more than 20,000,000 pounds of steel. Ice was a hazard, and the bridges and piers were protected with armored icebreakers consisting of old rails anchored into the concrete.

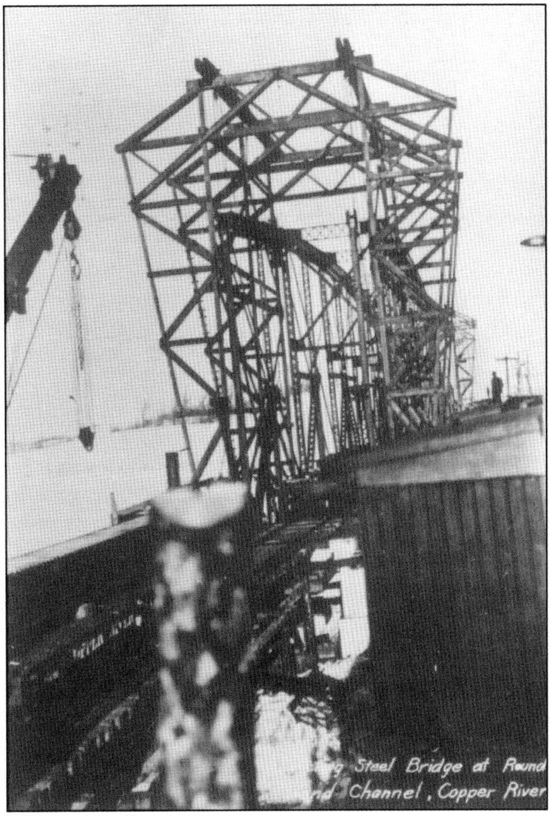

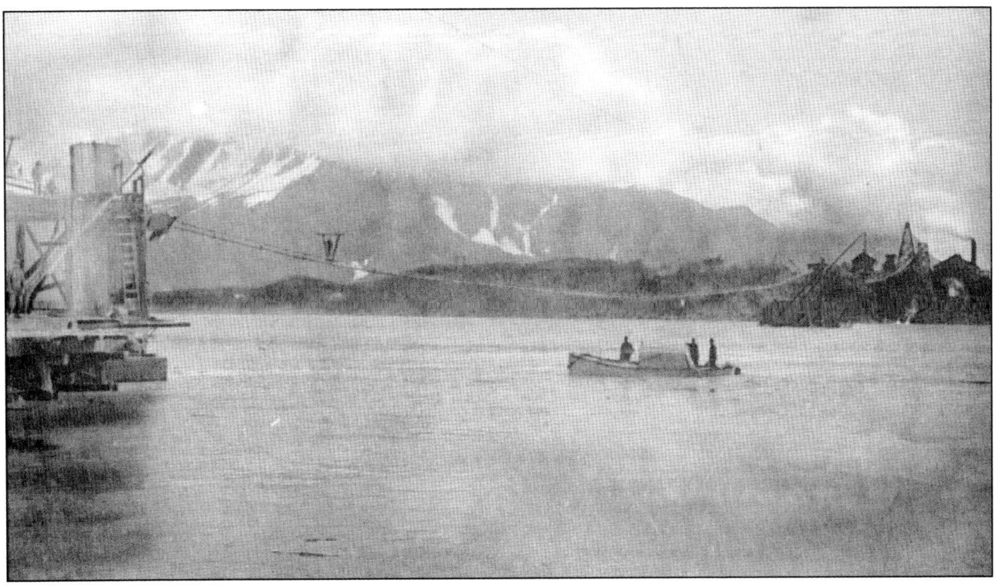

The bridge at mile 49, the Miles Glacier Bridge, was key to completion of the route. The channel was 1,500 feet wide between Childs and Miles Glaciers. Engineers chose an S curve between the two glaciers for the crossing and designed it to withstand the bombardment of icebergs and the onslaught of river ice breaking up. The glaciers were named by Lt. William Abercrombie after Washington Childs and Gen. Nelson Miles.

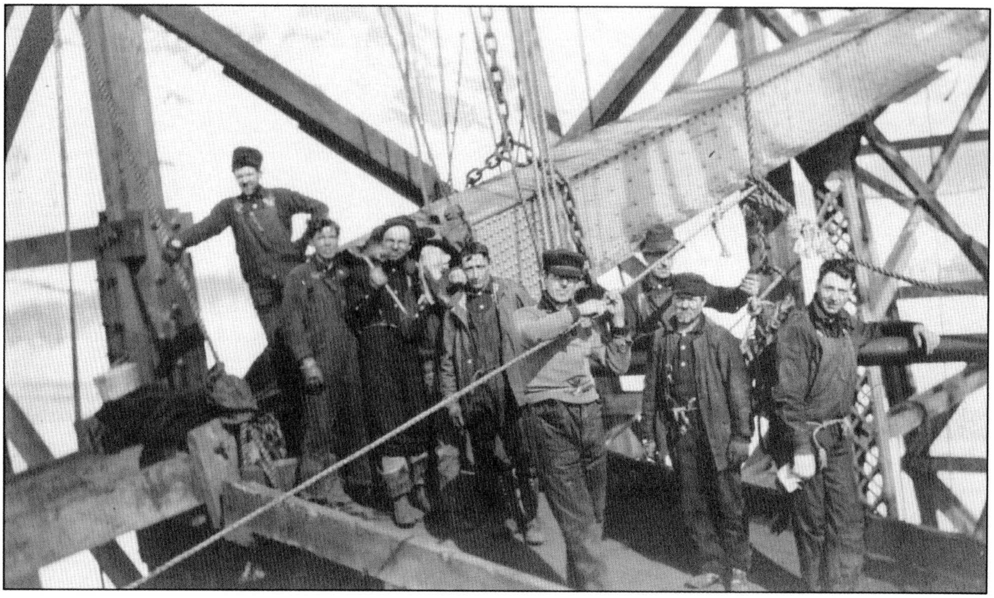

A full-scale camp housed the many workmen; a powerhouse was built to supply compressed air for the caisson construction and to power the machinery. Water for the six boilers had to be filtered because of the quantities of silt in the Copper River and because of the extreme cold weather; water heaters were installed to insure continuous operations. Rock-crusher and concrete-mixing plants were built. A barge was operated in Miles Lake during the summer to transport equipment and materials. Each day, huge shipments of rails, steel, equipment, and supplies were received at the Cordova docks. In spite of the tremendous number of parts and equipment that was required, relatively few delays were experienced. When necessary, the machine shop in Cordova made parts and fittings to maintain a continuous flow "up the line" for the construction crews.

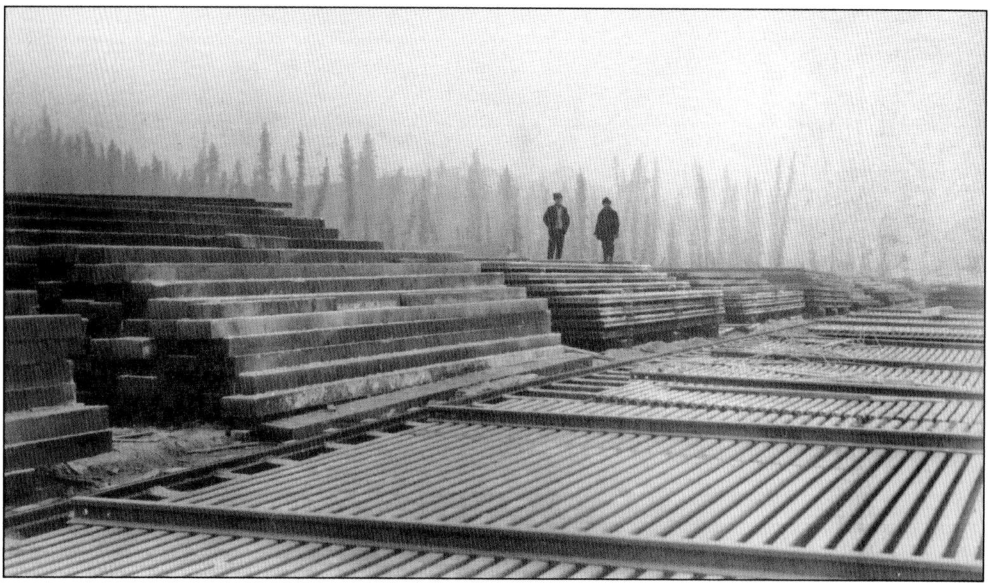

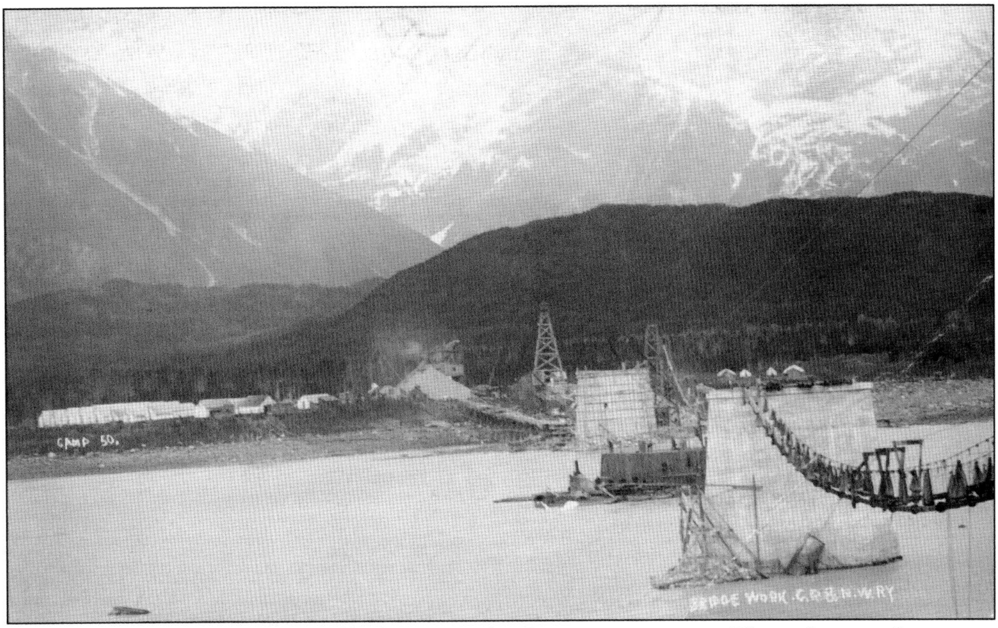

Miles Glacier Bridge was the world's first example of arctic engineering. The techniques for setting the foundations and steelwork for the bridge became standards for future arctic construction. Work started March 1909, and E.C. Hawkins, engineer for the CR&NW, kept it on schedule constantly reviewing the design for the tracks and structures. The piers and abutments were completed late in 1909; steel for the spans arrived in March 1910. Work continued throughout a snowy, wet April and May, with the men working round the clock to beat the rapidly breaking river ice. They literally finished with minutes to spare. By June 1910, the hardworking crews had completed the fourth and final span of this engineering feat. The bridge was in full service, transporting supplies farther north by July 1910. Now known as the Million Dollar Bridge, it actually cost $1,424,774.

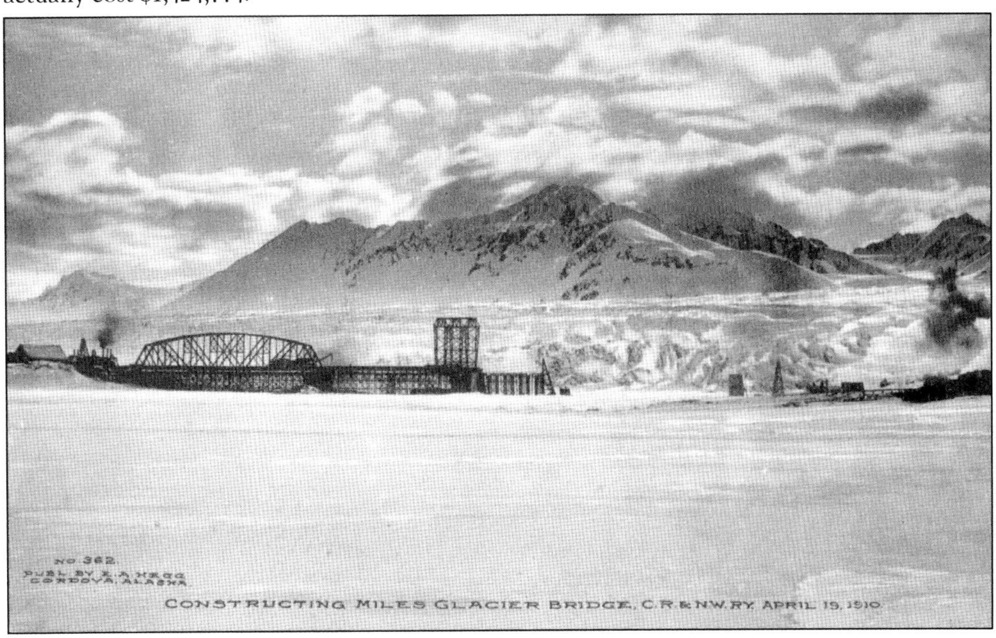

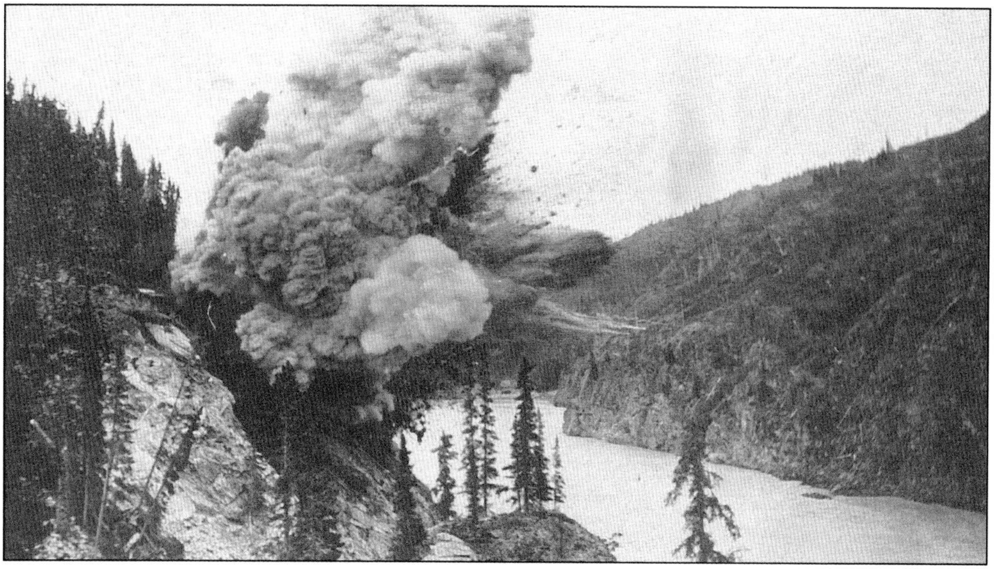

Blasting was common along the construction route, and a total of $375,000 was spent on explosives. Between miles 86 and 101, construction involved cliff work and one 400-foot tunnel with considerable curves. Strong winds, heavy snowslides, and rockslides often led to blocked tracks; operations were suspended until the section crews could dynamite and clear the tracks. Some of the most difficult work took place in Woods Canyon. (Courtesy of Geoff Bleakly.)

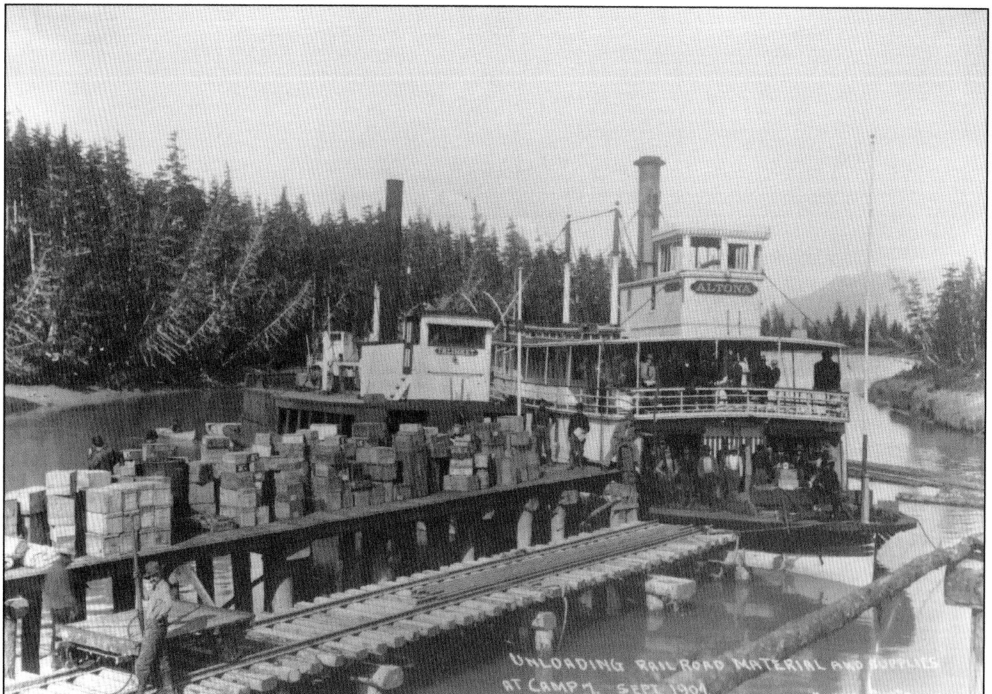

Steamboats plied the river busily during the summer of 1910, hauling great quantities of supplies and equipment, particularly bridge materials for the Kuskulana. The steamboats also brought up lumber and hardware to build the town of Chitina, originally designed as a railroad junction for the planned route to Fairbanks, which was never built, and a spur eastward to the copper mines.

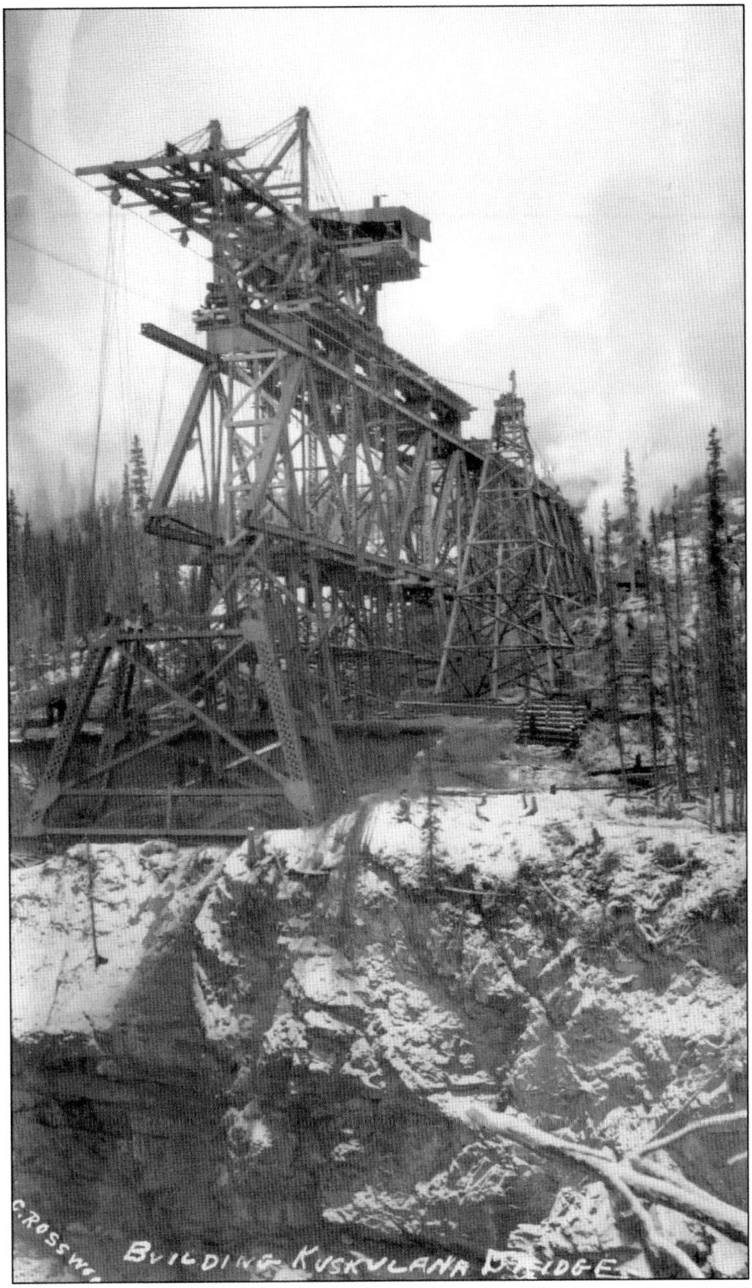

Work on the Kuskulana River Bridge, which spanned a gorge 190 feet wide and 175 feet deep at mile 144, began in October 1910. An assembly yard was established at the Miles Glacier Bridge, and components were moved by rail to Tiekel at mile 101. From there, materials were hauled overland on a rough wagon road or by sled on the river before the ice went out. Conditions were even worse at this bridge site where interior temperatures were far lower in winter (in 1910–1911, 67 degrees below zero) and higher in summer (96 degrees), with only about three hours of daylight during December. Steelwork erection was carried on simultaneously from each side. The ends of the cantilevered bridge were joined on January 1, 1911, with work not stopping during the cold, dark winter months. This bridge was converted to highway and was in use until 1987.

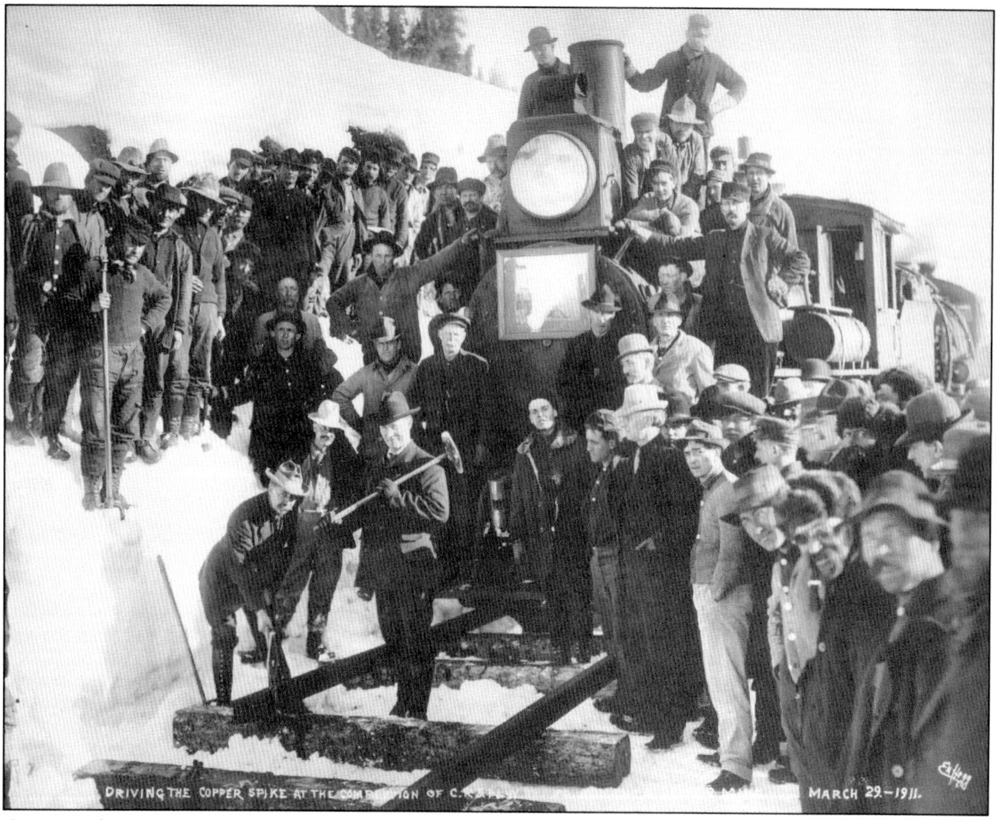

On March 29, 1911, a copper spike was driven to mark the completion of the 196-mile railroad; Michael Heney, the man behind it, never lived to see the final spike in place. Simultaneously, Stephen Birch and a crew were engaged in building a concentrator mill; a 15,000-foot aerial tramway to transport ore to the railroad; and ore bunkers, chutes, snowsheds, bunkhouses, shops, and a waterway system fed by a newly constructed dam. The six-story concentrator mill building was constructed using 200,000 board feet of lumber; it was and still is the dominant structure in Kennicott. Ore was concentrated into usable minerals (copper and silver) through a series of mechanical processes and dropped by gravity through the levels of the mill to the plant where the high-grade ore was placed in bags for shipment by rail to Cordova.

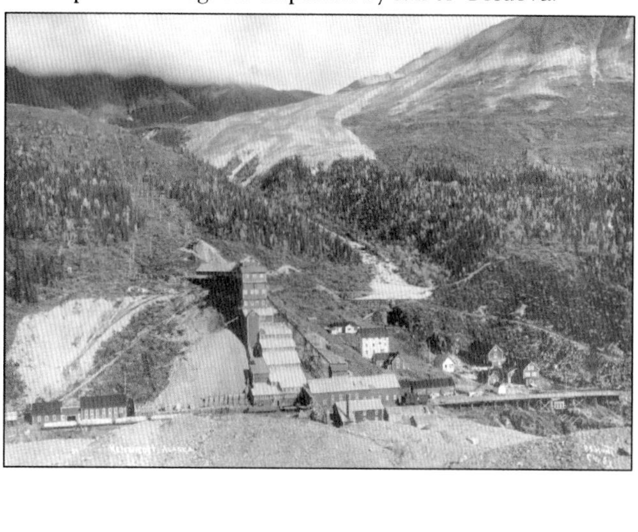

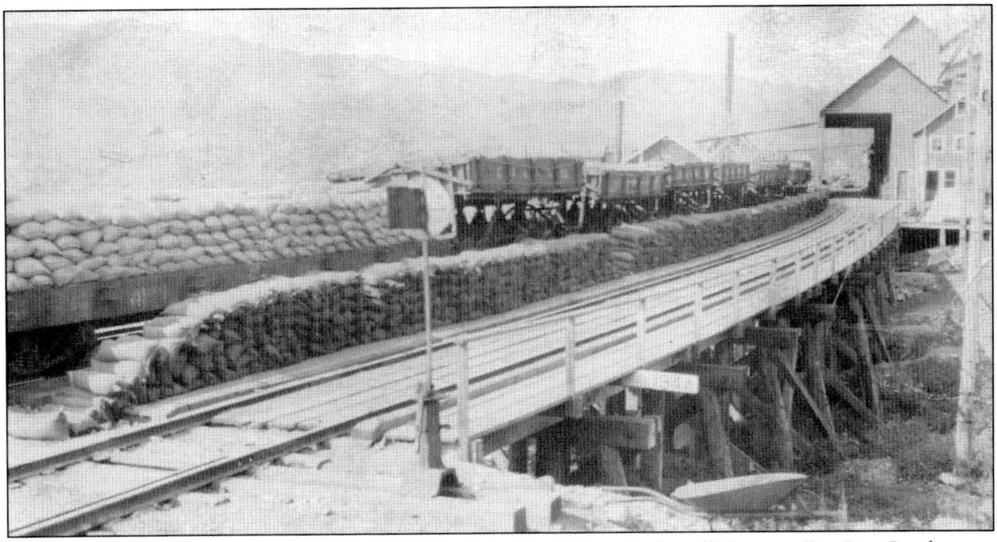

The first trainload of ore reached Cordova on April 8, 1911— declared "Copper Day" in Cordova— with 1,200 tons of high-grade copper ore with an estimated value of a quarter of a million dollars. A special train was sent to escort the ore train to the dock where the steamer *Northwestern* awaited the shipment. A reduced rate was given to the residents of Chitina to come to Cordova, and special excursions fares were made by the steamship companies to bring residents from neighboring towns to join the celebration. Five big steamships were in port, and all of Cordova turned out for the event. The Eagles Band played, church bells rang, and horns and engine whistles blared as the ore train approached town.

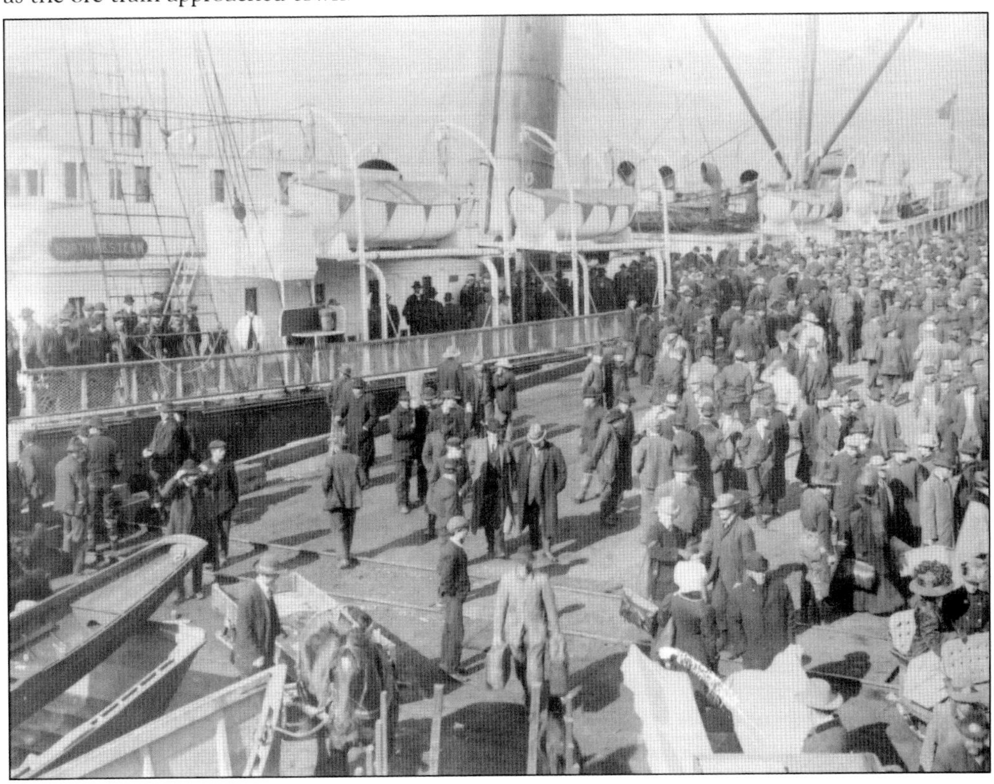

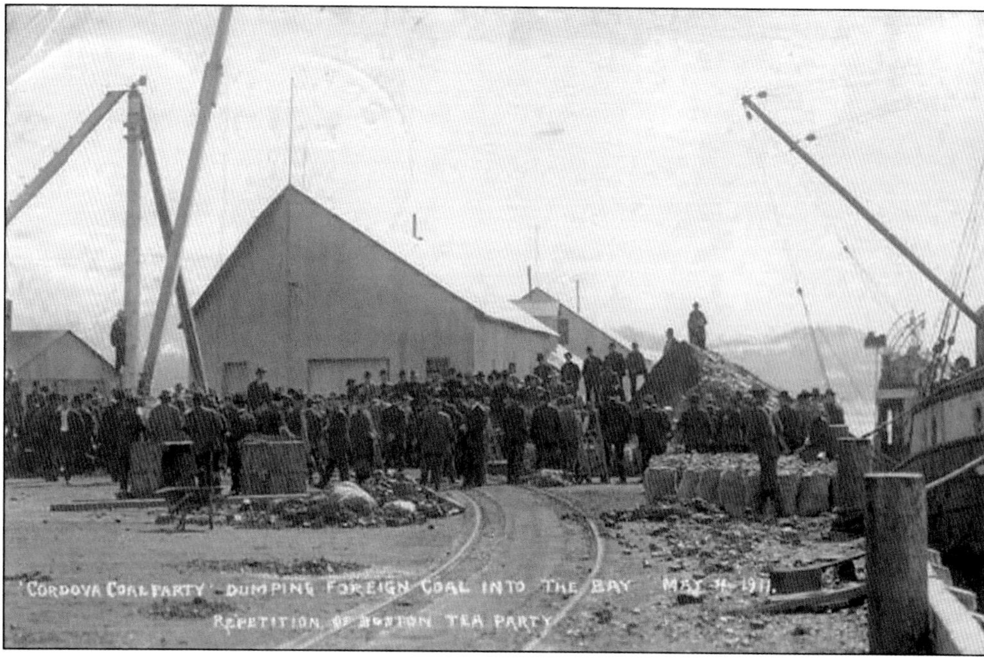

The success of moving copper ore to Cordova led residents to make sure politicians back east realized that they were still interested in accessing the coalfields in the Bering River region. The *Cordova Daily Alaskan* editorially reported that "the businessman, resident or prospector is refused the coal that should be his for $5 per ton, and is compelled to pay from $15 to $20 for the fuel that must be transported from British Columbia." On May 3, 1911, unhappy Cordovans staged a "Cordova Coal Party," fashioned after the famous Boston Tea Party. Chanting, "Give us Alaskan Coal," an organized group of citizens attacked a steamship loaded with Canadian coal and shoveled it directly from the ship into the harbor. It would not be the last time Cordovans were politically vociferous. (Above, courtesy Alaska State Library.)

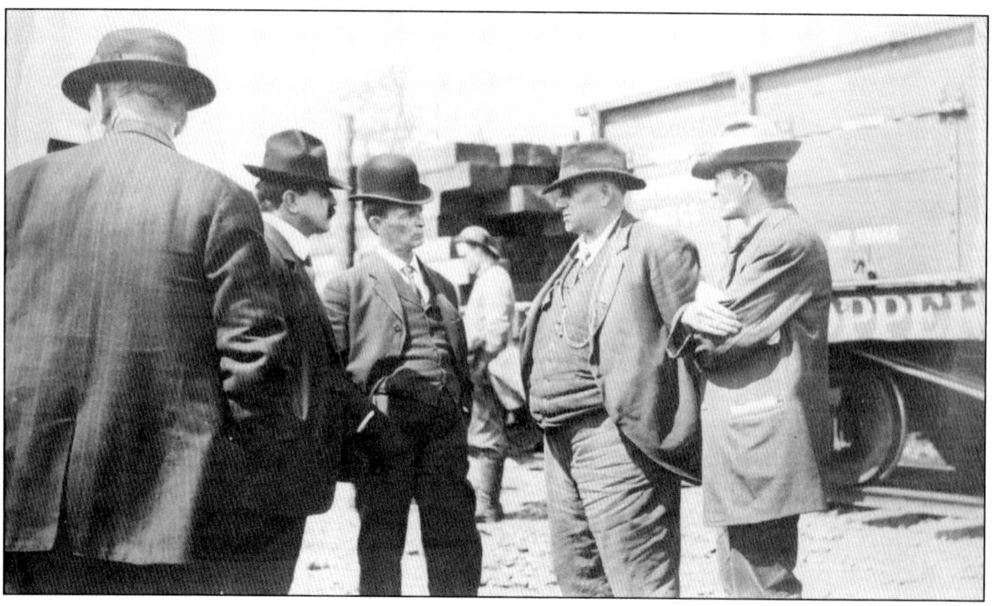

Three

The Boom Years 1915–1940

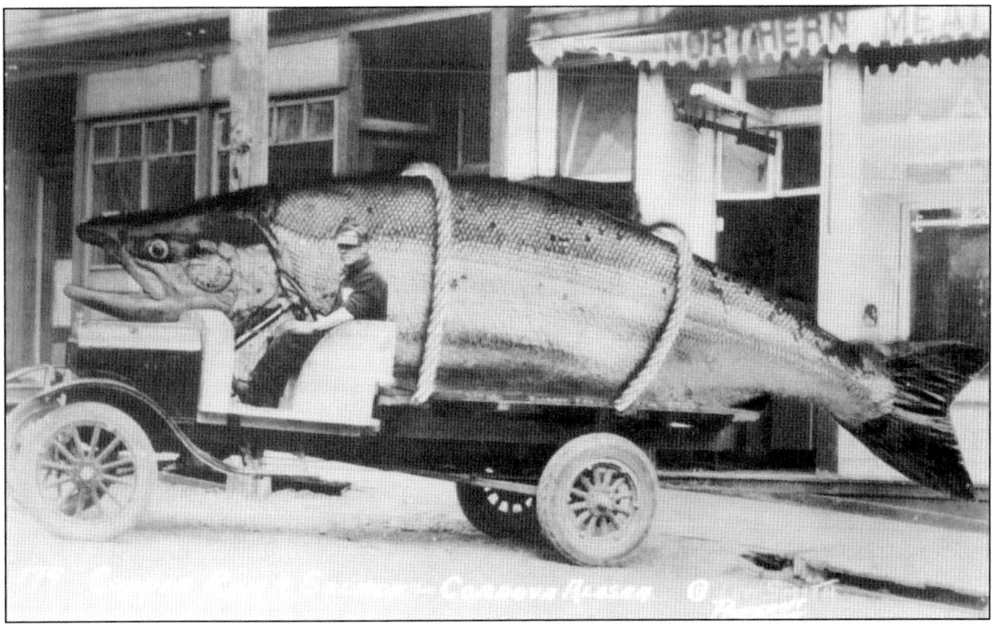

After the ceremony in Kennicott and the arrival of $250,000 worth of copper ore at the port, the founders were certain Cordova was destined to be the important seaport in the territory. Fishing was booming; mining was booming; steamships arrived every week with folks anxious to make their fortune in this "copper gateway." As more people arrived, more ships plied the waters, and more need for safety and communication began to arise.

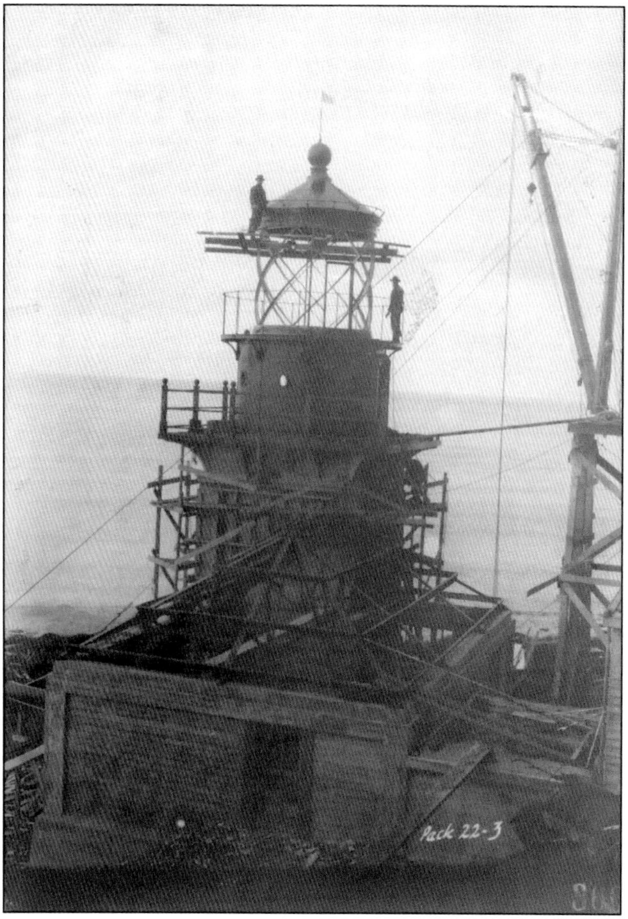

The rush to Alaska for gold, copper, coal, and salmon led to increased ship traffic and accidents at sea. In 1910, Congress authorized Alaska as a lighthouse district. On the list of lights were Cape Hinchinbrook and Cape St. Elias (left). Construction of the Cape St. Elias light began in the spring of 1915 on what is regarded as the most dangerous point along the Pacific Coast. St. Elias was a third-order double-flash group two Fresnel lens. It was manned by the US Coast Guard, and a one-year tour of duty at the Alaskan lighthouses was a challenge. "A year, day by day, is a terribly long time," remarked one Coast Guard keeper, "especially at age 19." Lit in September 1916 and maintained by the US Coast Guard cutters *Haida* (below) and *Sedge*, the light was decommissioned in 1974.

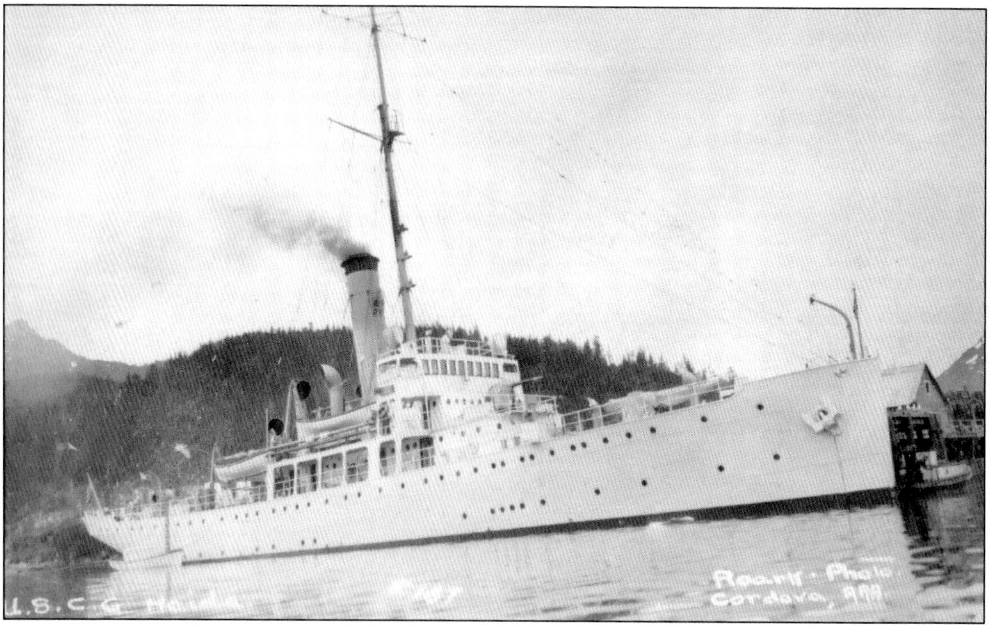

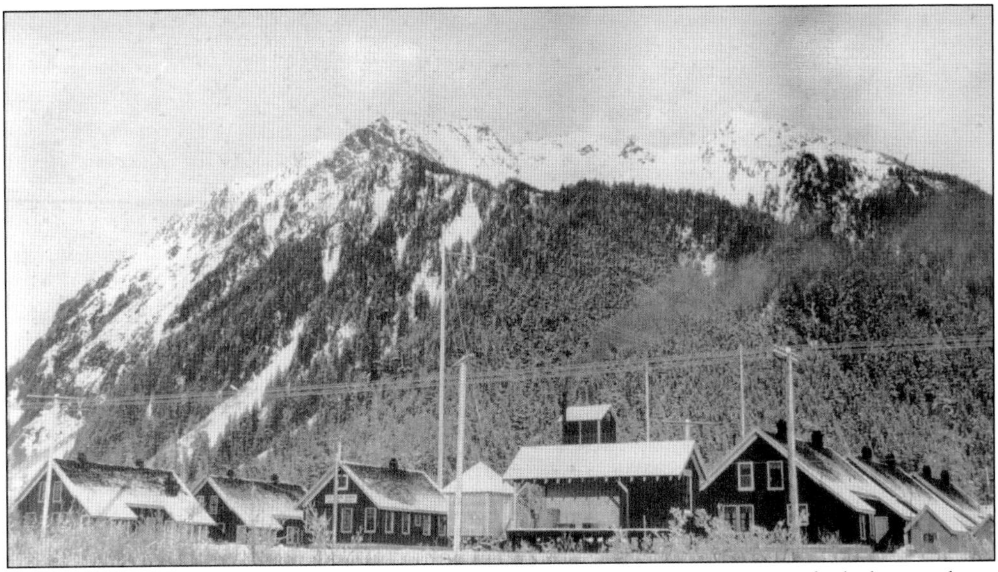

Communication technology was advancing and critical to the development of Alaska, resulting in another huge influx of population. Pres. Theodore Roosevelt decreed all governmental radio messages would be the responsibility of the US Navy. The Navy was also permitted to receive and transmit messages from ship to shore. The Navy established a radio station at Point Whitshed, nine miles from Cordova, and stations at miles 7 (above) and 14.

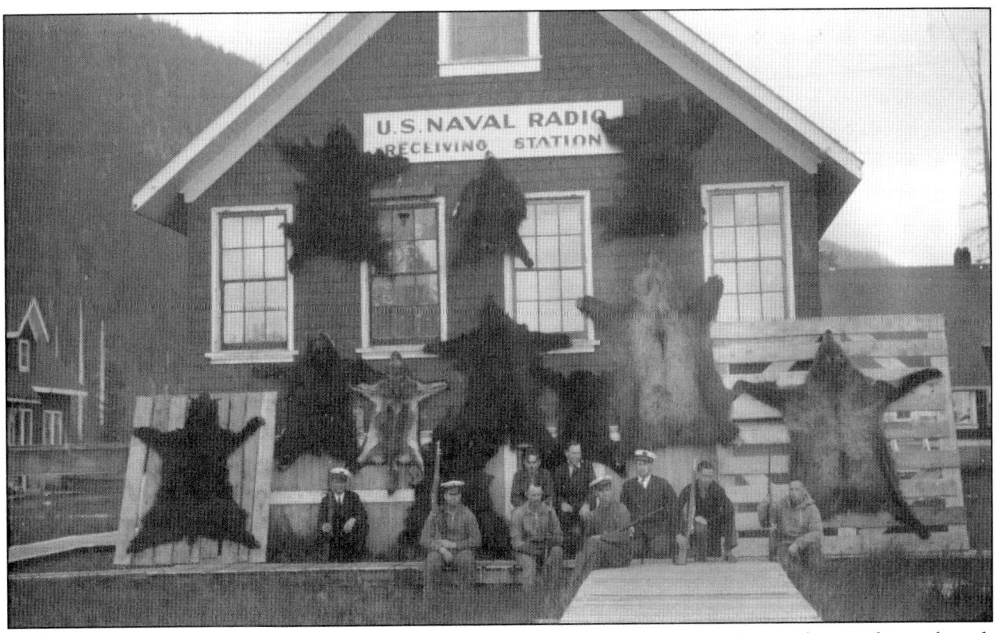

No roads went into these areas, so all freight to the stations had to be shipped over the railroad. The mile 7 structures were located near streams from the nearby glaciers. It became a rather large site, and during its active life, the number of personnel at the station averaged about 20, with never less than a cadre of two officers and 10 other ranks.

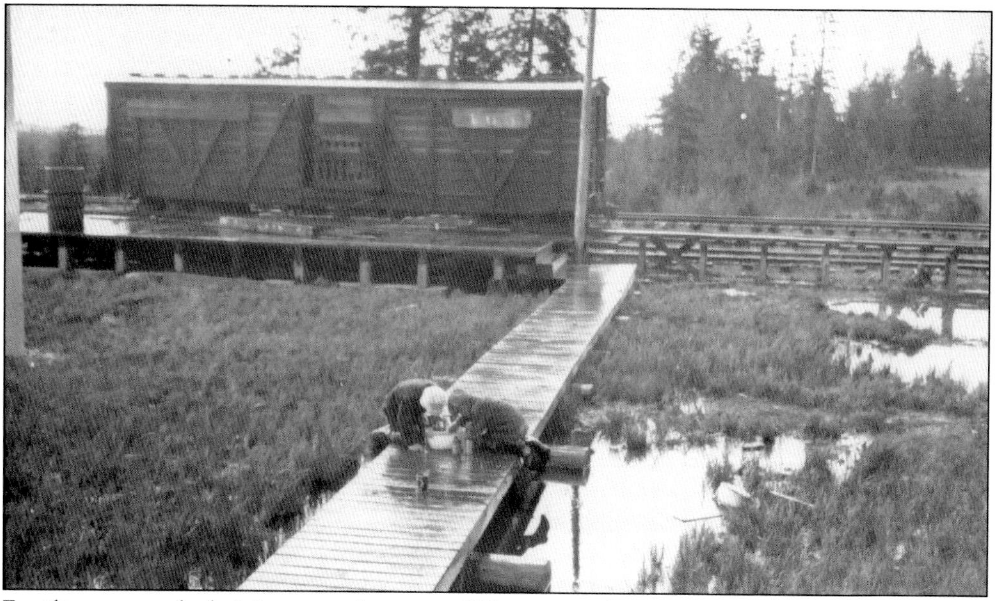

Families, too, made their homes at the station. When it was first commissioned, it had five wooden 1.5-story double cottages with a total of 10 rooms. These buildings were used to house personnel and had a capacity of two families each. Another cottage housed the officer in charge. The terrain was glacial moraine, swampy and impossible to traverse on foot.

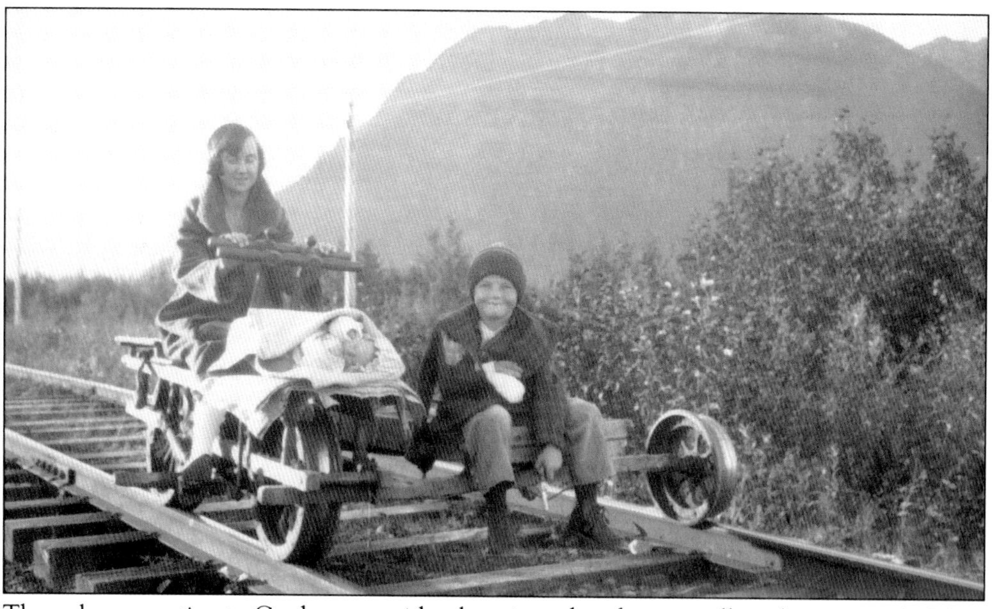

The only connection to Cordova was either by using a handcar or walking between rails. Mary Ferree Garwood (the infant shown above) grew up there along with her brother John. The railroad charged the Navy a per-trip fee for the use of its rails. In 1933, a decision to place the Eyak Station in inactive status marked the beginning of the end for the mile 7 station; in 1938, it was decommissioned.

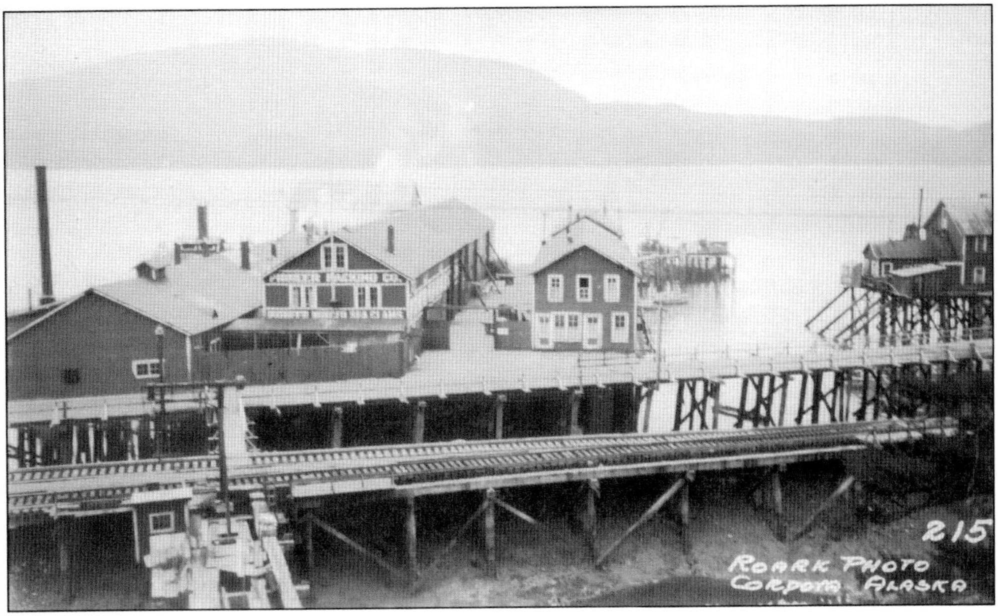

The fishing boom in Cordova did not revolve just around salmon. Clamming began in the mid-1910s with the opening of the Lighthouse Canning and Packing Co., which was quickly followed by G.P. Halferty, who completed a two-line cannery in 1916. Together these plants heralded the commencement of the Alaska razor clam industry. In 1916, 35 diggers dug nearly half a million pounds of clams, and in the following year, which was the peak for the industry, 135 diggers unburied three and a half million pounds of razor clams. The heavy exploitation of Cordova's beaches led to the nickname of "Razor Clam Capital of the World" and the distinction of generating over half the clam pack produced for the entire United States.

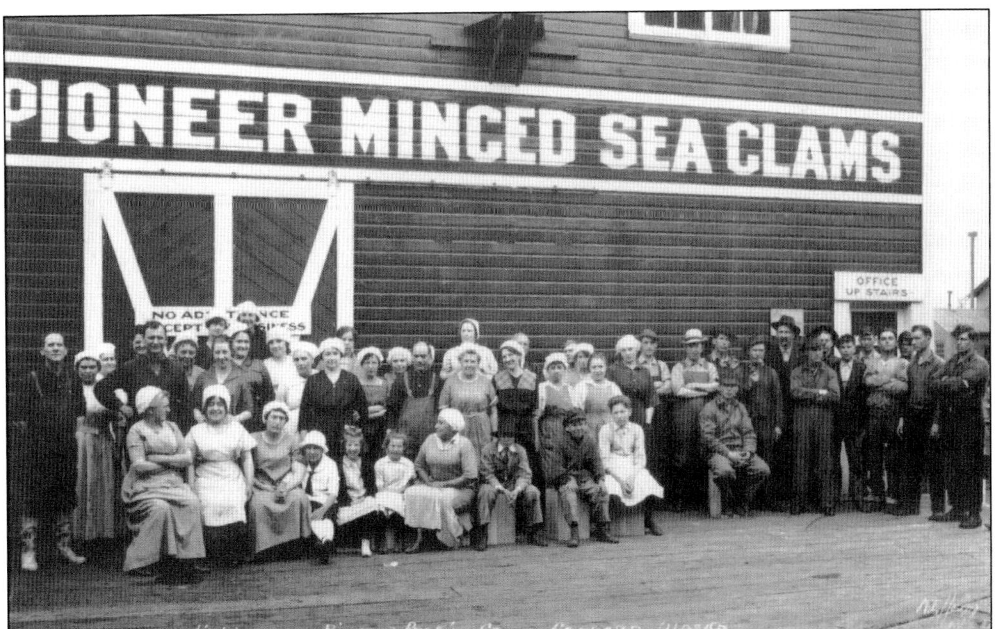

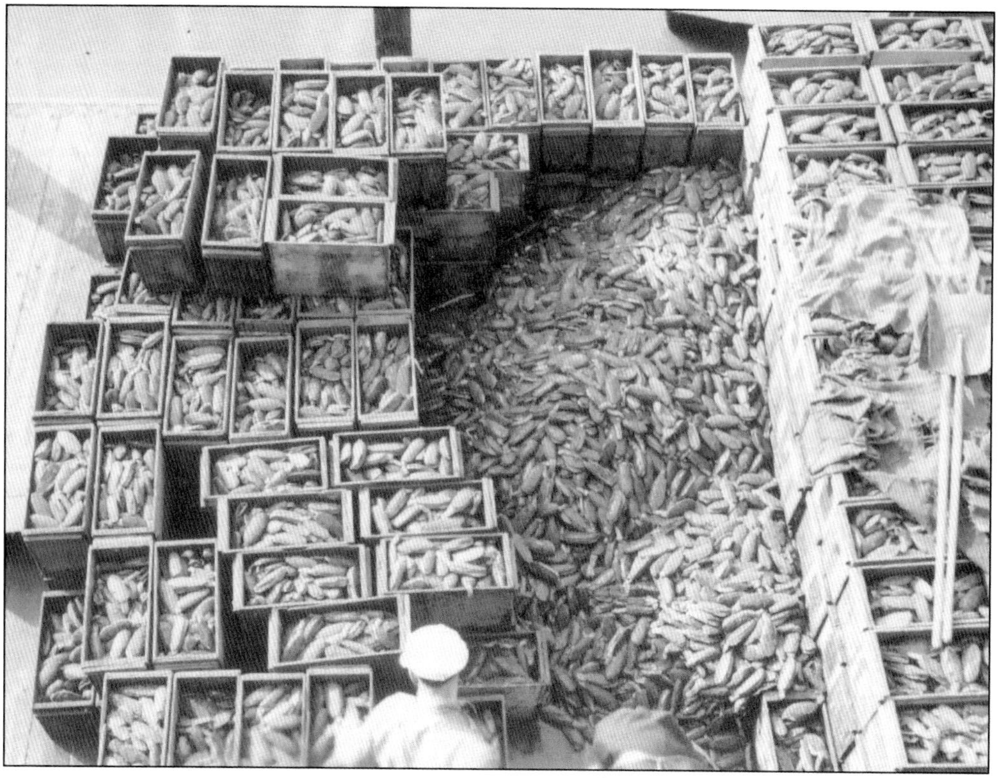

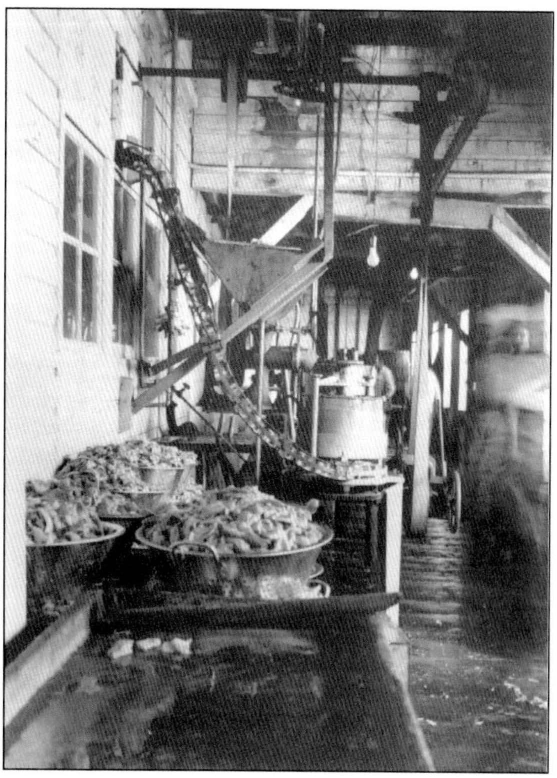

The steady work to keep the "clam capital" title took its toll on the habitat and production rate for Cordova clam canneries. Quotas placed by fishery regulations were barely met, and a scientific investigation of the condition of the razor clam fishery showed a depletion of stocks. That factor and competition from Atlantic-canned clams nearly suspended activities in Alaska. The 1964 earthquake and the reintroduction of sea otters in the Prince William Sound area ended large-scale commercial production of razor clams. Today, clamming is only a memory for the children who once dug with their families to earn a living and a recreational hobby for Cordovans.

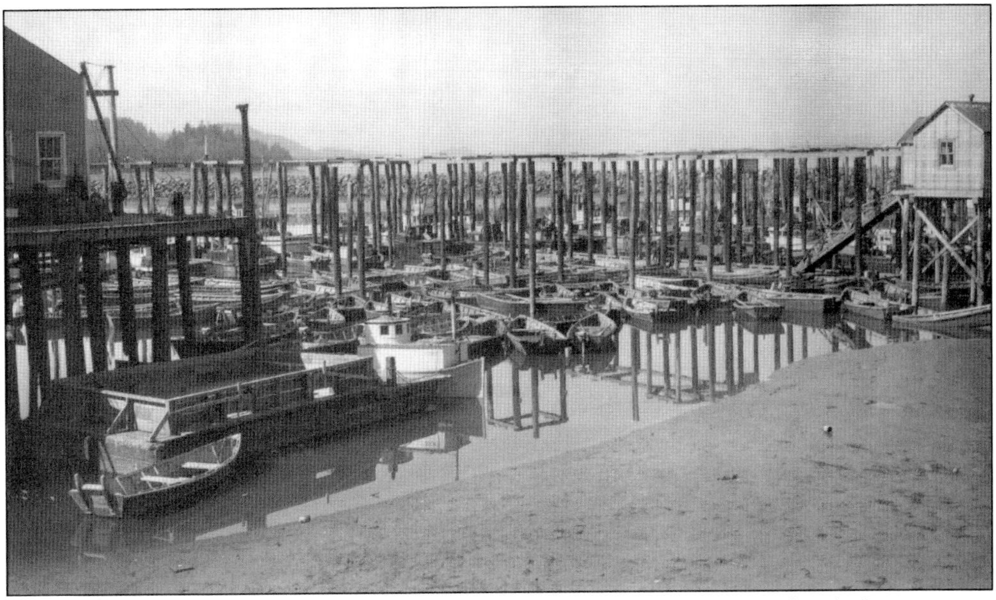

By 1920, Cordova had constructed a wharf to support small boats associated with the canneries that now lined the railroad tracks along the busy waterfront. Within another decade, the harbor was expanded for the growing fishing industry, and several breakwaters were added to provide more protection to the mostly open-skiff wooden fleet, including the locally built *Tiedeman* skiff.

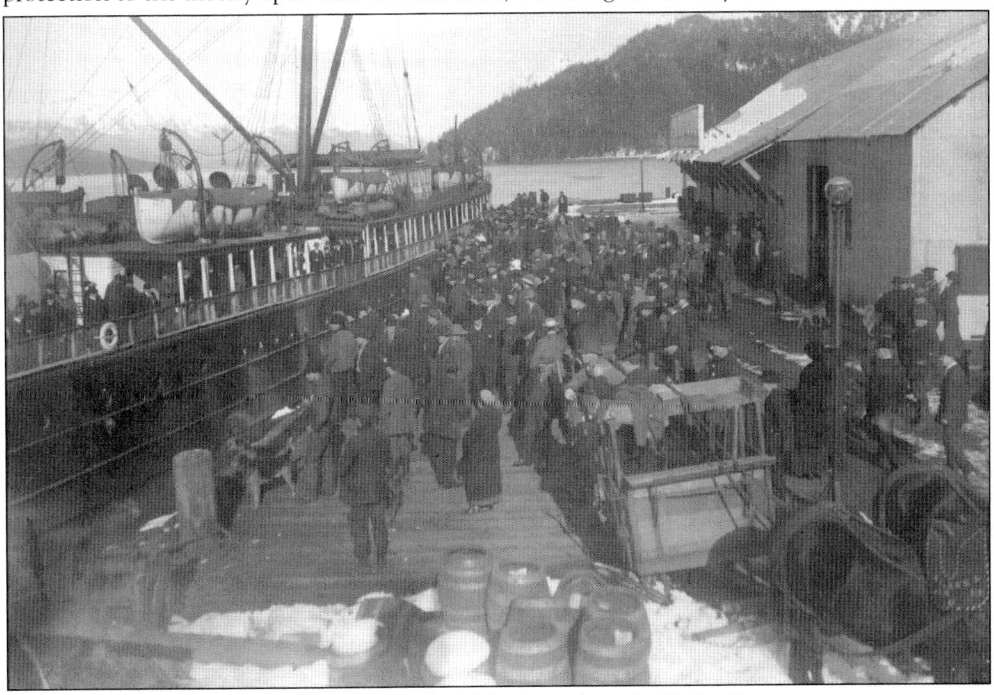

The syndicate had completed its railroad and had purchased Alaska Steam to transport ore to the smelters. Cordova's wharf was one of only two in Alaska with a capacity for larger vessels. Passenger lists dominated by brawling glory-seekers now consisted of men and women who were professional people, tourists, and others from a prosperous layer of society. The syndicate redesigned the steamships and arranged special excursions featuring a railroad trip.

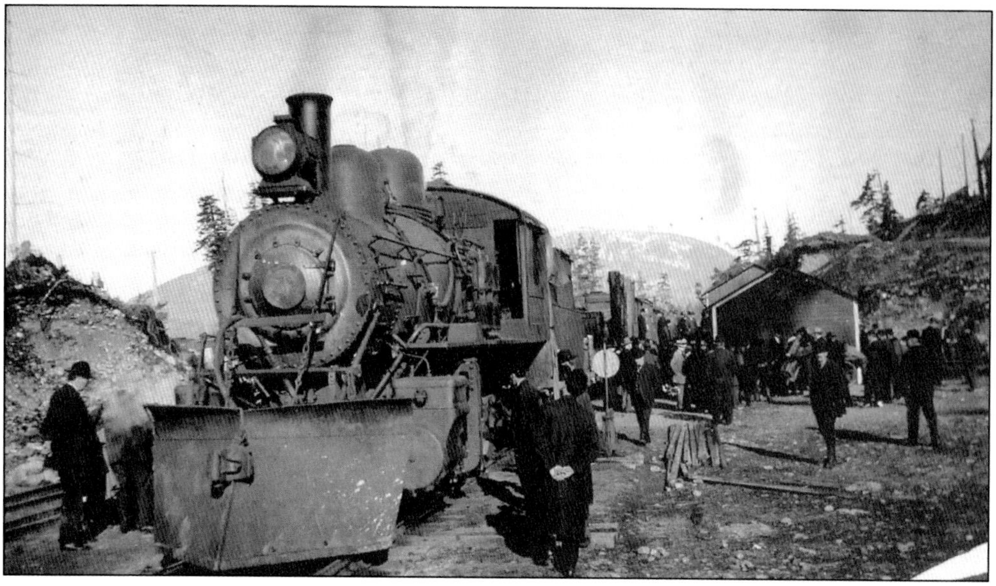

The passenger depot, located 1.5 miles from the wharf, was the start of a daily train run each way between Cordova and Chitina to provide freight and passenger service and two weekly ore trains from Kennicott to Cordova. A dining car service was acclaimed to be the best for appetizing meals and comfortable service. Workmen traveled to and from Cordova and Kennicott, and the communities shared events and friendships. Tourists that summer were treated to the awe-inspiring sight of 300-foot tower of ice looming over the train and the bridge. Excursion trains stopped for an hour and half to view the spectacular performance of the glaciers; according to the chamber of commerce brochure, the cost in 1932 of this 50-mile trip was $10.

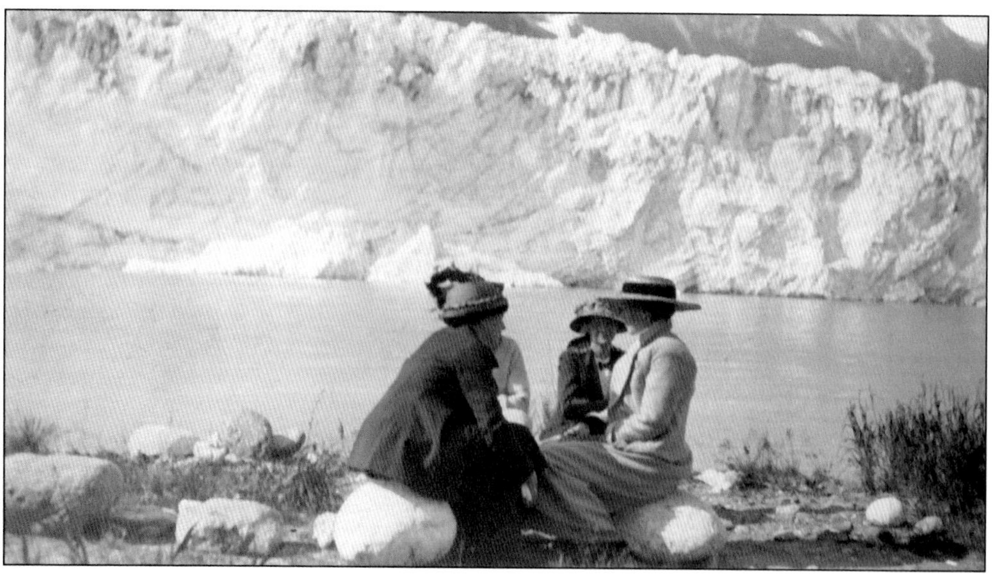

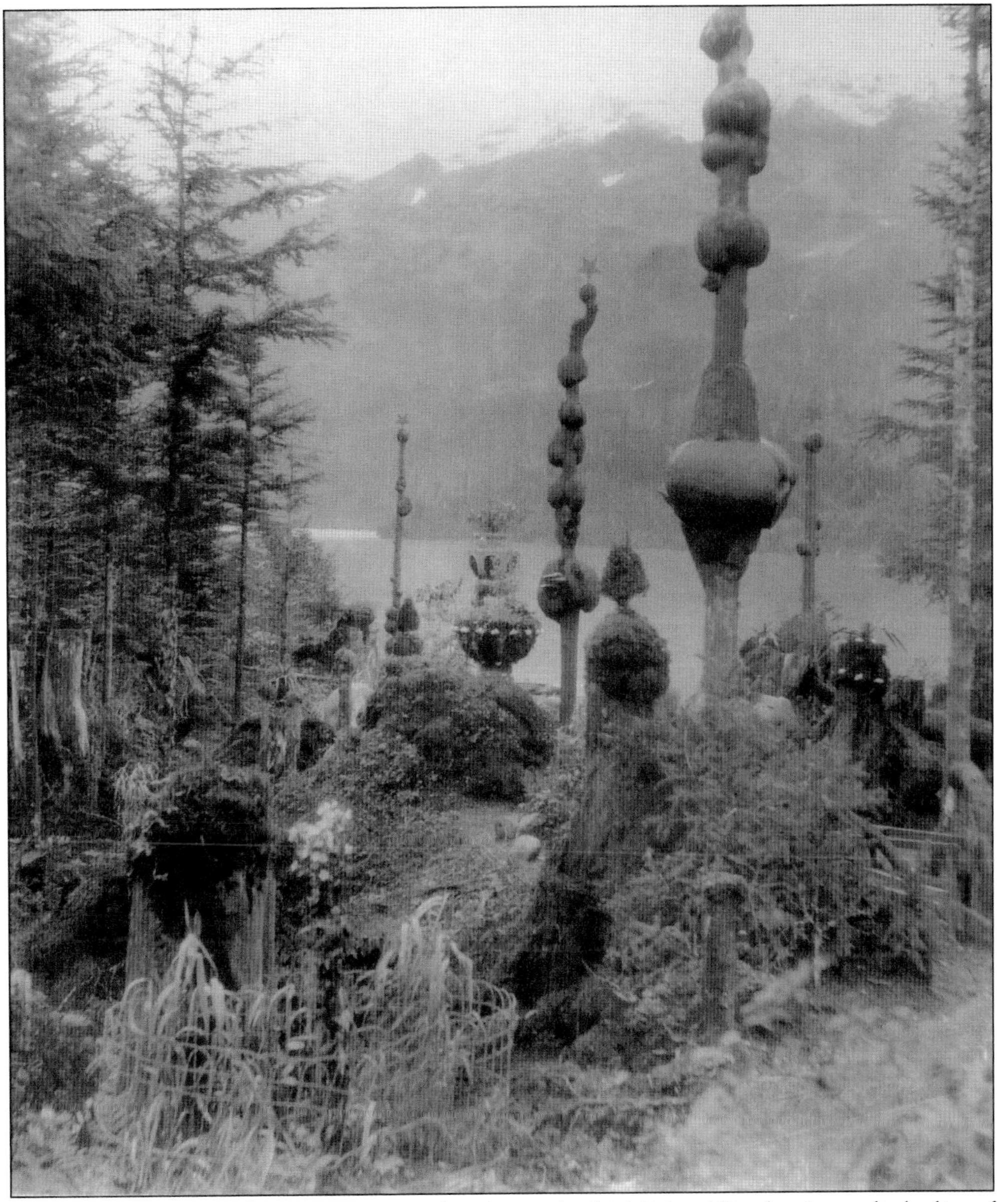

Those same chamber of commerce tourist brochures also highlighted Cordova's own little slice of heaven—Nirvana Park, originally a native cemetery. In 1909, the newspaper noted the difficulty of reaching the graveyard, since there was no road, and expressed concern about the poor conditions. The transformation of this spot began with the arrival of German immigrant Henry C. Feldman, who followed the mining rush to Cordova but instead began operating the Northwestern Hardware Co. Feldman had a great interest in Buddhism, and this was reflected in the name he chose and the peaceful wanderings throughout his hand-scaped park. Distinguished by its trails, interesting fences and bridges, statues, sculptures, and fountains all created out of nature's bounty, the park became a pleasant place for residents and visitors to frequent. In a tourist brochure titled *Cordova – Shortcut to the Interior of Alaska*, the park is described as follows: "a sylvan retreat, built and maintained by an old pioneer who devotes his entire time to this fairyland. . . . a ten-minute walk from the center of town, a perfect stroll while the steamer is in port."

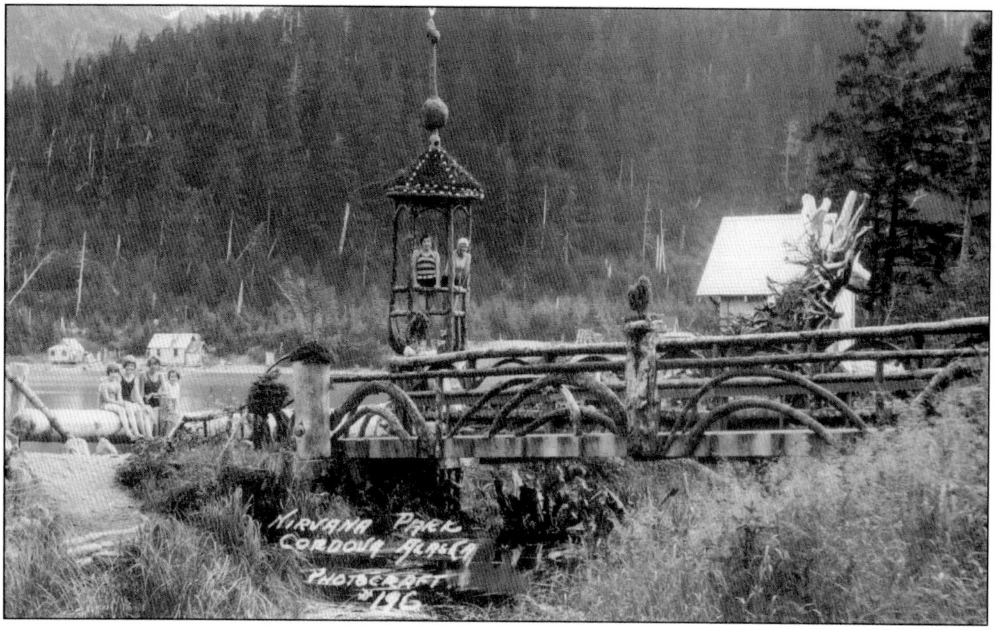

Two wooden gates in Hindu-style architecture guarded the park. Ponds and streams were used for children as safe places to swim. Wooden bridges with hand-carved rails guided visitors to the two bathhouses, which were provided for swimmers to discreetly change attire. The flowers bordering the paths were wild flowers that Feldman had collected. Somewhere in the park, a Buddha watched the proceedings, created from a strangely shaped piece of wood encrusted with many different kinds of stones. During the Depression, Feldman paid a bonus to anyone who found an interestingly shaped piece of wood or rock. Nirvana Park became one of Cordova's biggest attractions in the 1930s.

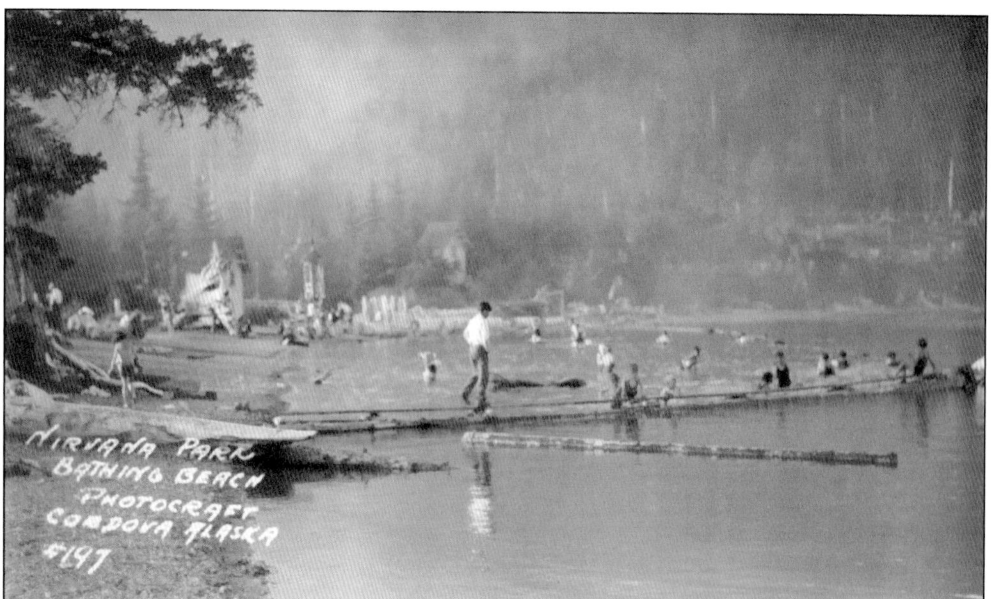

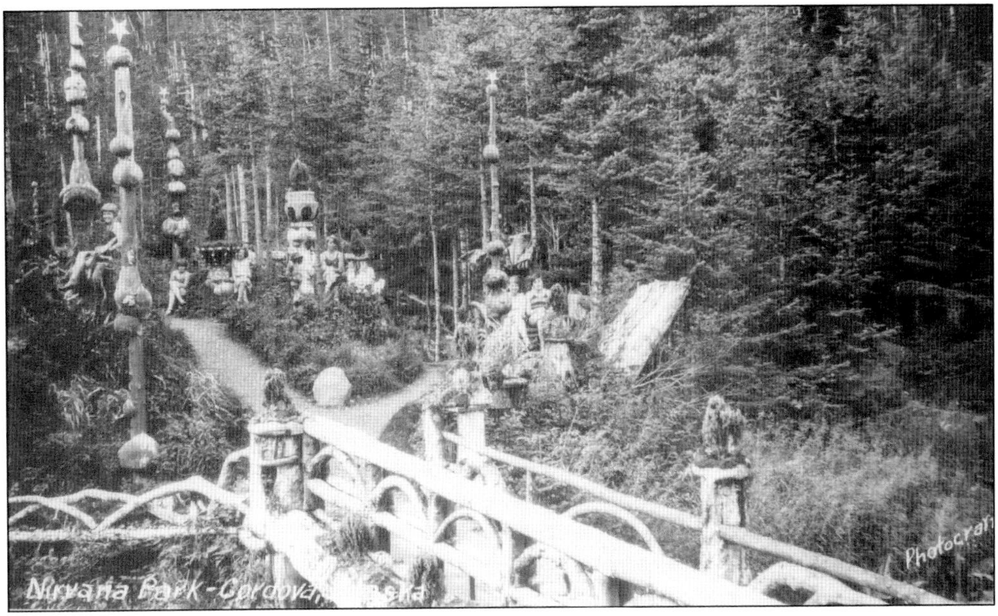

Nirvana Park drew many visitors in its heyday; few places in the territory had a fountain that could compare with Feldman's creations. Feldman left Cordova for a few years but came back to retire and mind the park; he was seen going to the park nearly every day, rain or shine. The Civilian Conservation Corps helped maintain the park in the early 1940s after Feldman became frail and less able to care for his ornate creations. Cordovans still enjoy the natural paths and scenery, but the fancy fences, bridges, and fountains have been reclaimed by both time and the weather. Henry Feldman, however, rests peacefully in the park of his own creation.

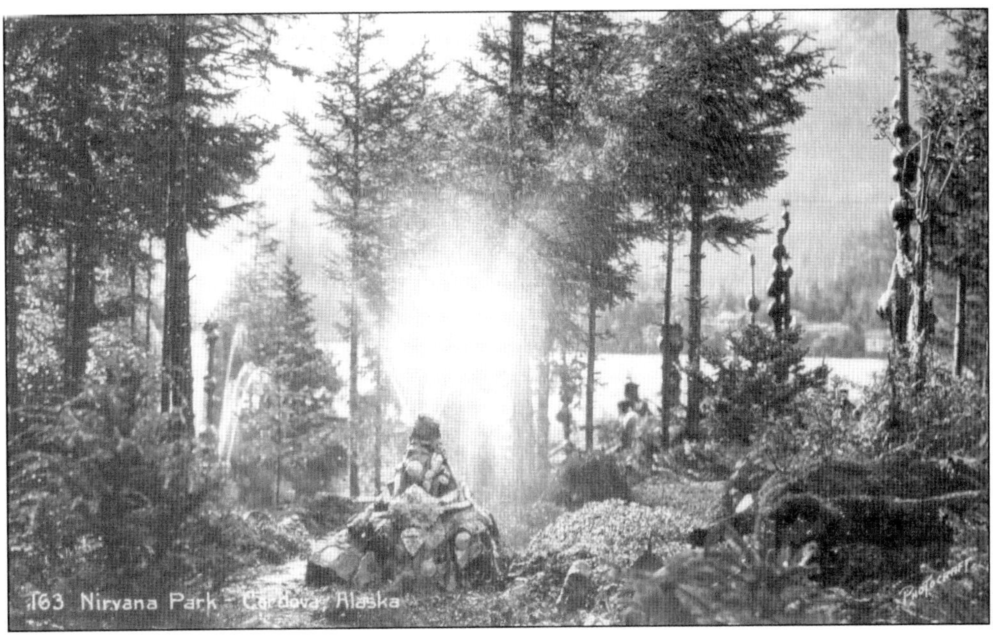

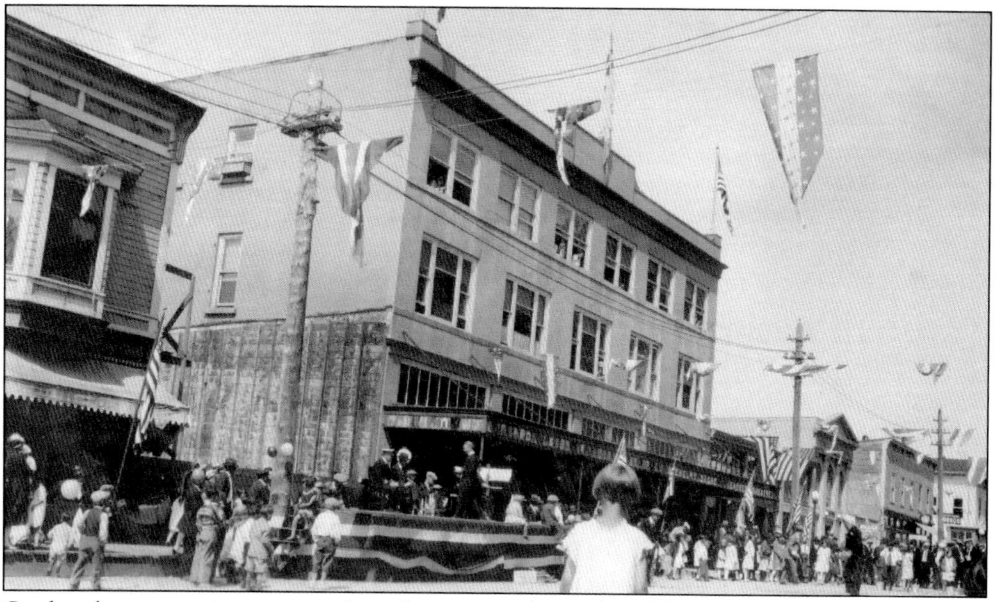

Cordova began creating its warm, friendly image in this era by celebrating holidays like the Fourth of July with parades and pie-eating contests, holding dances with Coast Guard crews, and even by playing America's favorite pastime—baseball. Local merchants, railroad workers, and miners all made up various teams and even traveled to Valdez to play. The first baseball field was created in the very early 1900s and was within sight of the railroad depot and local sawmill. Adjacent to the waterfront, the field included a grandstand to hold the well-dressed audience and a lovely picket fence. Today, children and adults play in nearly the same location.

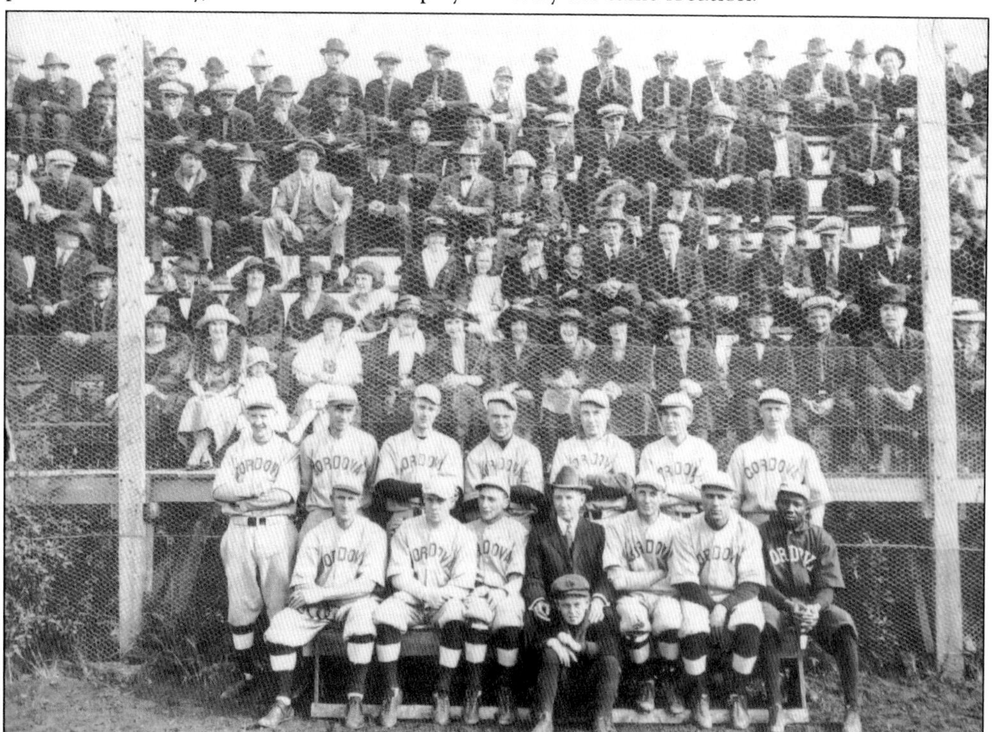

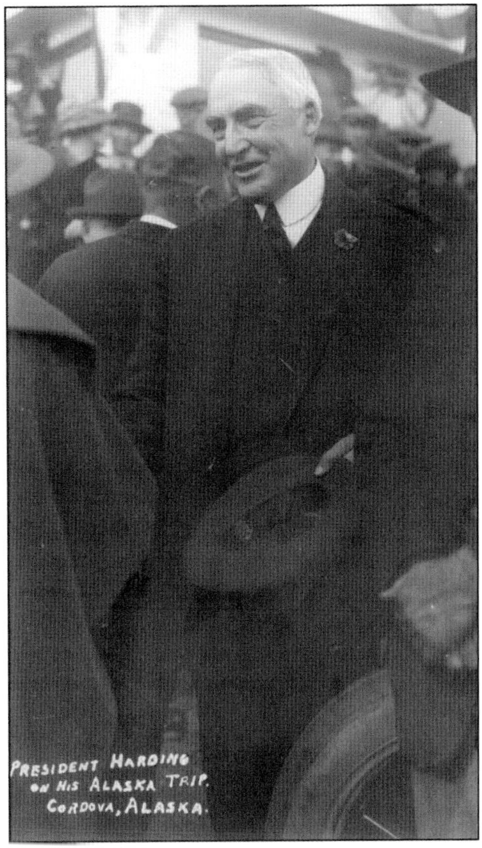

Even Pres. Warren Harding became one of Cordova's visitors in the booming era of resource extraction. During his 1923 visit to Alaska, Harding arrived via steamship and traveled on the Copper River & Northwest Railway to see Childs and Miles Glaciers, where the Secret Service men fired their guns in an effort to make the glacier calve. The president also spoke to the gathering of Cordovans from their newly built bandstand placed at the end of First Street, adjacent to the community's World War I memorial flagpole and cannon. The memorial honored those Cordovan veterans who had lost their lives in battle. Unfortunately, President Harding succumbed to illness just three days after visiting the territory.

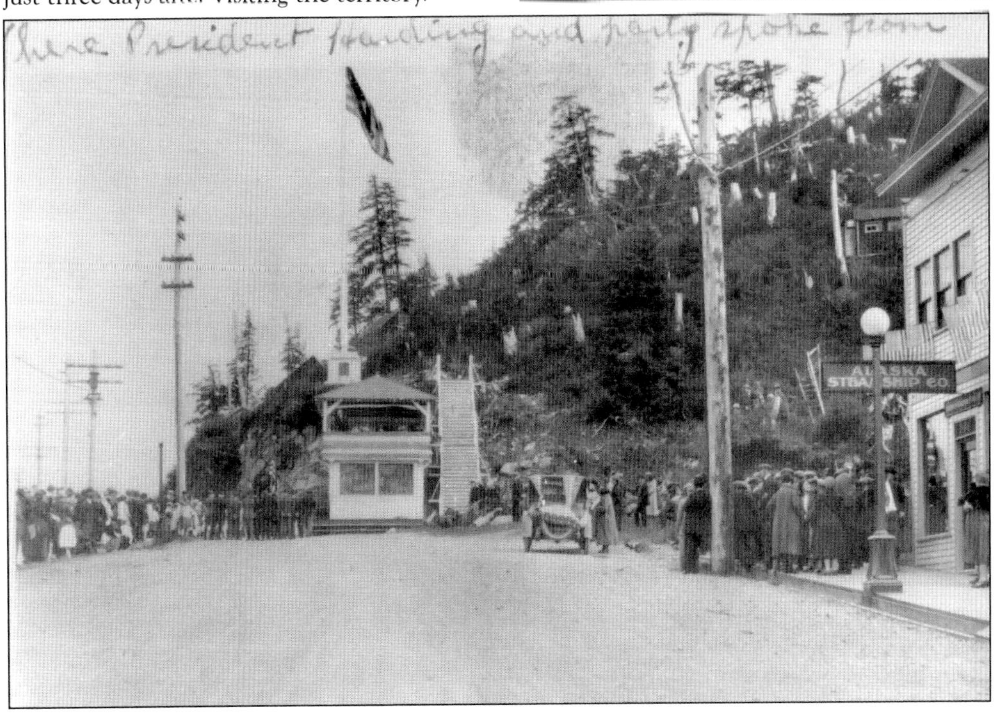

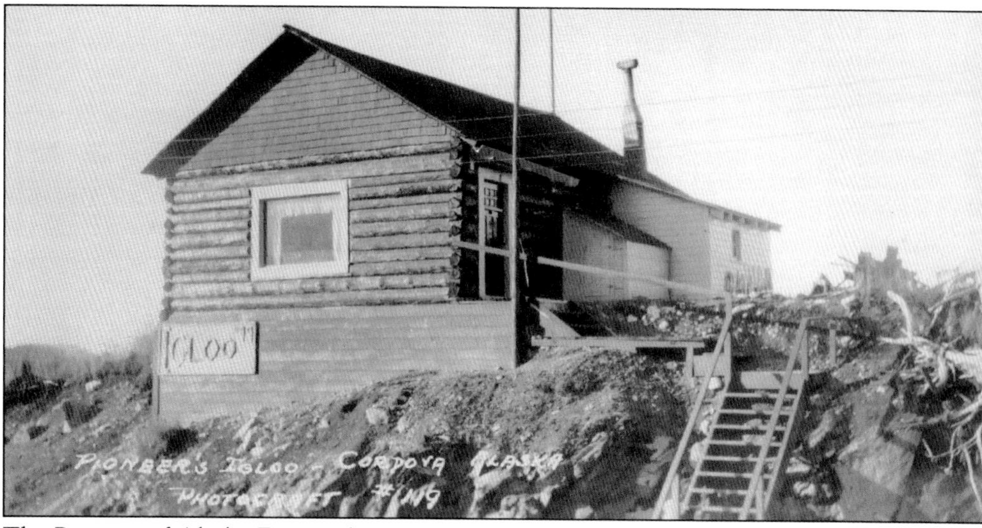

The Pioneers of Alaska Fraternal Organization was founded on February 20, 1907, in Nome, Alaska, where Igloo No. 1 was established to "to preserve the names of all Alaska's pioneers on its rolls; to collect and preserve the literature and incidents of Alaska's history, and to promote the best interests of Alaska." The Pioneers eventually established 35 igloos throughout the state, each serving as an important social center for the community it represented. Pioneer Igloo No. 17 was established in Cordova in 1918 and was officially chartered in 1920. Construction of the hall was initiated in 1928 on a prominent site in Cordova's downtown, donated by longtime resident doctor, multiple-term mayor, and Pioneer member William Chase. The hall was constructed of local spruce logs from Power Creek and was designed to represent a typical Alaskan trapper cabin.

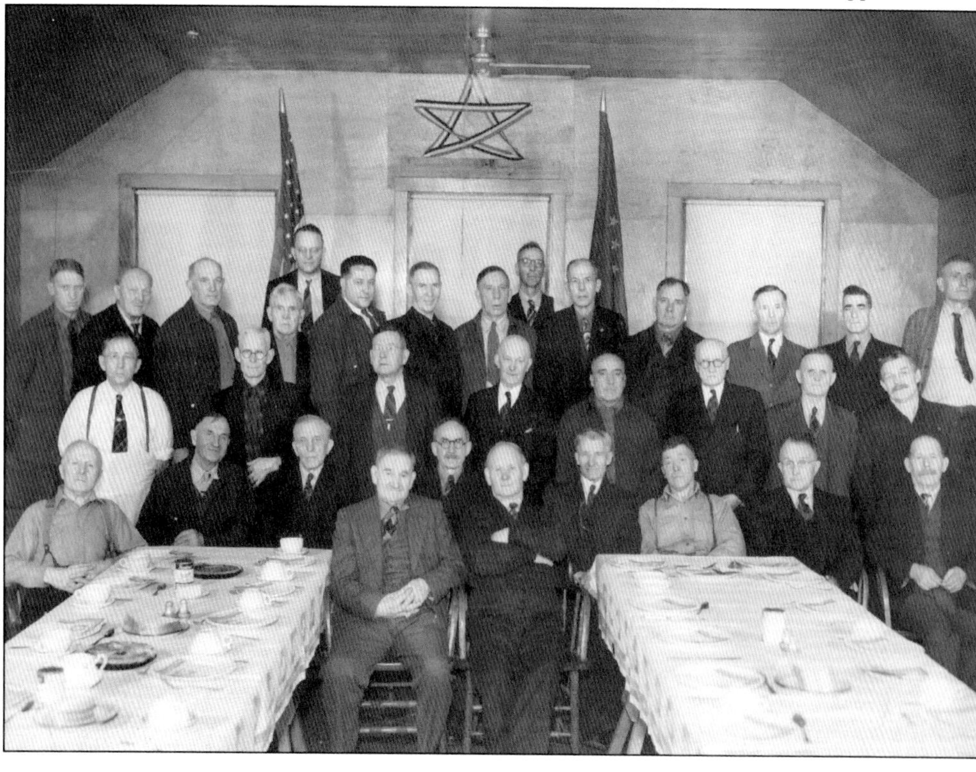

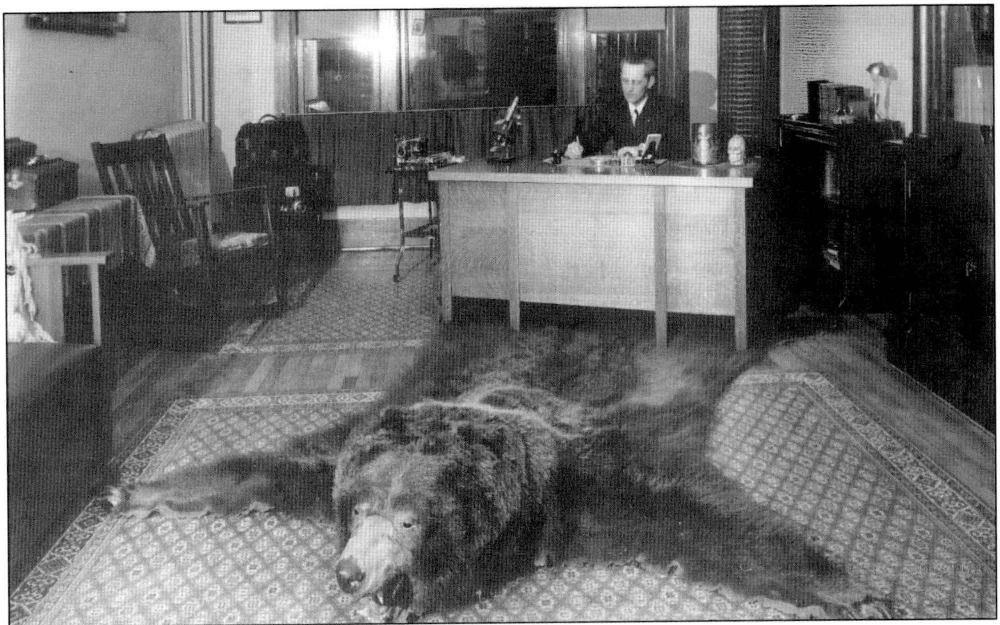

Will Chase, a larger-than-life figure in Cordova, attended medical school as a young man for only a few months but practiced medicine on gold miners. In 1906, aboard an Alaska Packers boat, Chase met Dr. J.H. Romig, another Alaska pioneer physician, and together they started the Alaska Medical Association. Dr. Chase was granted a medical license under the "grandfather" laws of the territory and opened an office in Cordova.

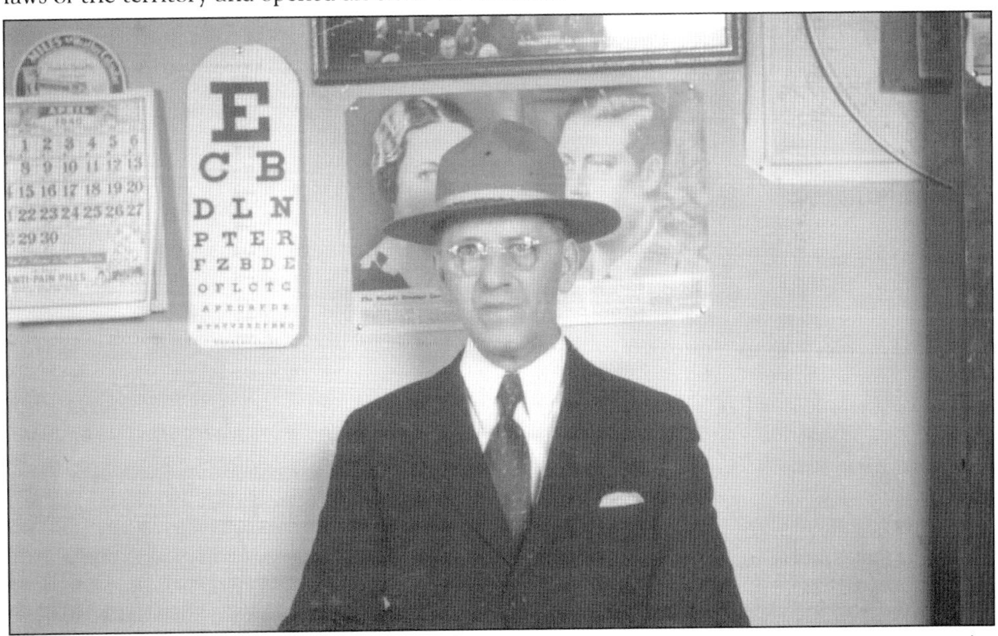

While he was busy delivering hundreds of babies, Dr. Chase also served in many other roles during his lifetime, like mayor of Cordova 24 times and Alaska's first health commissioner. Dr. Chase built up a circle of acquaintances who knew him as an outdoorsman, guide, author, and authority on Alaskan lore and wildlife. He served as a museum field-worker providing many rare specimen of Alaskan wildlife to museums and zoological parks.

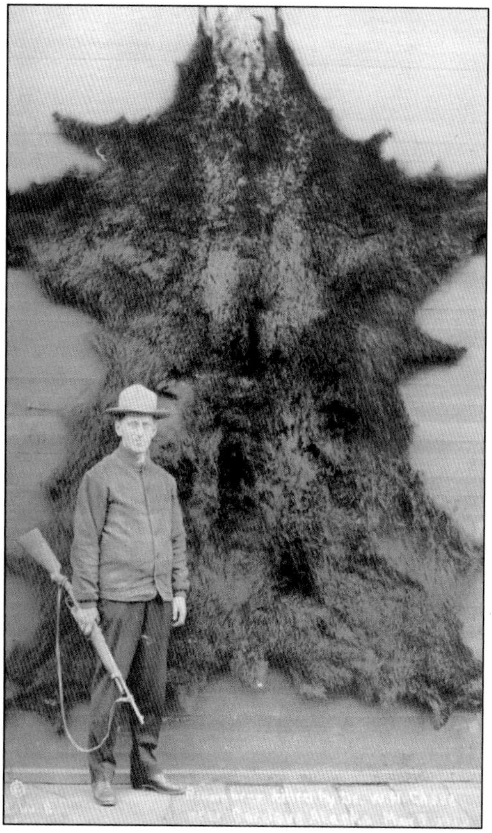

Doc Chase was an original member of the Alaska Game Commission serving as commissioner for six years. Chase loved the outdoors and was an avid hunter who proudly displayed "the biggest brown bear shot in Alaska." The Hinchinbrook Island bear had been dispatched with two shots from a 401 Winchester. Locals jokingly referred it to as "some mammoth that strayed down from the prehistoric ages." Doc Chase became known as an authority on bears and wrote scientific papers on Alaskan brown bears. He also wrote hunting stories for the *Alaska Sportsman* magazine and authored five books. He was an avid Pioneer of Alaska and chronicled the territorial history of the organization.

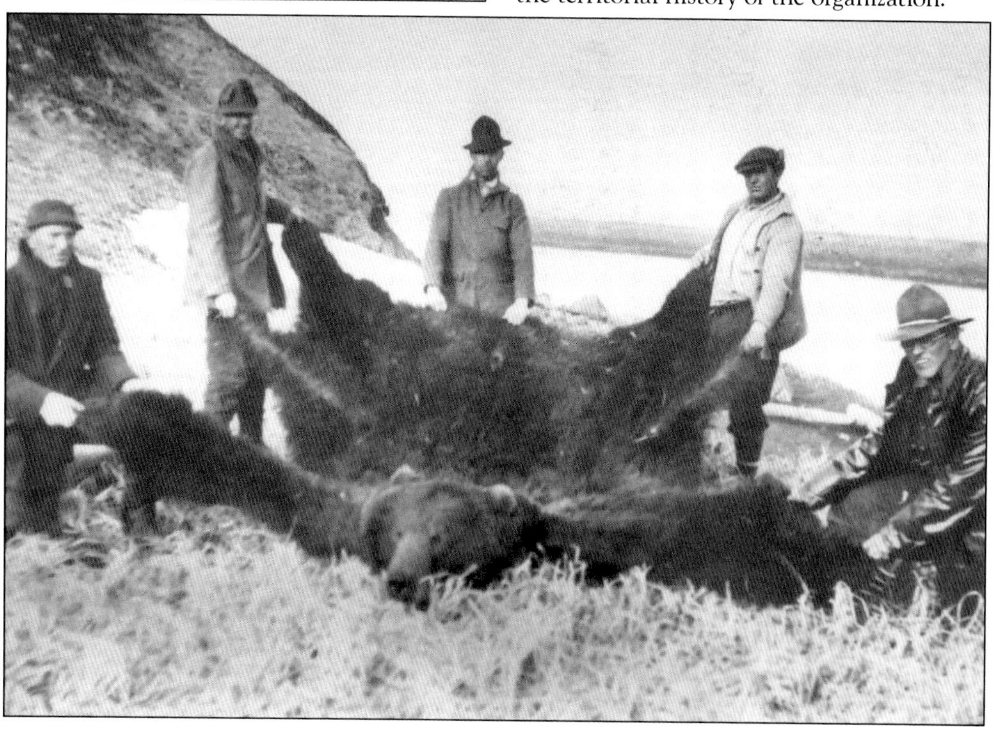

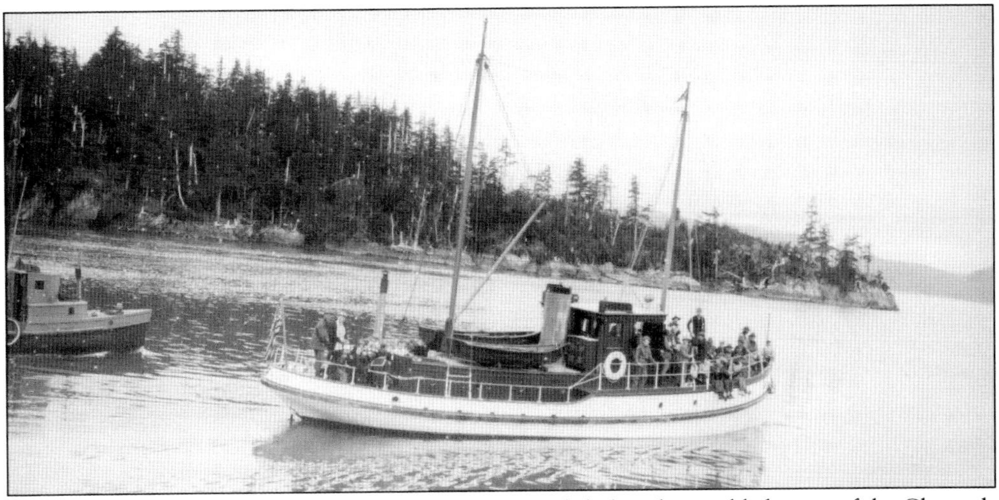

The push for conservation by Pres. Theodore Roosevelt led to the establishment of the Chugach National Forest surrounding the Cordova area, totaling over six million acres. US Forest Service employees spent years in Cordova with their families, maintaining lengthy relationships with the community. The Cordova office had a gas-powered vessel, the *Chugach*. The *Chugach* was one of the largest of the Forest Service vessels in Alaska. It was 60 feet long with a 14-foot beam and sleeping accommodations for eight in the bow—a four-berth stateroom, three berths in the salon, and one berth in the pilot house. The *Chugach* operated year-round throughout Prince William Sound, carrying out a myriad of tasks such as scaling timber, administering permits for fox farms, clam cabins, trapping cabins, and transporting Civilian Conservation Corps members to work camps.

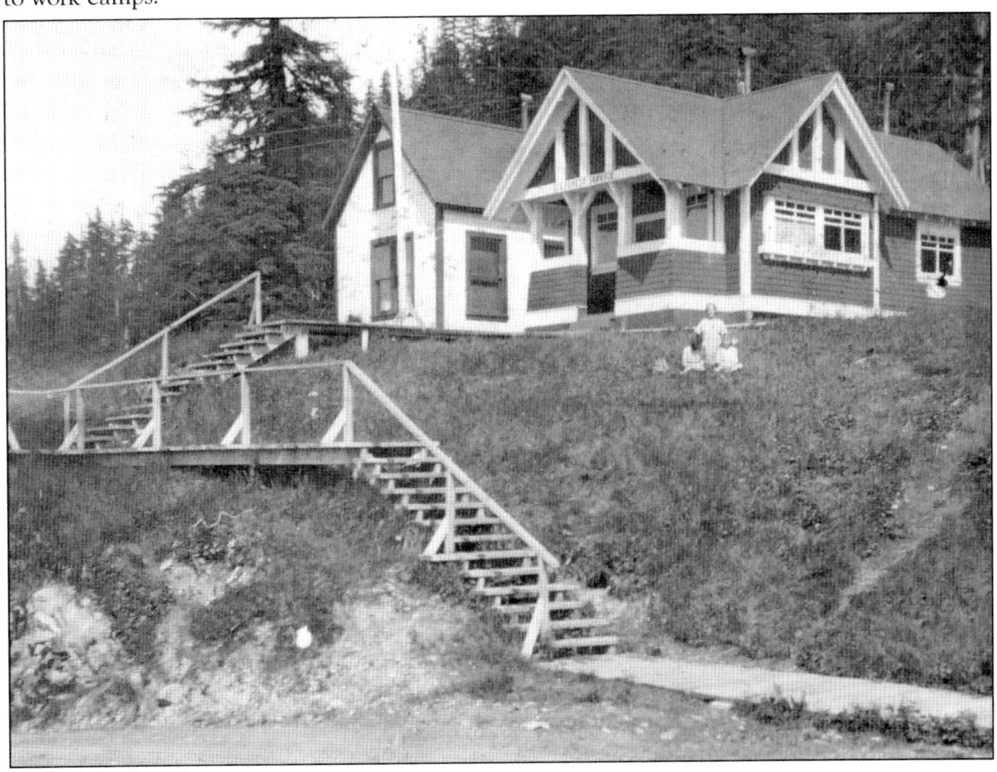

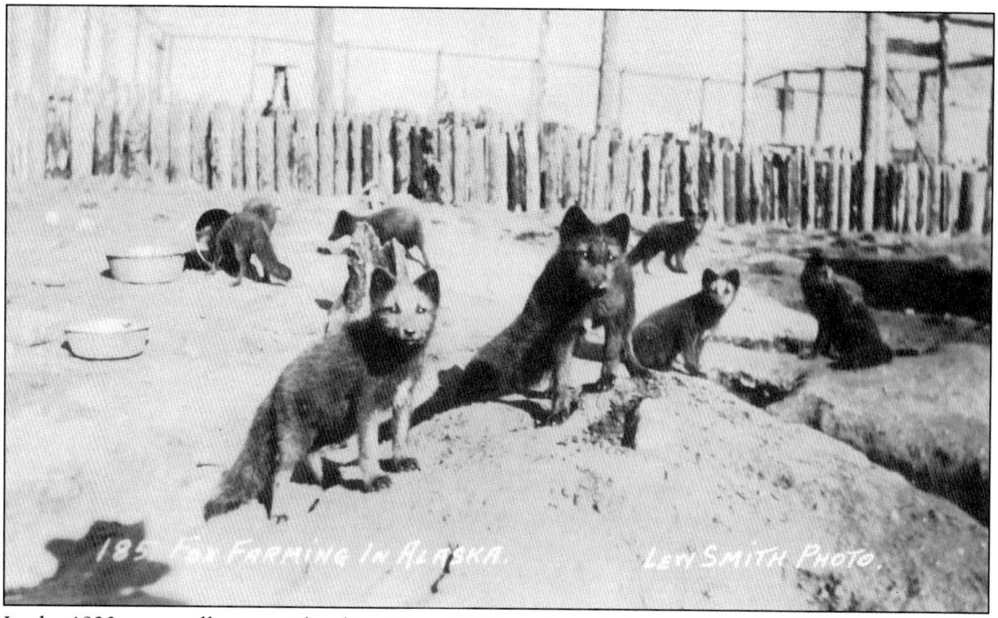

In the 1920s, virtually every island in Prince William Sound that was suitable for raising foxes was under permit with the US Forest Service. In 1922, the Forest Service organized and sponsored the very first fox farmers' convention, which led to the development of the Fox Farmer's Association. During that year alone, 581 skins were harvested with an estimated value of $70,000.

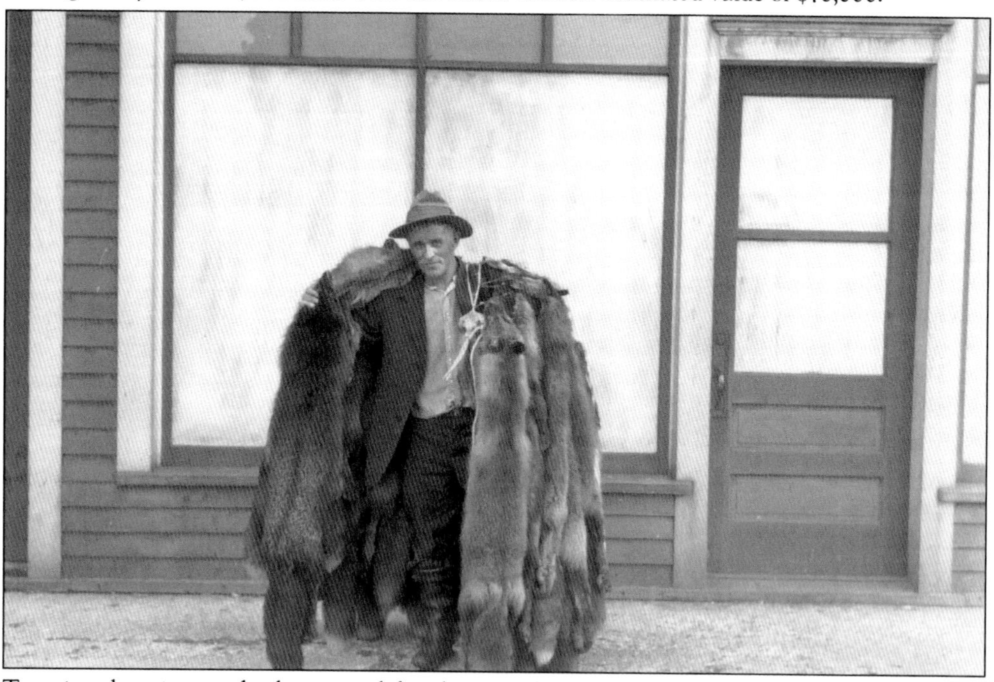

Trapping, hunting, and subsistence lifestyles were less regulated in the territorial days before statehood. Actually, a lot of things were less regulated before statehood; even eagles were considered predators and swans delicacies. Marten, mink, wolverine, coyote, fox, lynx, and river otter were all trapped, harvested, and sold and were a major factor in the early economy of Cordova and the Prince William Sound islands in the region.

A subsistence lifestyle for all who called Cordova home has been a way of life for as long as anyone can remember. The migratory waterfowl that passed through the Copper River delta region or the waterfowl that called the delta home provided an early abundance of sustenance and continue to provide to through the present.

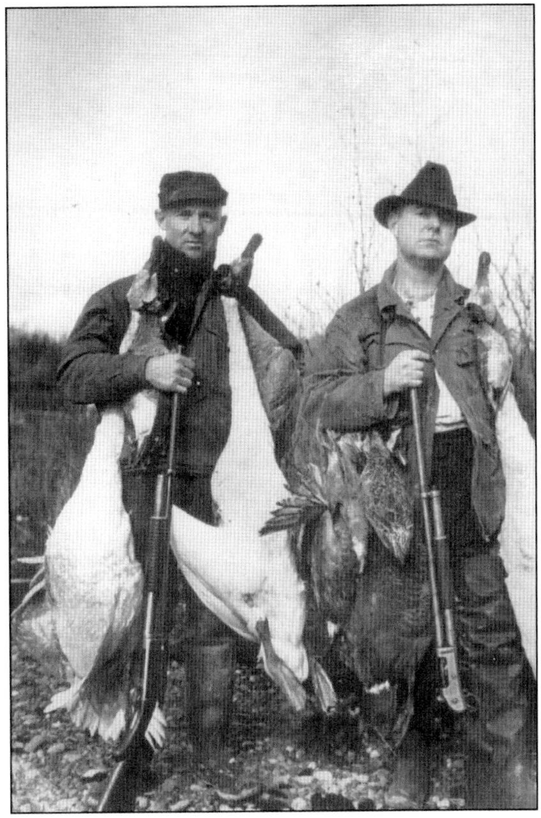

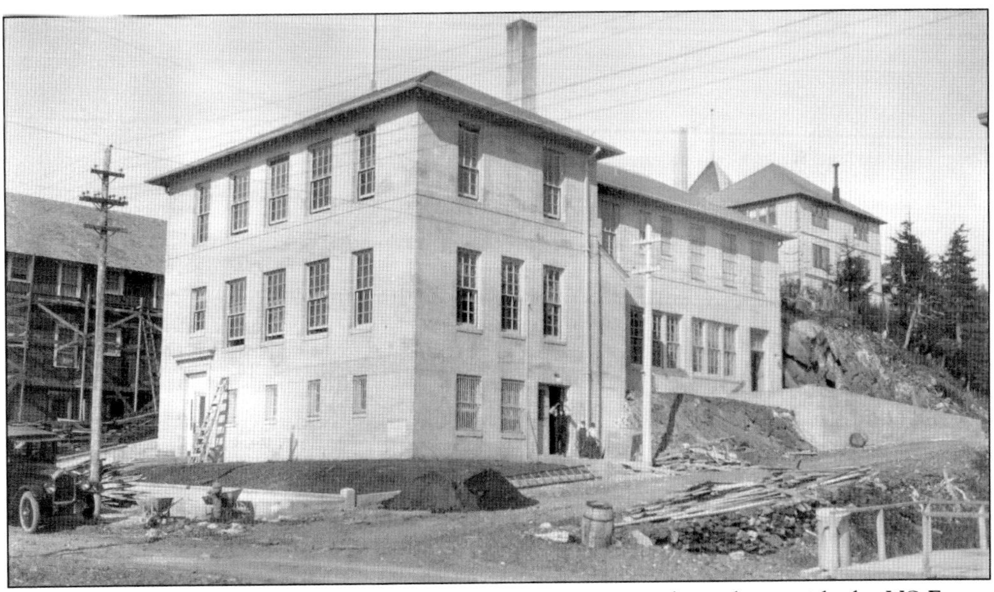

Territorial game wardens oversaw hunting in conjunction with working with the US Forest Service officers. US marshals arrived in Cordova in the mid-1920s. Cordova's Federal Building was completed in 1927 and served as a post office, federal courthouse, and jail. Now listed in the National Register of Historic Places, the Federal Building still provides a work facility for the employees of the US Forest Service on the Cordova Ranger District.

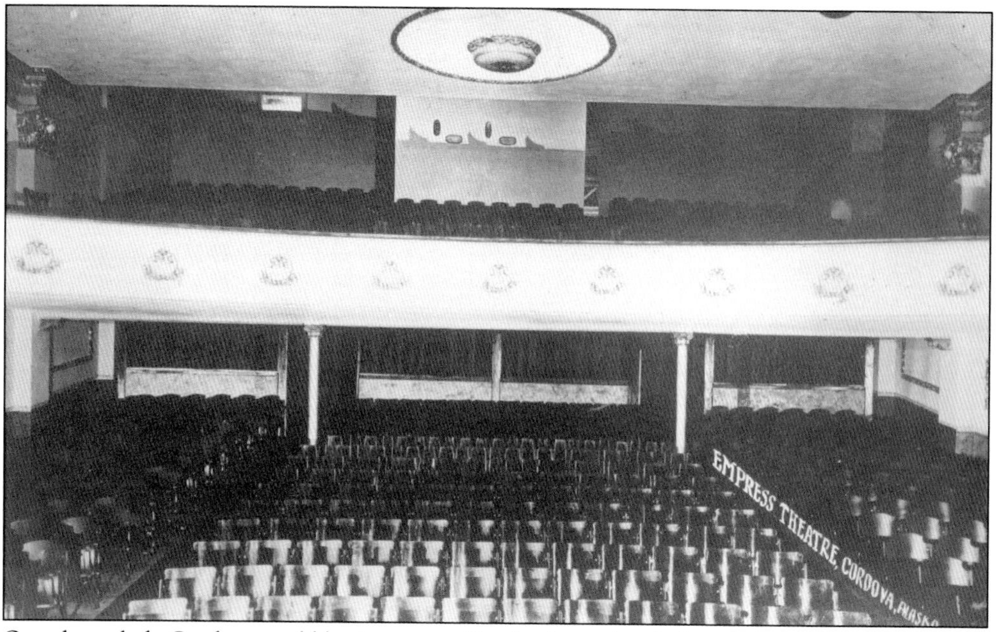

One day, a lady Cordovan told businessman Cap Lathrop that "what this place needs is a place for men and women to relax in the evenings." Never one to let a good suggestion go unheeded, he began to build his first motion picture theater. Comprised of both concrete and wood, it was at the time one of the finest and certainly fanciest structures of its kind in Alaska.

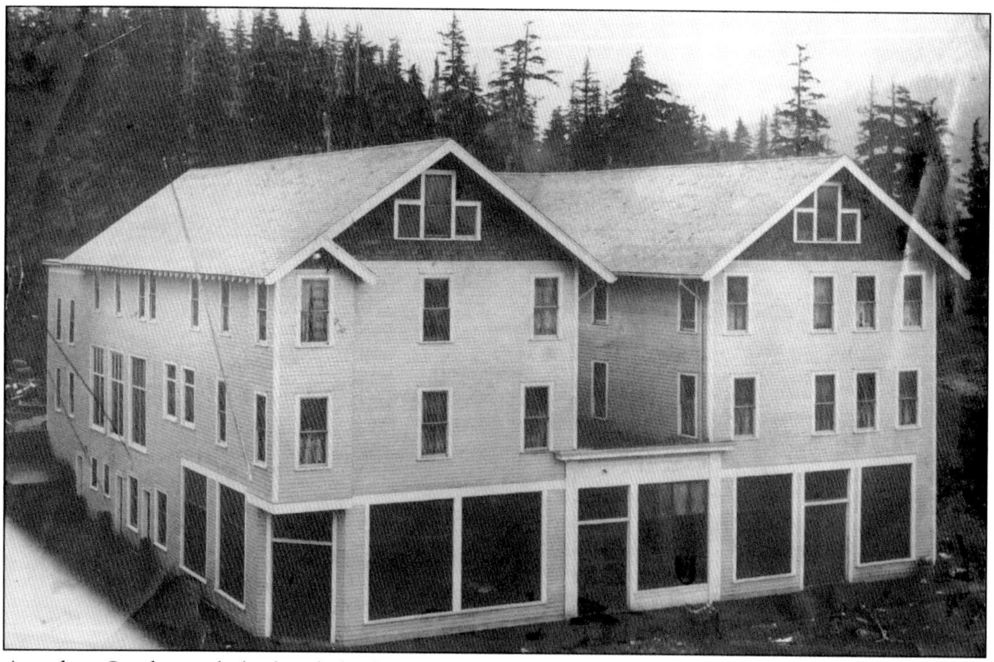
Another Cordovan lady decided what the town needed was a majestic and classy hotel and restaurant, so Miss L.A. Burke built the largest and most costly structure in early Cordova. Three stories high, the Burke Hotel, later called the Windsor, was steam heated and electrically lit, with all the modern conveniences. During its life, the hotel also housed the public library but was, sadly, demolished in 1972.

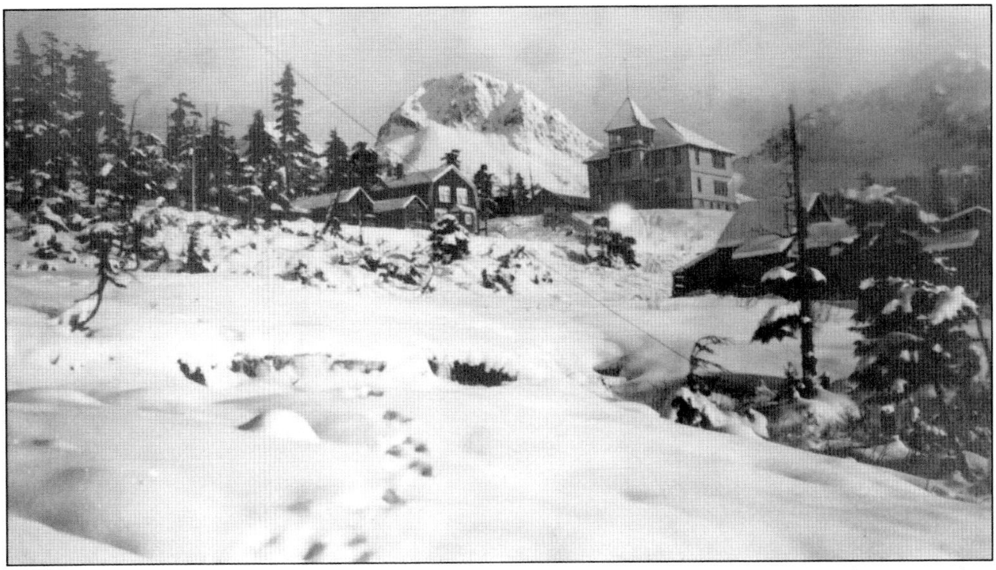

Cordovans established a school board in 1908 and began operating a school with one teacher by 1908, but an actual school building was not completed for a few more years. The first was built on the hill overlooking the growing town. It consisted of four large rooms with adjoining cloakrooms and sat on the side of a hill behind Second Avenue. The Nelson Act of 1905 specified that the territory's schools should be devoted to the education of white children and children of mixed blood who lead a civilized life. The education of the natives in the territory fell to federal hands, and in Cordova, that was the Bureau of Indian Affairs. A native school was created in a converted apartment house across from the ballpark, but then a new school was built in Eyak or Old Town.

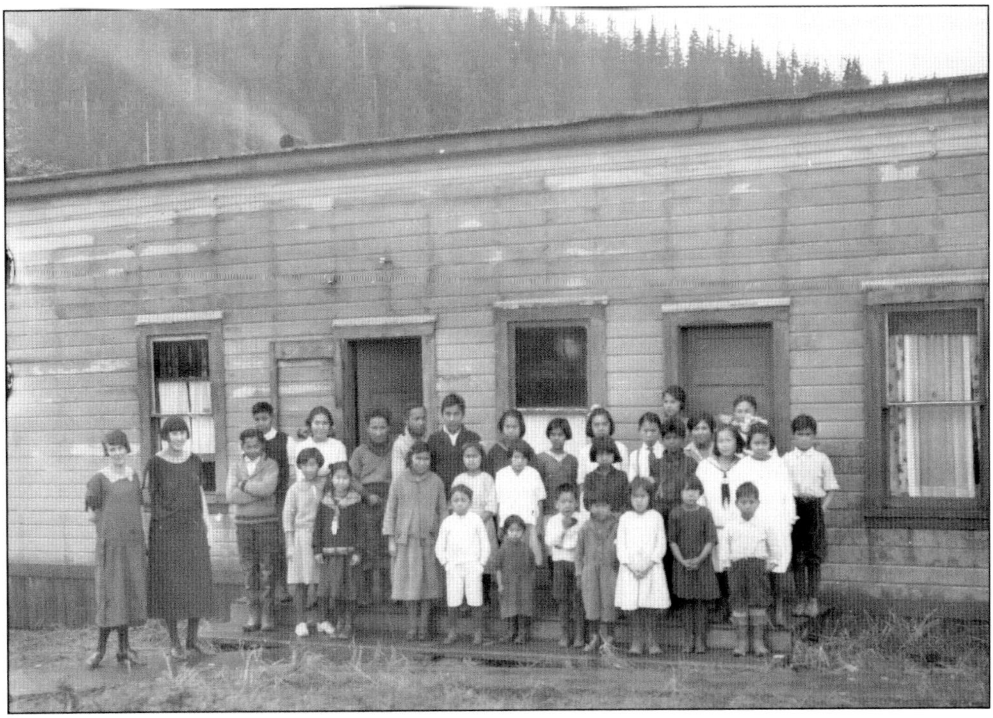

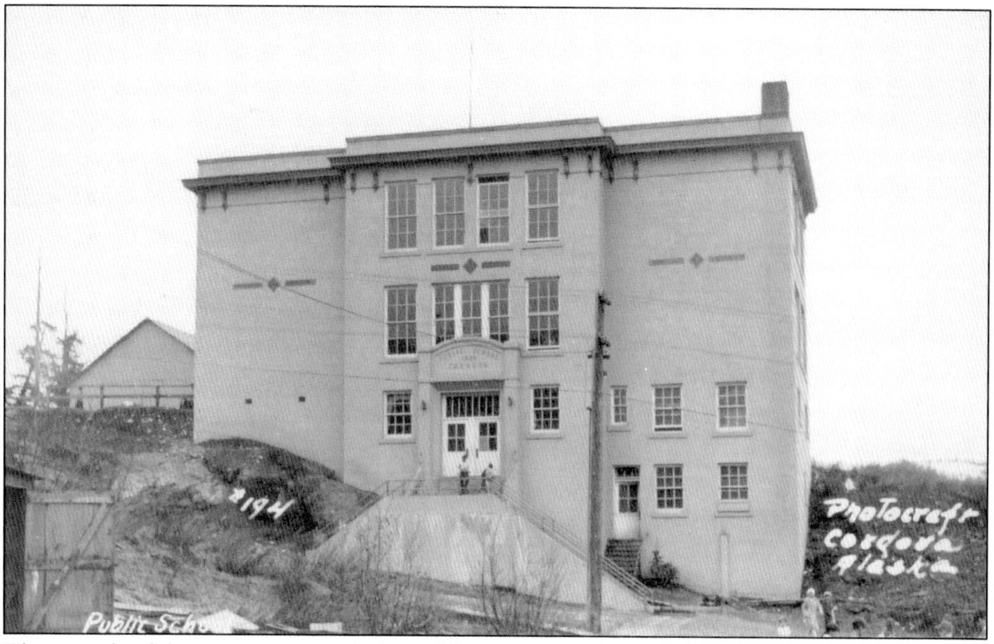

The growth of the town was steady; by 1920, the senior class numbered two and included John Rosswog, who would become a member of the statehood convention that drew up Alaska's constitution. Bonds issued a few years later for $50,000 made it possible to build a larger concrete building adjacent to the old school. By 1925, it was ready for occupancy; school enrollment was now 161 students with 10 teachers.

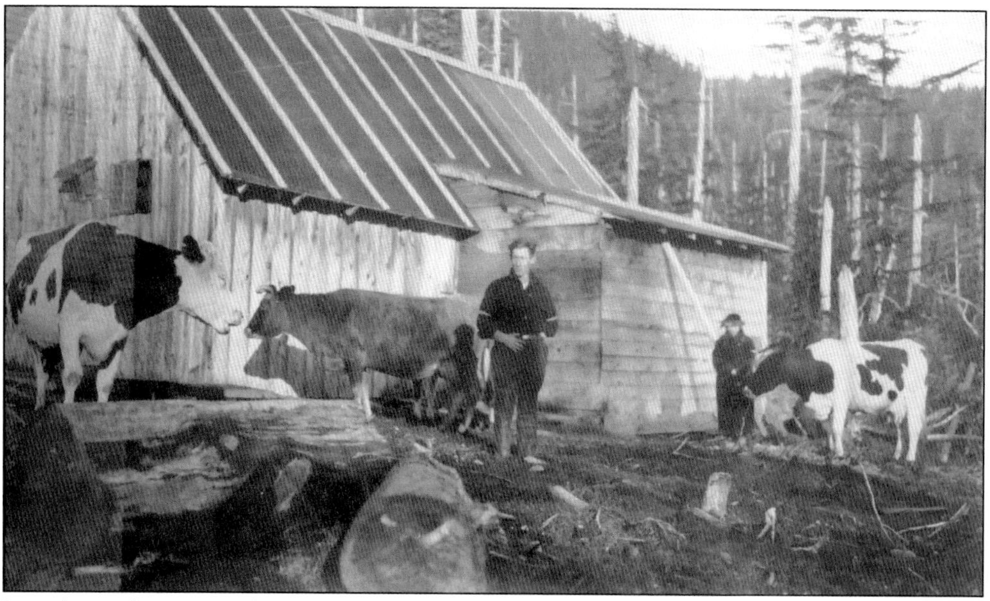

In early Cordova, a couple of dairies provided fresh milk to the residents. At Vina Young's Dairy, each cow had its own personalized drinking cup. Young delivered milk by horse-drawn wagon and got her first cow, named Goldie, from Kennicott. The dairy served 235 customers with milk and cream, including half-pint bottles for local restaurants to offer.

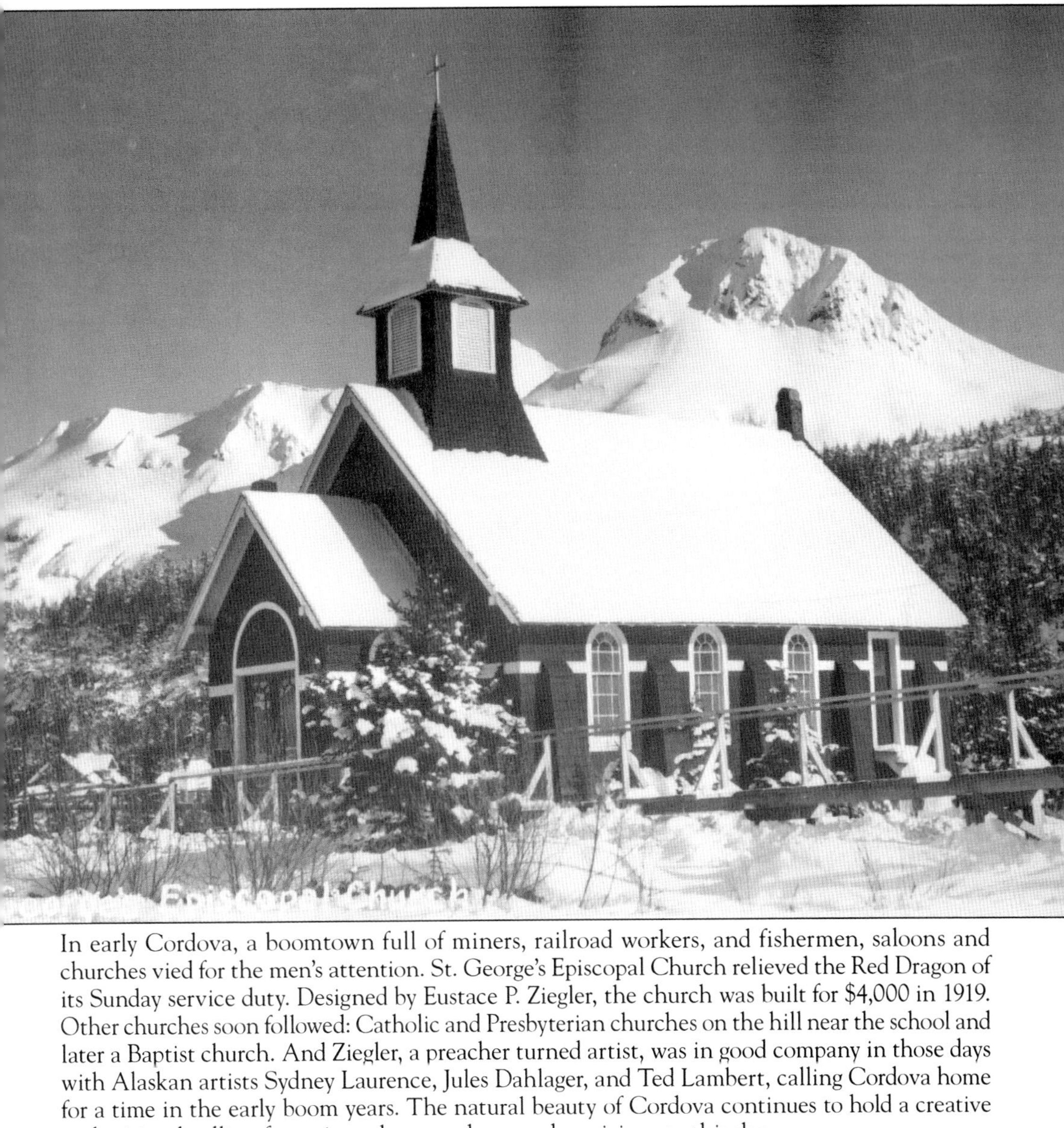

In early Cordova, a boomtown full of miners, railroad workers, and fishermen, saloons and churches vied for the men's attention. St. George's Episcopal Church relieved the Red Dragon of its Sunday service duty. Designed by Eustace P. Ziegler, the church was built for $4,000 in 1919. Other churches soon followed: Catholic and Presbyterian churches on the hill near the school and later a Baptist church. And Ziegler, a preacher turned artist, was in good company in those days with Alaskan artists Sydney Laurence, Jules Dahlager, and Ted Lambert, calling Cordova home for a time in the early boom years. The natural beauty of Cordova continues to hold a creative and spiritual calling for artists, photographers, and musicians to this day.

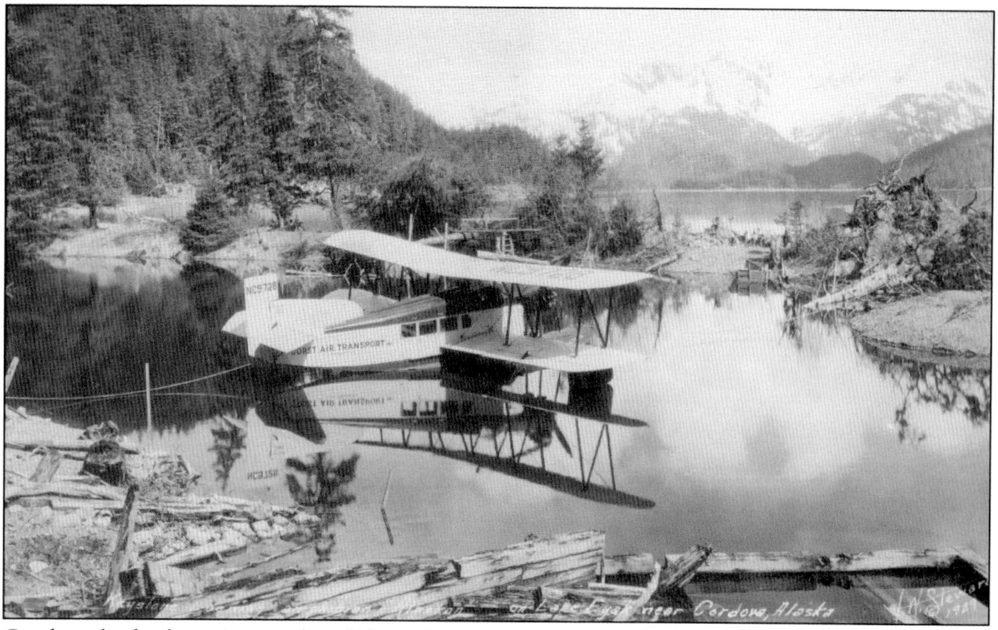

Cordova had a lot going on but did not have air service until 1929, when the first airplane, a Gorst Air Loening amphibious plane, piloted by Clayton Scott, flew in from Juneau. The plane, named *Alaskan*, was greeted by steam whistles, sirens, and bells ringing as Cordovans came down to the dock. Scott stayed for a time in Cordova providing flights to residents, service to Valdez, and even performing a marriage aloft.

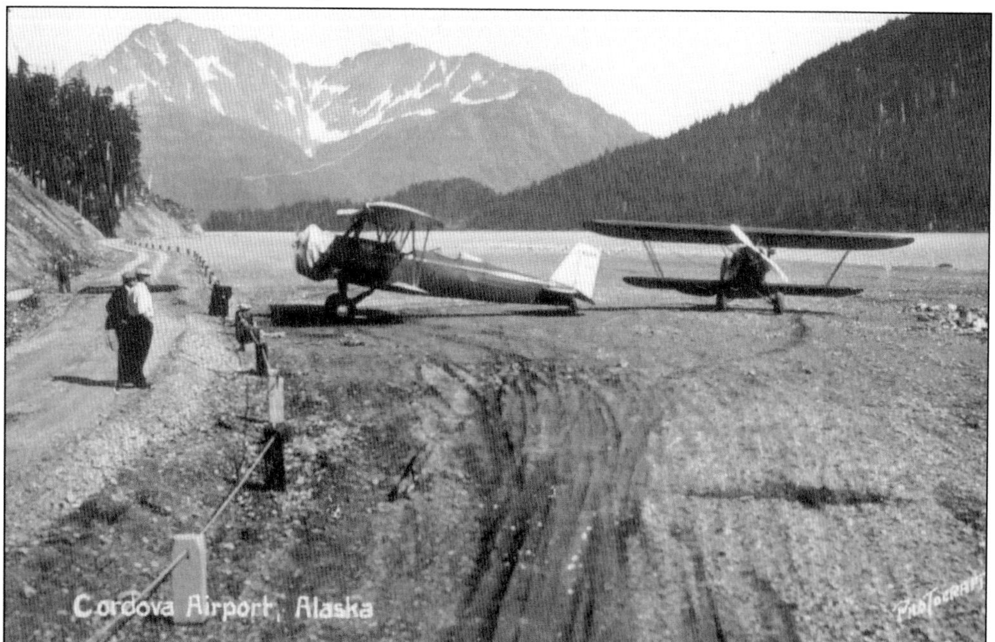

After a taste of air service, Cordovans were not about to give it up. Bush pilots, like M.D. Kirkpatrick and Harold "Thrill-em, Spill-em, No Kill-em" Gillam, began landing on the sandbars near mile 17. In 1934, Cordova dedicated its city airstrip. The landing field parallel to the lake was great for wheeled planes and pontoons, and in the winter, the freezing lake made it perfect for skis.

There were two labor forces in the early Alaskan fishing industry—the fishermen and cannery workers. Cannery work offered few opportunities for local labor as the packers and syndicate had a pool of cheap immigrant labor in the ports of Seattle and San Francisco. Shipped off to the Alaskan canneries, the workers were charged for their passage, and then room, board, and clothing were deducted from their wages. The Alaskan Fishermen's Union based out of San Francisco began to represent the canneries and the fishermen in the 1930s, but this union was still primarily controlled by nonresidents. To escape the grasping tentacles of the packers monopoly, fishermen staged strikes of their own. Locally, an organization known as the Alaska Fish Cannery Workers Union formed in 1935 and included cannery workers, clam diggers, and fishermen, eventually developing into Cordova District Fishermen United.

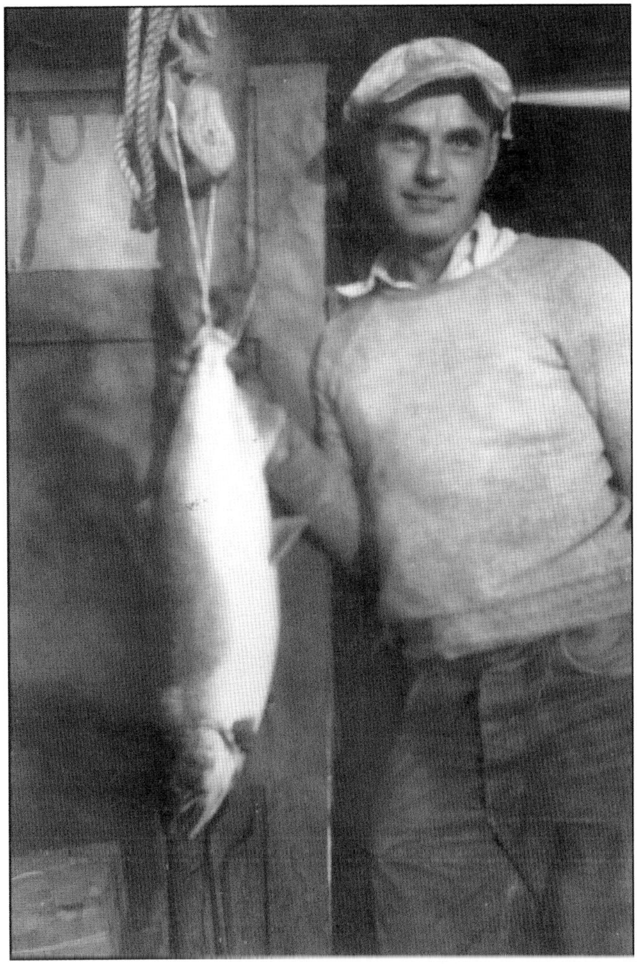

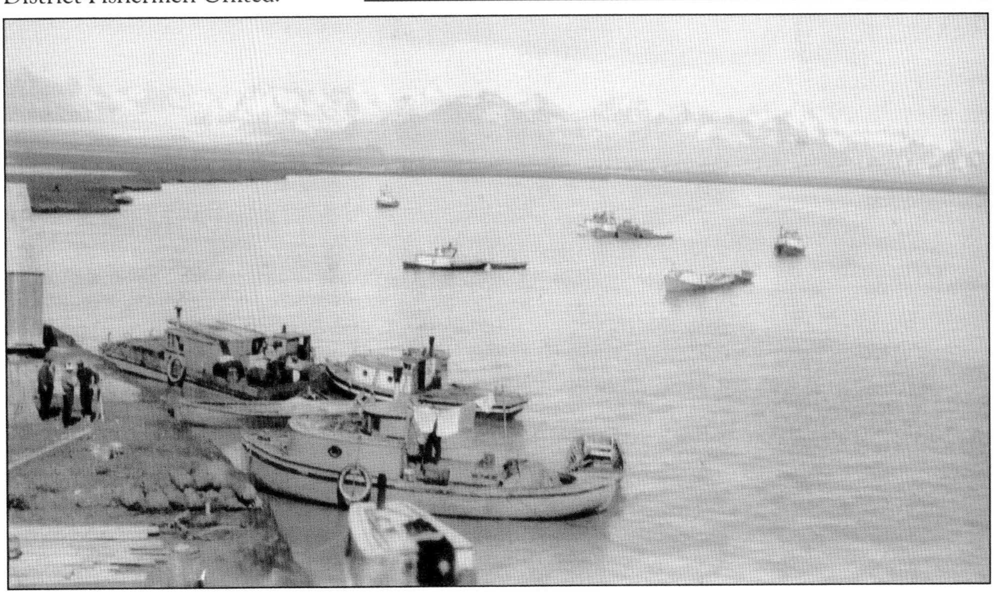

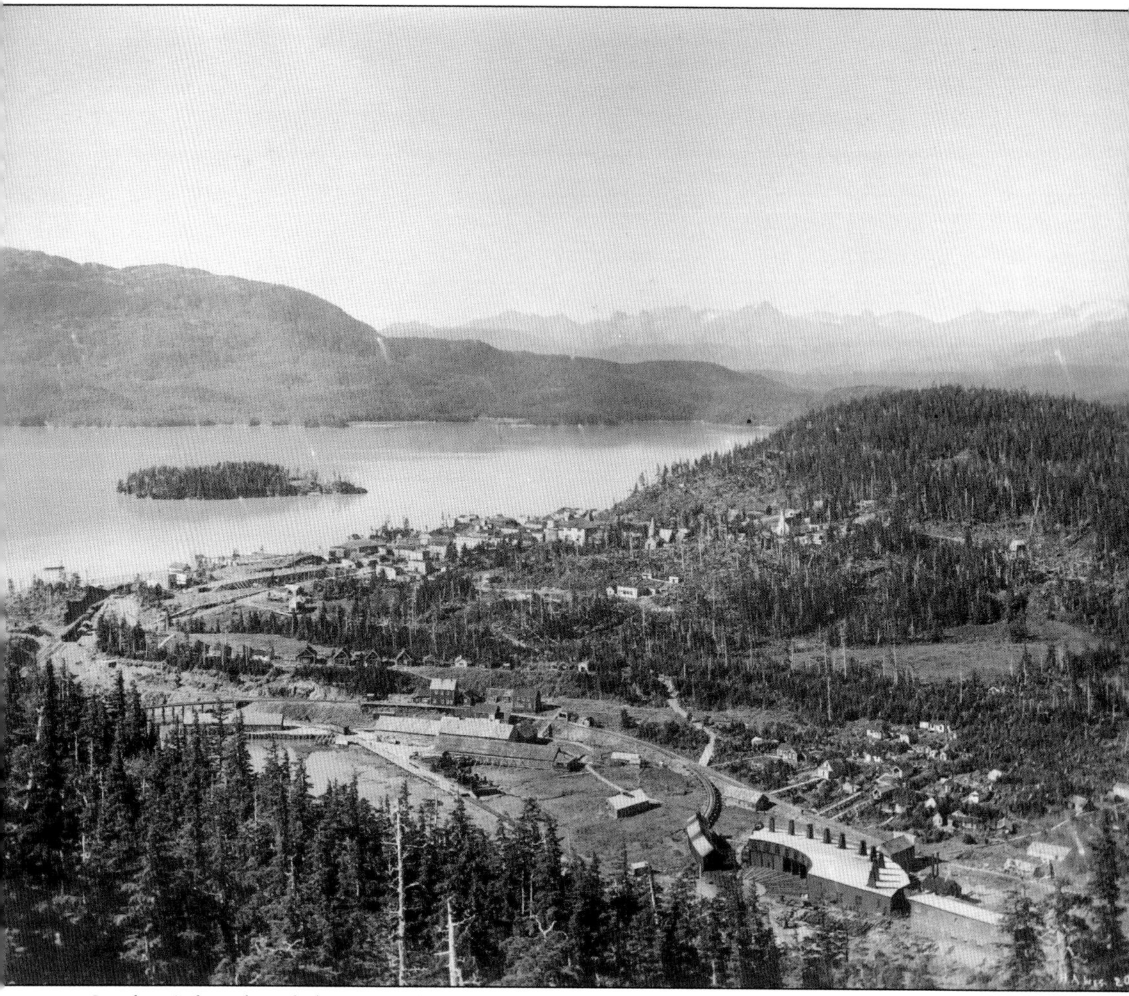

Cordova's founding fathers were bursting with pride in the 1920s and 1930s, but soon as it always does, the tide was about to turn. While Cordova escaped the tough Depression years with the demand for the relatively inexpensive canned salmon, this unmeasured assault on the region's bounty would soon begin to cause a backlash. The unregulated fish traps were taking a heavy toll on the industry. After World War I, the price of copper fell flat, forcing the Kennecott Corporation to make plans to close the mine. In 1933 and 1934, very little copper was mined at all, and the last train left Kennicott on November 11, 1938. Cordovans feared the worst that, with the demise of the railroad and the copper mine, the town would soon become nothing more than an Alaskan ghost town. With another world war on the horizon, what once was a bright future seemed to be eluding the determined residents, and little did they know that some of the community's most difficult struggles lay ahead.

Four

Growing Pains 1940–1959

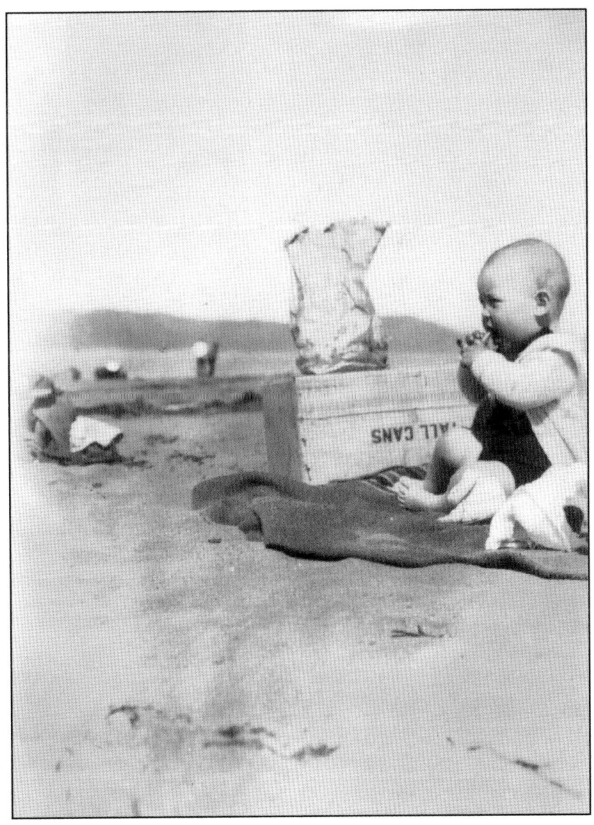

Cordova, the town raised on fish and copper, was about to experience growing pains. Fishing harvests were declining, the copper mine had closed, and the railroad stopped running. Luckily, Cordova built a strong foundation on the backs of gritty individuals with convictions determined to maintain a vibrant place in the history of Alaska. The biggest struggles were yet to come, with statehood, devastating fires, and new regulations.

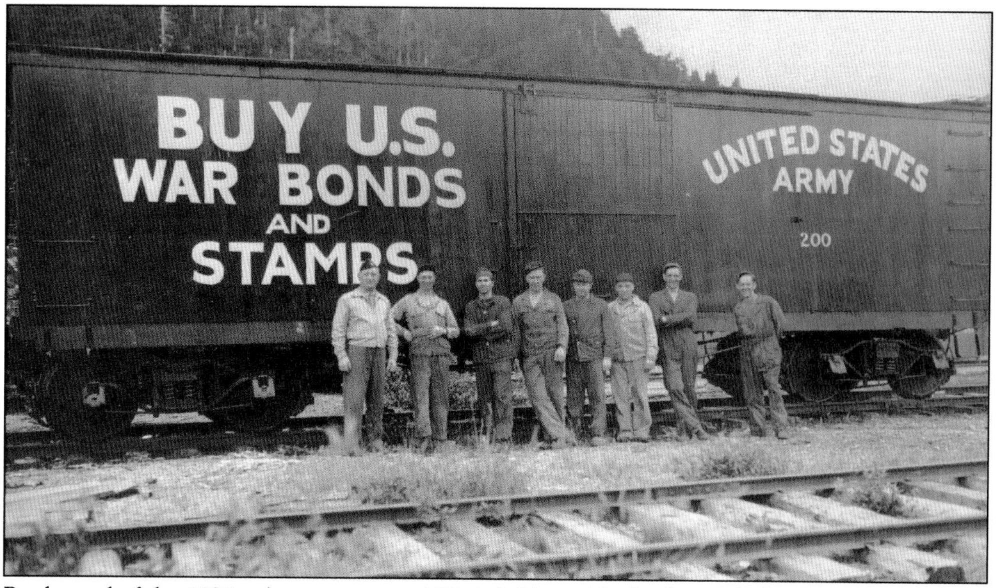

By the end of the 1930s, there were over 100 airfields in Alaska, but only four were adequate for modern aircraft. The Civil Aeronautics Act created an authority to regulate air traffic, and in 1940, as World War II raged in Europe, Congress seriously considered its Alaskan defenses. The Army began a program of building airfields along the coastal route in Alaska. The Chugach National Forest announced it would use funds to convert the railway bed to a highway between Cordova and the preferred airfield site at mile 13. Soon, Cordova learned it would be the base for the 42nd Engineer Regiment. It would assist with airfield construction and provide a military presence as World War II escalated. Cordovans welcomed the 42nd, and the soldiers became a part of the community.

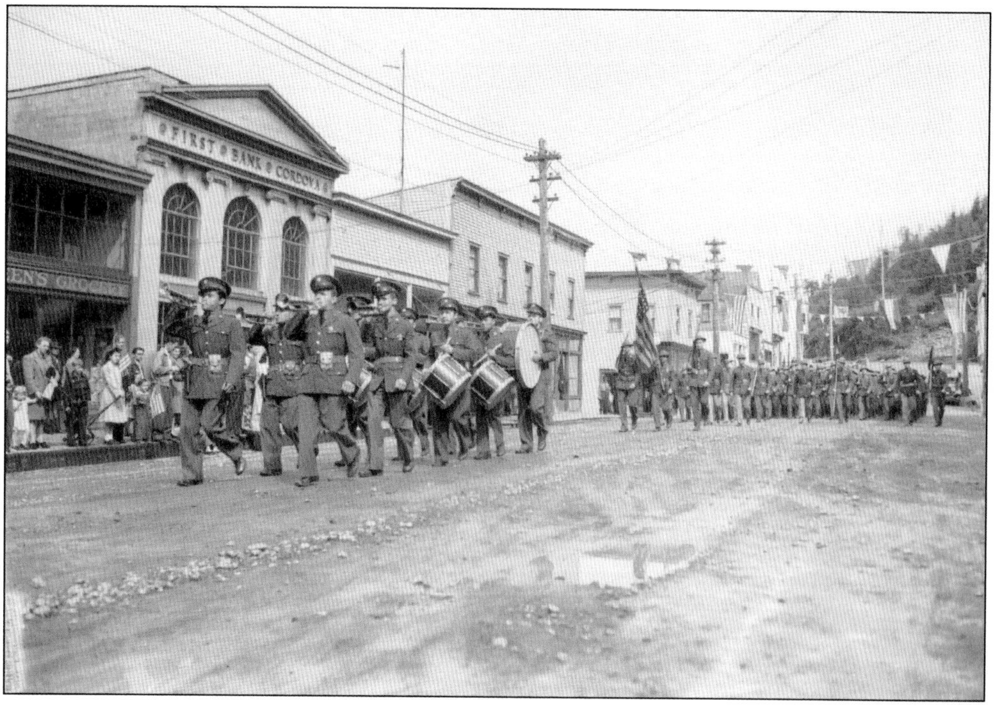

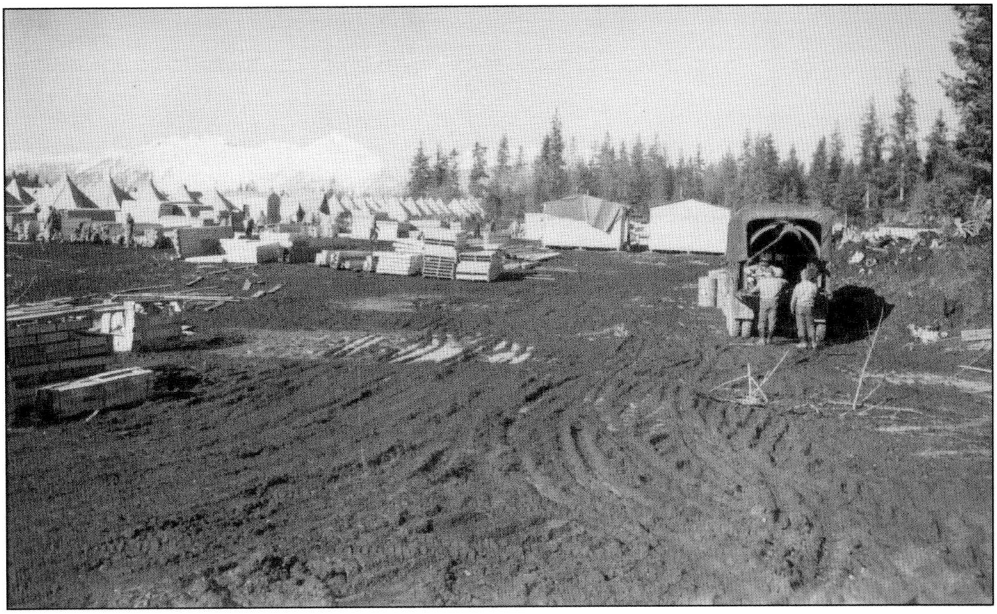

In the spring of 1941, the Army arranged to pull rail from the abandoned Copper River & Northwestern Railway for use at Fort Richardson in Anchorage; however, rail was left in place as far as mile 13. It was decided to use a leftover CR&NW locomotive to move heavy equipment out to mile 13, where members of D Company would put up their pyramidal tents. E Company would remain in Cordova stationed at the old CR&NW headquarters and would utilize the roundhouse as its own headquarters. In the first few months of the camp at mile 13, there was no mechanical refrigeration, so a truck would be sent up to Sheridan glacier and shoveled full of glacial ice.

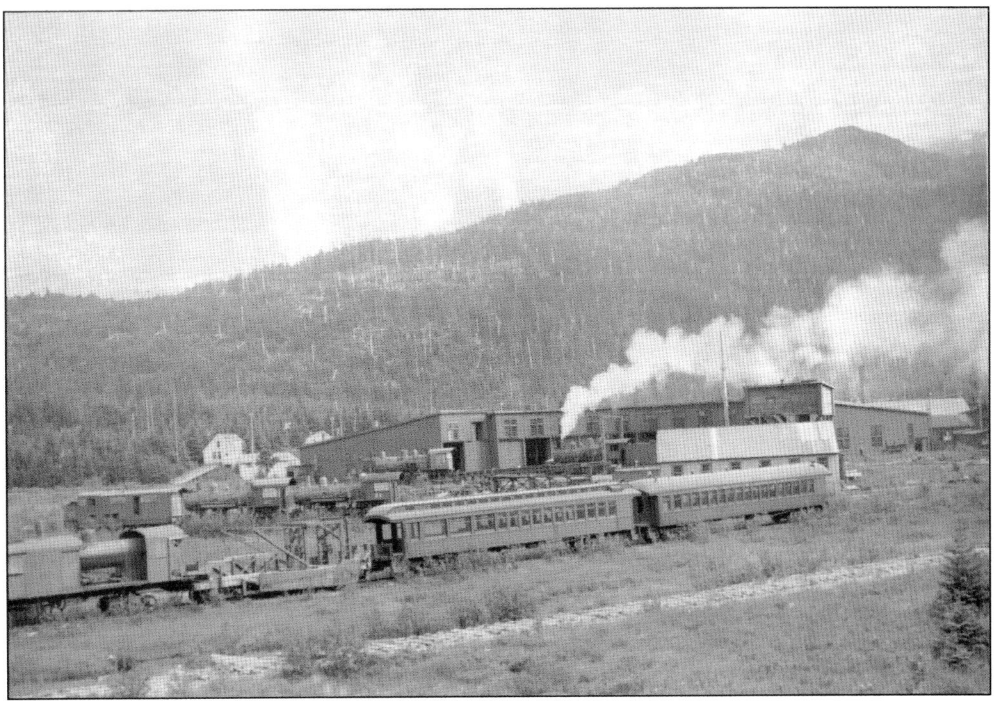

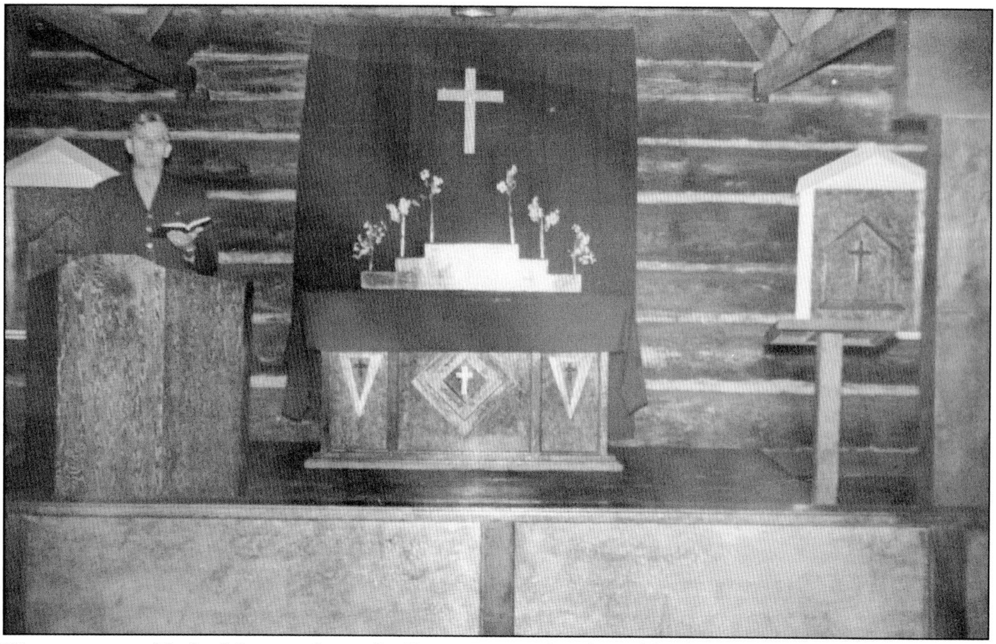

The most notable building at the mile 13 camp was the chapel built by E Company. Most of the buildings were prefabricated kits, but not the chapel. It was built of heavy spruce and hemlock logs and was a substantial, beautiful building. With the actions of the Japanese in the Aleutians, the war moved west, and more and more troops were moved away from mile 13. By June 1944, the garrison was down to fewer than 100 men; by 1945, almost all the regiment was gone except for a few fellows who decided they liked Cordova so much that they stayed—like Bob Taylor, who married Edith Nicholet of Cordova.

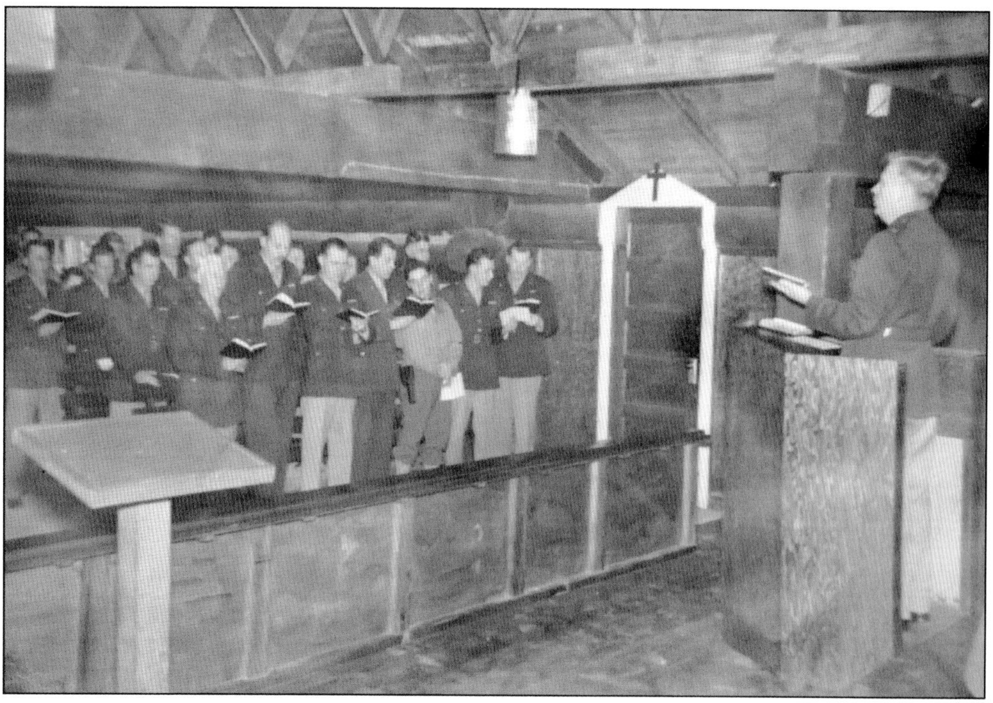

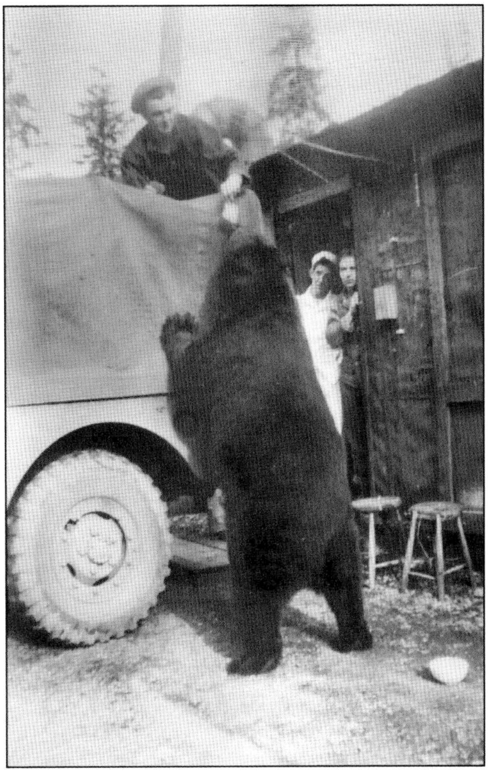

It was a total war effort at the mile 13 base, and even the bears pitched in. Cpl. Edgar Mueller adopted this bear and named her Suzi. She grew to be a rather large, one-person bear, sleeping on Mueller's bed and following him around like a dog. Her best trick, however, was honking the horn of the truck knowing the soldiers would come out and feed her. Getting into a major's barracks bag and eating up the candy that had been shipped in to him from his home folks was Suzi's fatal and last move. The major shot Suzi. Mueller hailed from Texas and noted of his time in Cordova that the weather was as unpredictable as in his home state of Texas. He was convinced that it rained at least 40 days in June and July 1942.

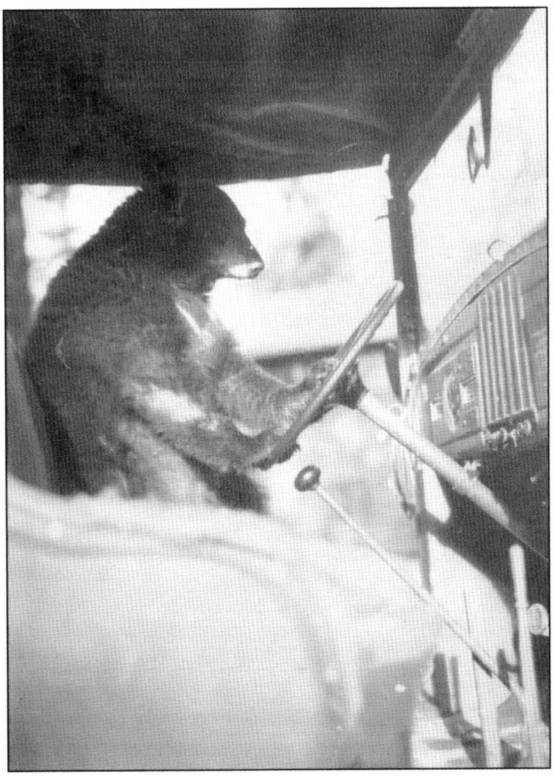

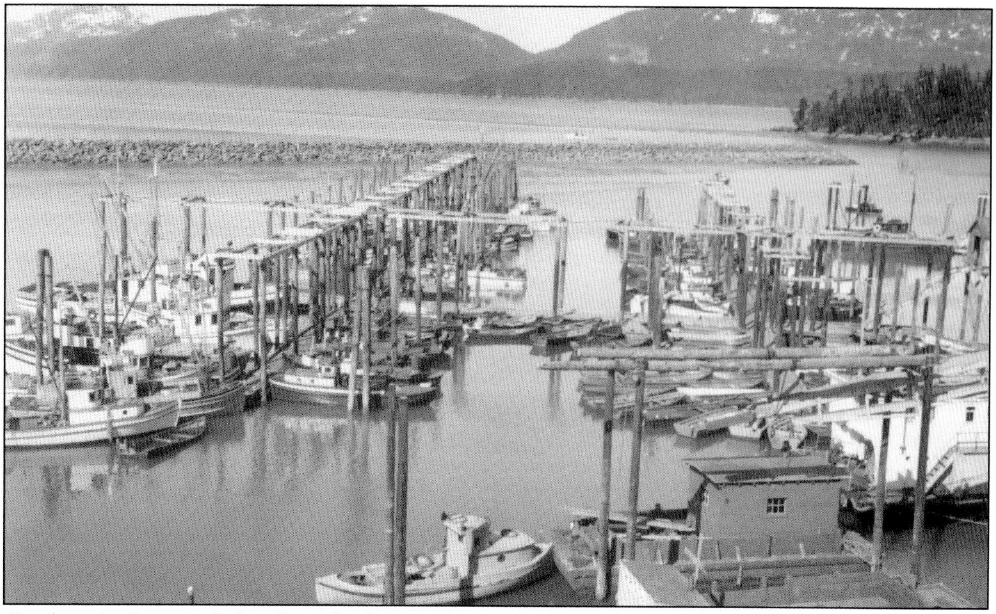

Cordova had expanded its boat harbor in the mid-1930s, and now with the throes of statehood upon the territory, many debated how that would affect the fisheries. Prior to World War II, the canneries owned the majority of the small gillnetters and the big fish-trap tenders. By the 1950s, however, 80 to 90 percent of the boats were now financed by the canneries but owned by independent fishermen.

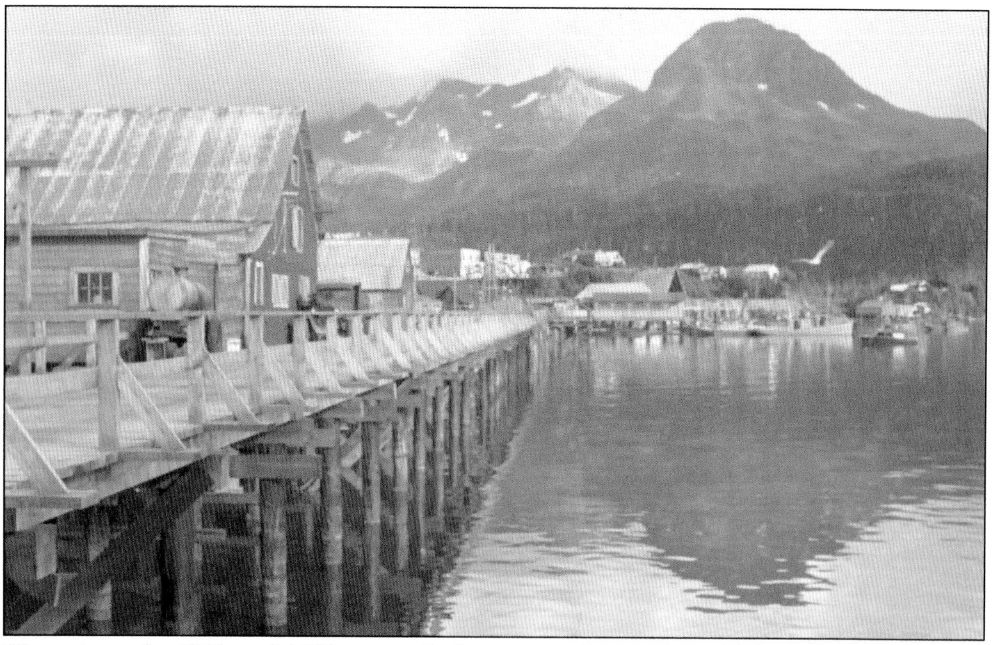

Throughout the 1940s and 1950s, a steady decrease in the number of fish taken statewide was noticed. In the Cordova region, canneries packed from 527,000 cases in 1947 to a low of 100,000 cases in 1955. In 1954 and 1955, there were essentially no pink and chum fisheries in the sound after two no-shows in prior years. Fish traps were seen as directly responsible, and pleas for their elimination were heard at statehood, when they were abolished.

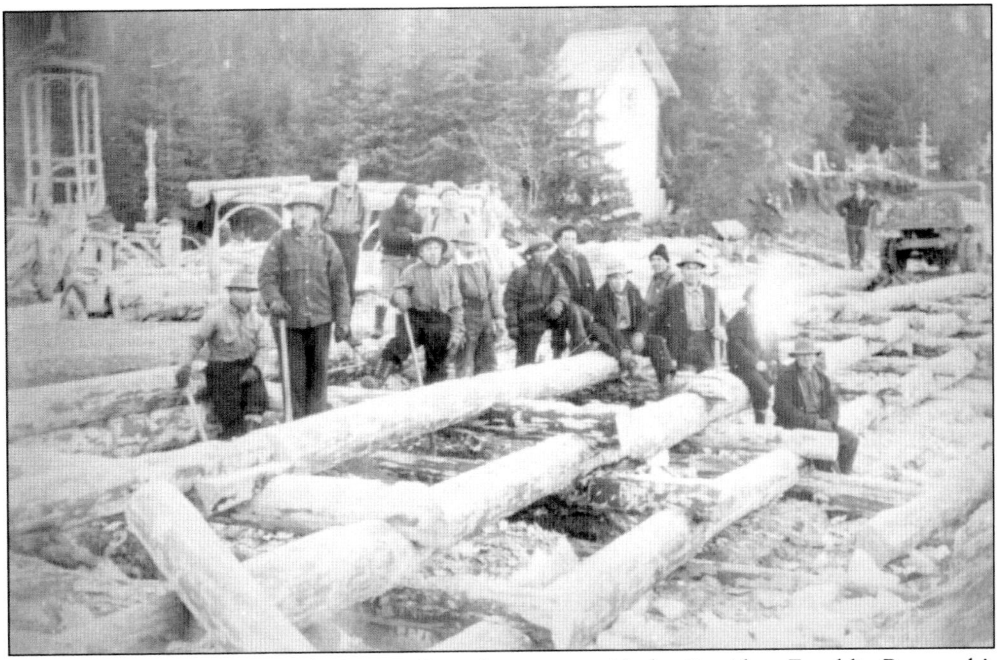

The lingering Depression in the Lower 48 made its way to Alaska. President Franklin Roosevelt's sincere interest in conservation was an impetus in developing the Civilian Conservation Corps. In Alaska, the CCC program was unique in that the US Forest Service was given authority to lead the program. The first CCC enrollment got under way in Cordova on May 23, 1933, and the three-mile Bay Trail was completed as its first project that summer. After that project was completed, the camp was moved to the old fish hatchery building at the head of Eyak Lake, and work was started on the Power Creek truck trail, which included a sturdy craftsman bridge to the American Legion Cabin. The CCC also worked on a revetment at Nirvana Park, creating a retaining wall to protect all the gravesites and artistic structures created by Henry Feldman.

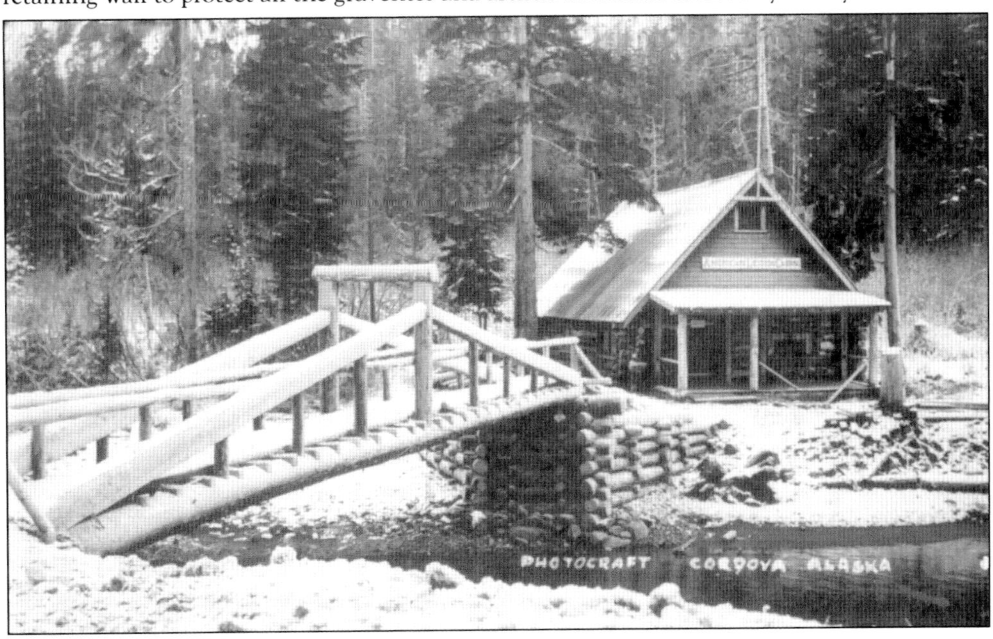

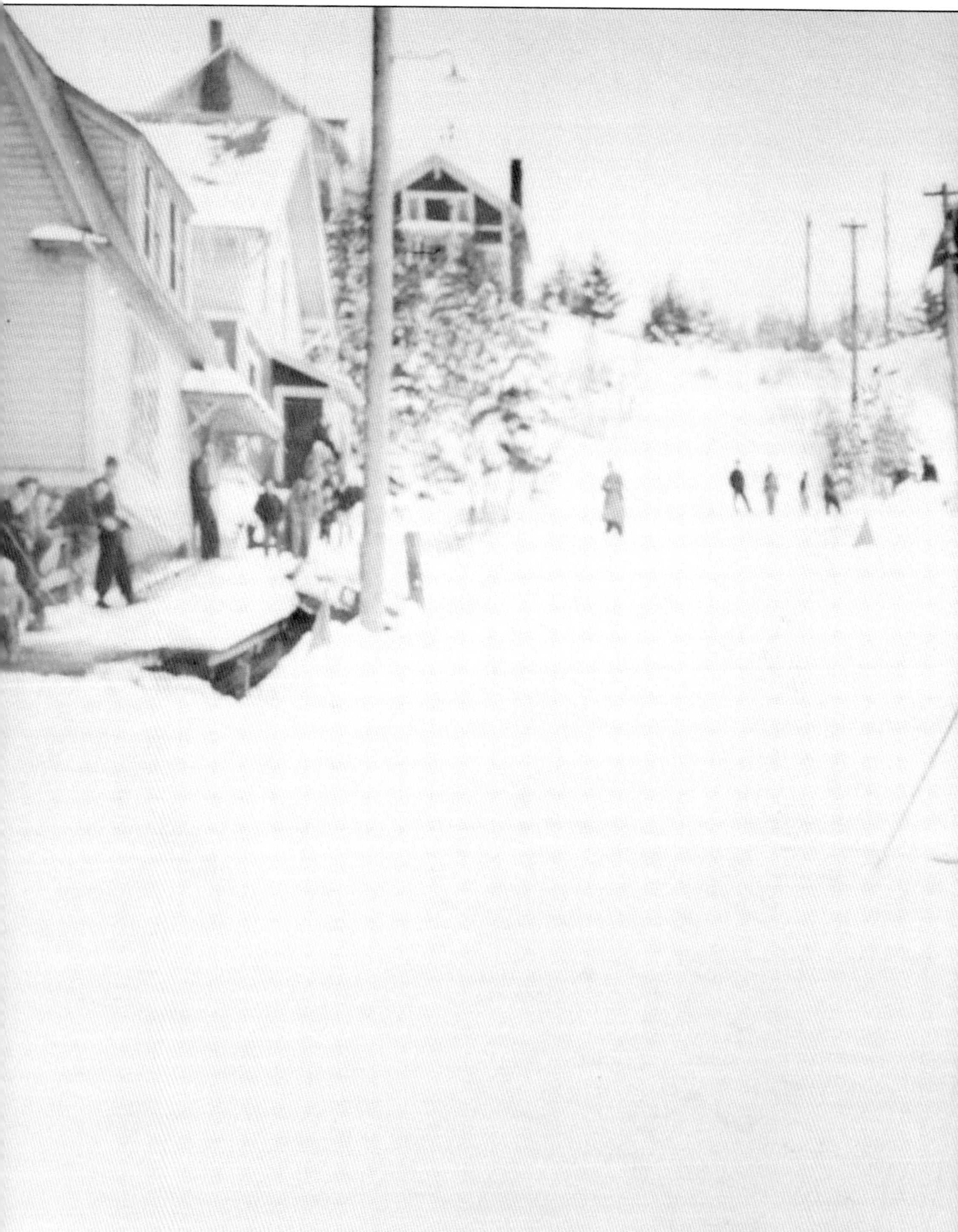

The very first ski club in the Cordova area was started about 1920 by Ben Osborne. The early fishing fleet was composed of many a Scandinavian immigrant, so skiing was not an uncommon hobby for many. Formed in 1948, the Sheridan Ski Club created a ski jump on C Street (Council

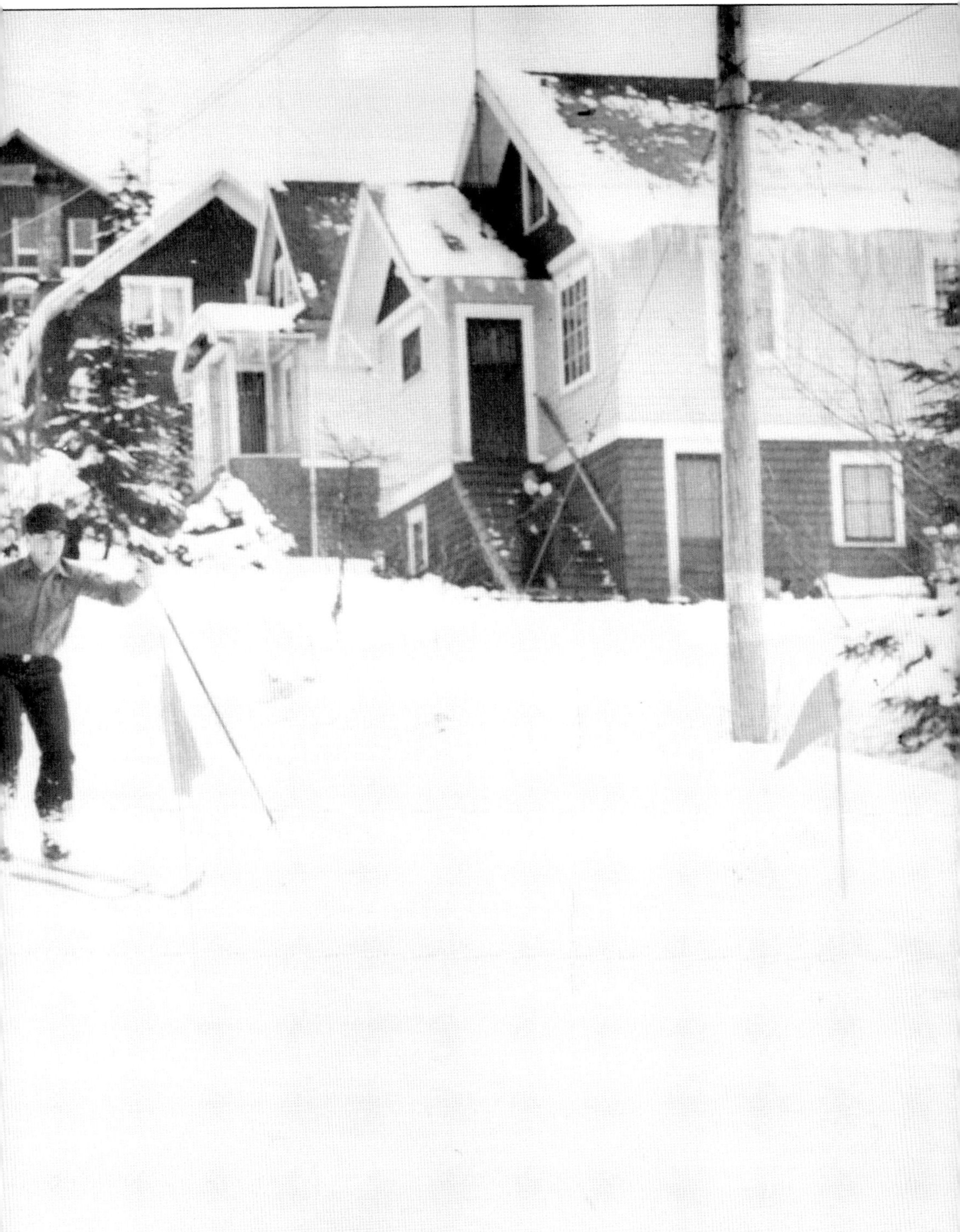

Street) between Smith's house and Mary Nicholoff's house. The Cordova townspeople could easily view the ski-jumping activities.

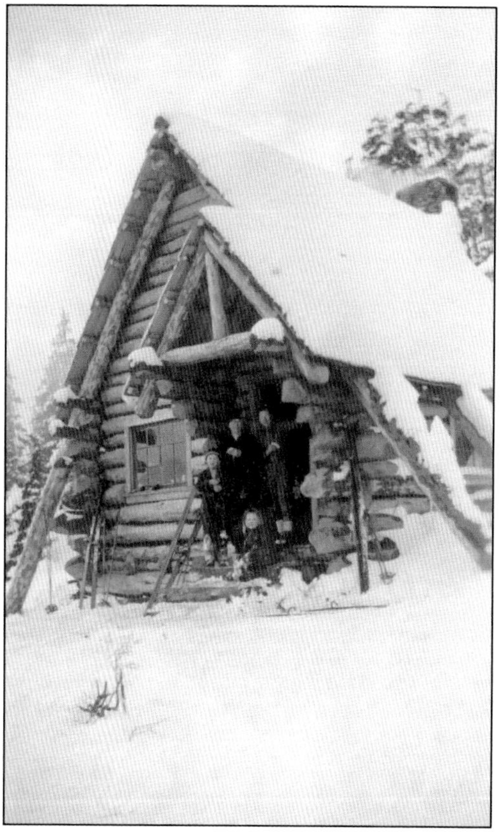

The CCC also worked on the Tripod Trail leading from town to the ski area on Mount Eyak. In July, workers began brushing out the trail to the Tripod; budget cuts delayed work on the Tripod Trail project, but progress was eventually made, and by snowfall, Cordovans were enjoying the fruits of their labor.

Crewmen from the Coast Guard cutter *Haida*, one of the earliest ships stationed in Cordova, were also active skiers. A favorite skiing locale was above the "'Golden Stairs" near the reservoir area, where coffee was served over a campfire. Skiing and skating were and are important wintertime activities for Cordovans who never let the weather deter them from outdoor adventures.

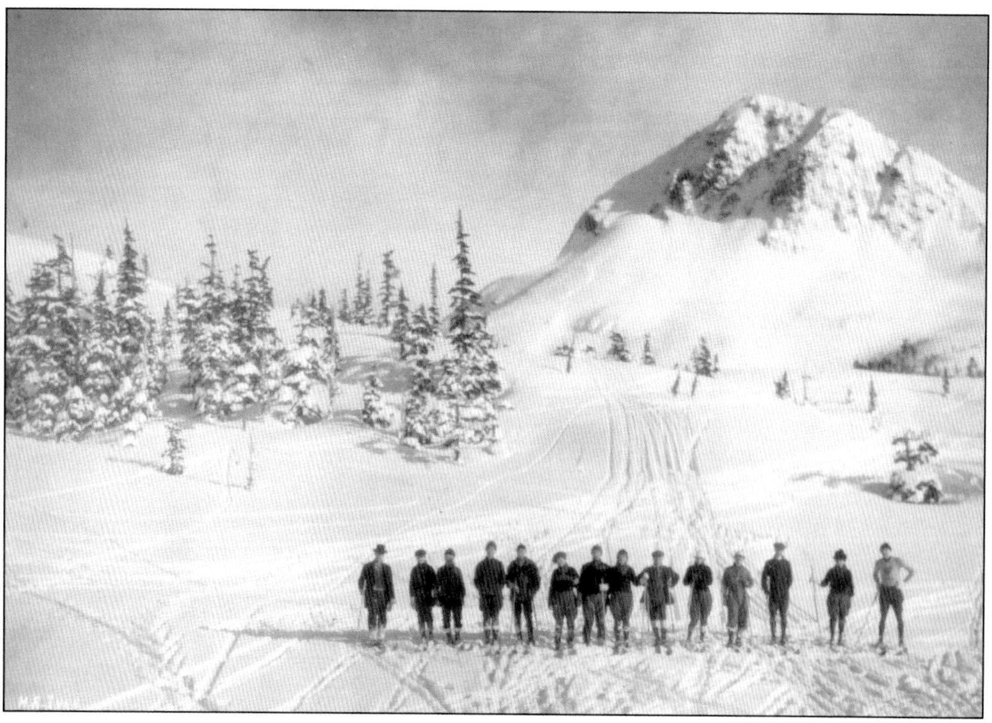

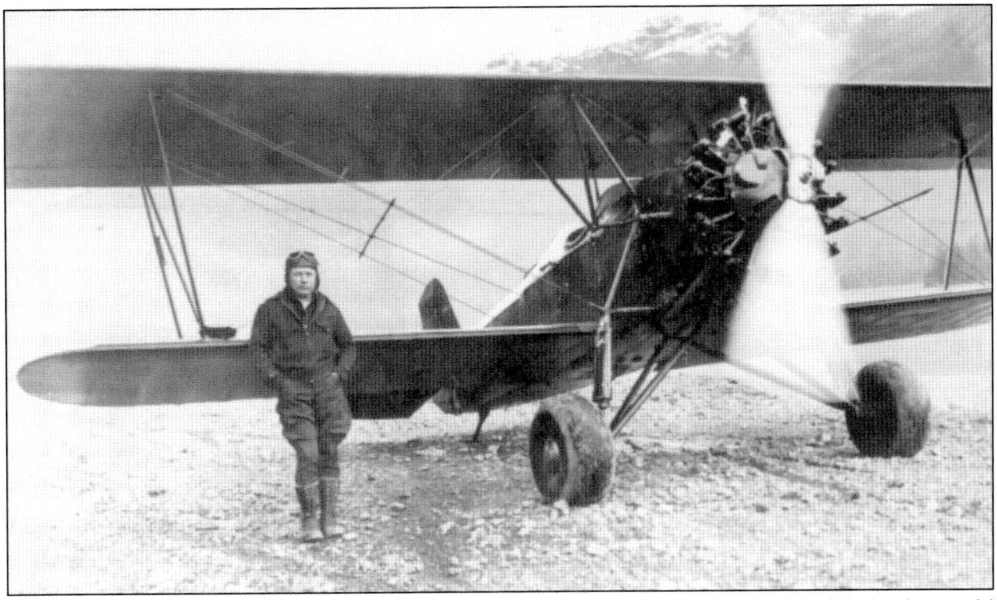

Merle Smith was born to fly; hanging around pilots, listening, and dreaming of flight, he could not remember a time when he did not want to fly. Smitty met "Kirk" Kirkpatrick, who was full of stories about legendary Alaskan bush pilots. A Cordova job with "Kirk" gave Smitty his bush pilot status. When Kirkpatrick was killed in a crash, Smitty was asked to manage Cordova Air Service, which he did with an ambitious program of expansion.

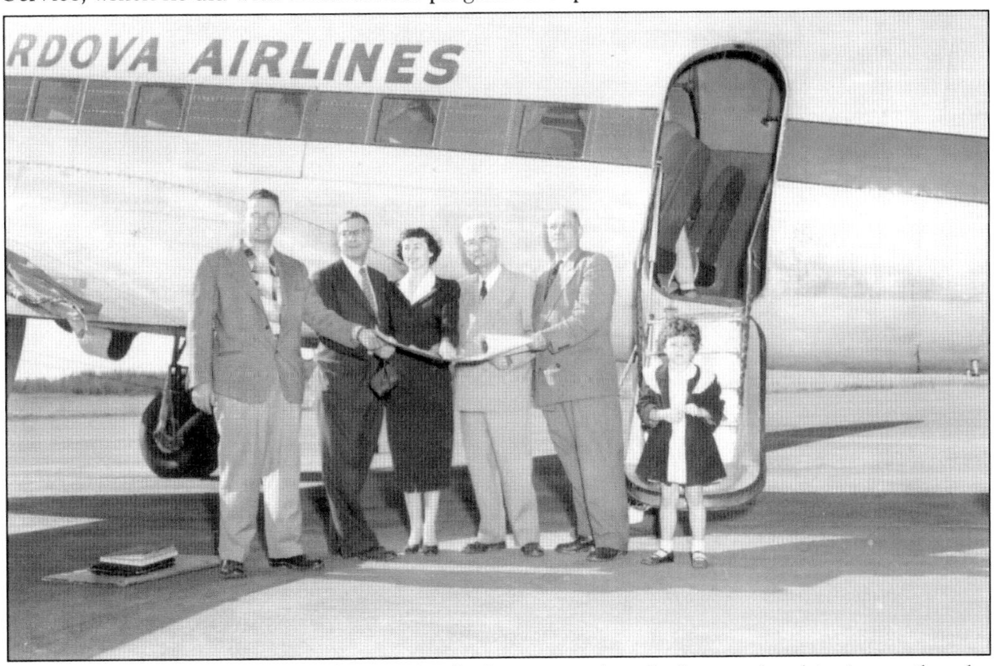

Cordova Air Service purchased a DC-3, which came in handy during the shipping strike; the Alaska Steamship Company strike meant no food shipments. Smitty began a nonstop grocery run, carrying 3.5 tons of food each trip and supplying the town for 69 days. In 1968, Cordova Airlines merged with Alaska Airlines, bringing jets to Cordova. Alaska Airlines brought Boeing 727s to Cordova, and the first person to step off one of these was Merle K. Smith.

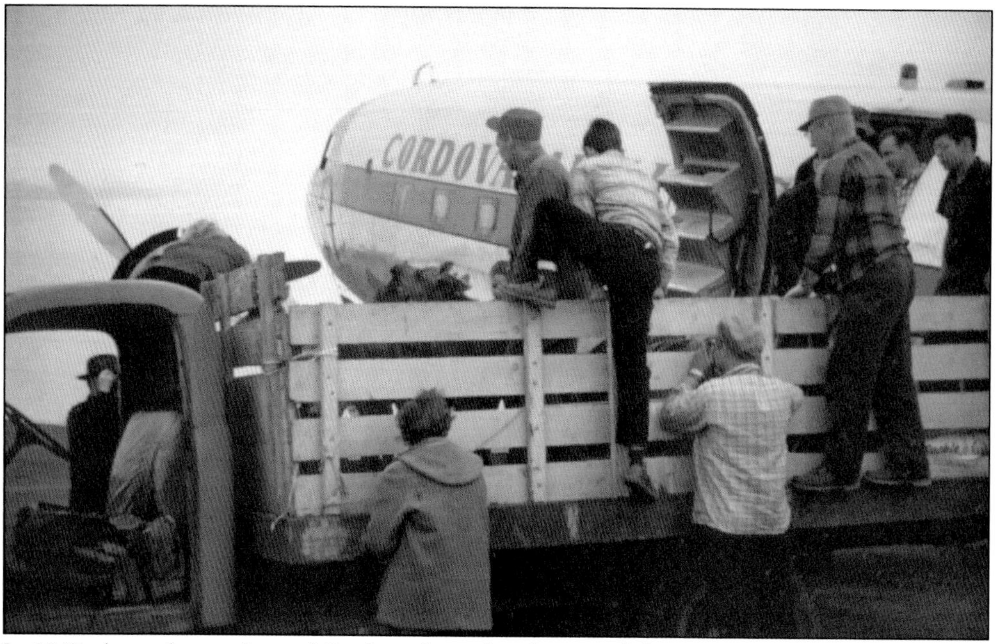

In 1947, the early members of Cordova formed a chapter of the Izaak Walton League because Cordova was determined to bring moose to the Copper River delta. Merle K. Smith brought the first moose calves to Cordova in his DC-3. Smitty recounted on the first flight that the moose calves escaped their corral and wandered into the cockpit with the pilots. After that trip, chicken wire was installed behind the cockpit.

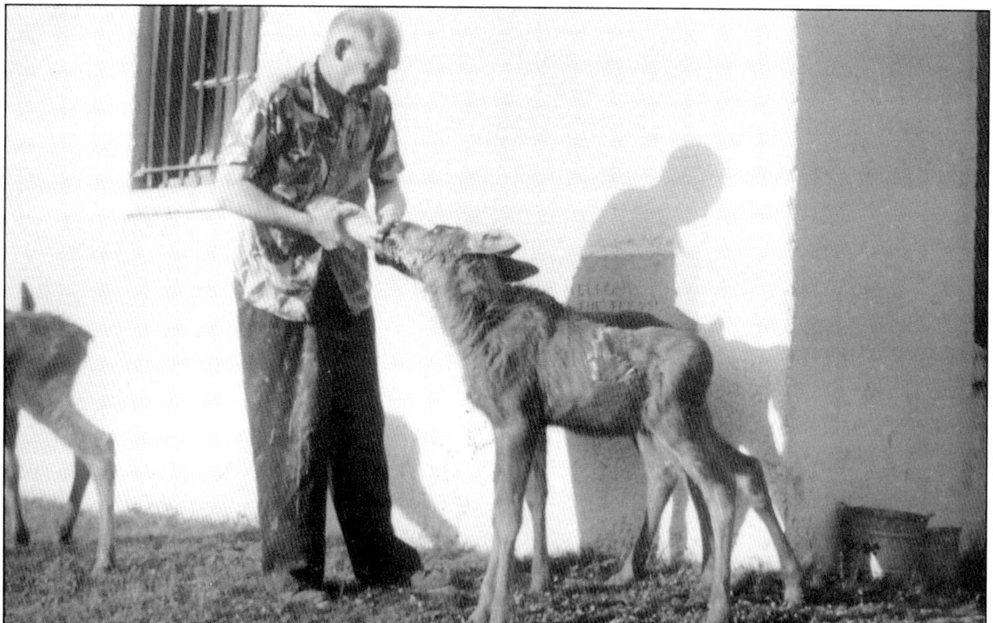

Hollis Heinrich, the local postmaster, was the spark plug for the whole deal and kept the moose in the grassy front yard of the post office. Heinrich also volunteered to act as nursemaid for the gangly-legged baby moose calves that arrived. It was a challenge; two of the calves died right away as the volunteers had trouble devising a proper formula to feed them.

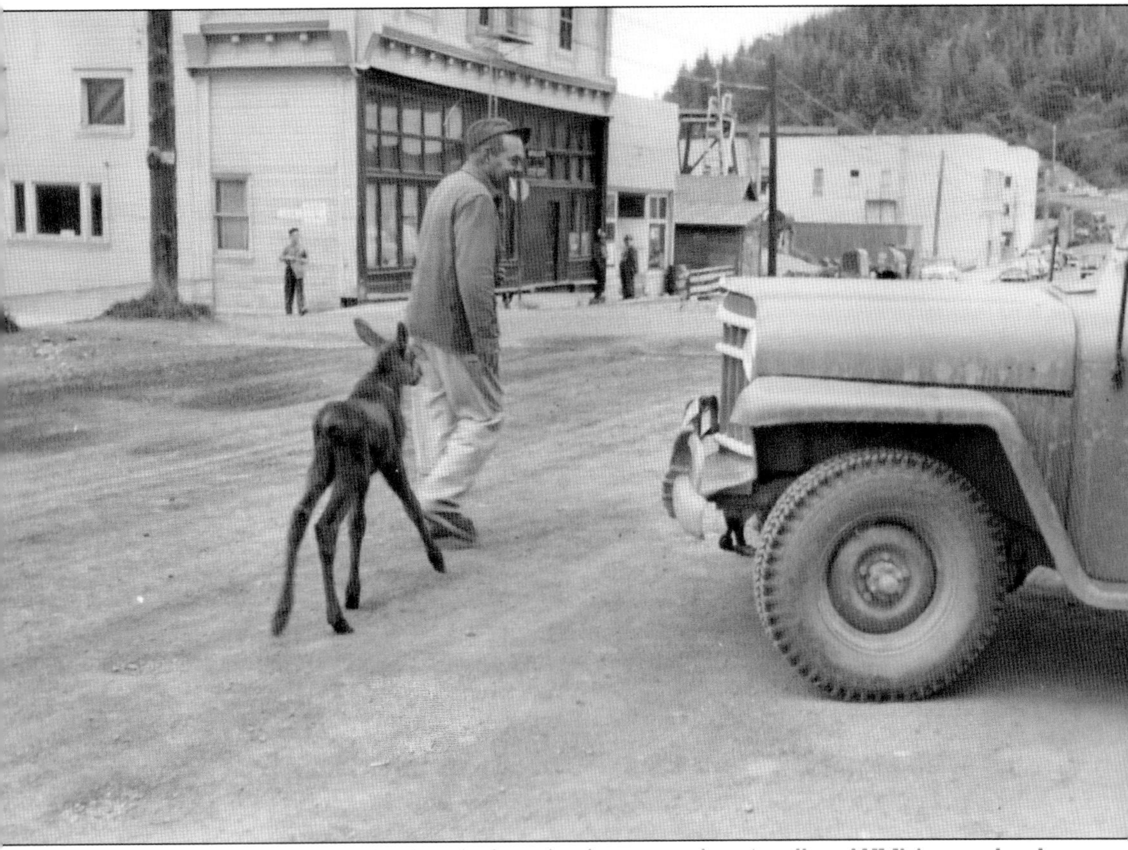

Finally, the determined group developed a formula of evaporated cow's milk and KLIM, a powdered-milk mix. The entire town became so attached to the moose that their social lives became a regular column in the *Cordova Times*. Mike Moose and Miss Minnie were the first to marry. Others were named Matilda, Lucy, and Phyllis. The children of Cordova were reprimanded for feeding the moose bubble gum and chocolate. It took until 1951 for the first calves to be released on the delta. The first successful calf born on the Copper River delta was in 1953. The Izaak Walton League continued the program until 1958 and succeeded in releasing 24 calf moose, 20 of which survived. With a thriving moose population on the delta, hunting began in 1965 and continues to this day.

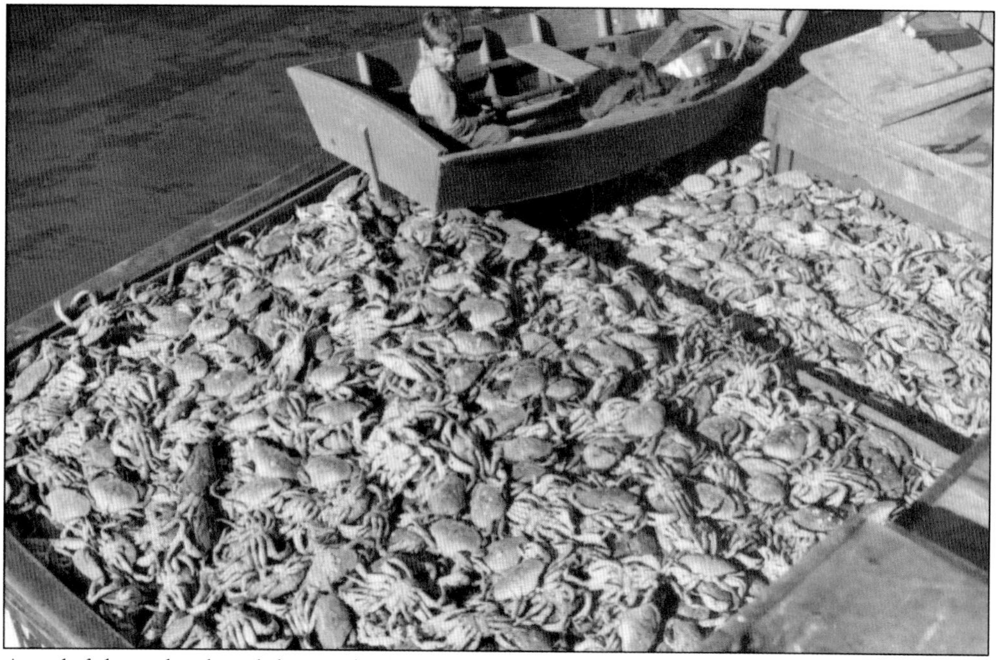

A crab fishery developed during the late 1920s, and in 1929, a record shipment of crab left on the SS *Alaska* from Cordova's port. Between 1935 and 1940, half a million pounds of crab were processed at the seven area plants. King crab, Dungeness crab, and Tanner (now marketed as snow) crab were all abundant in Orca Inlet.

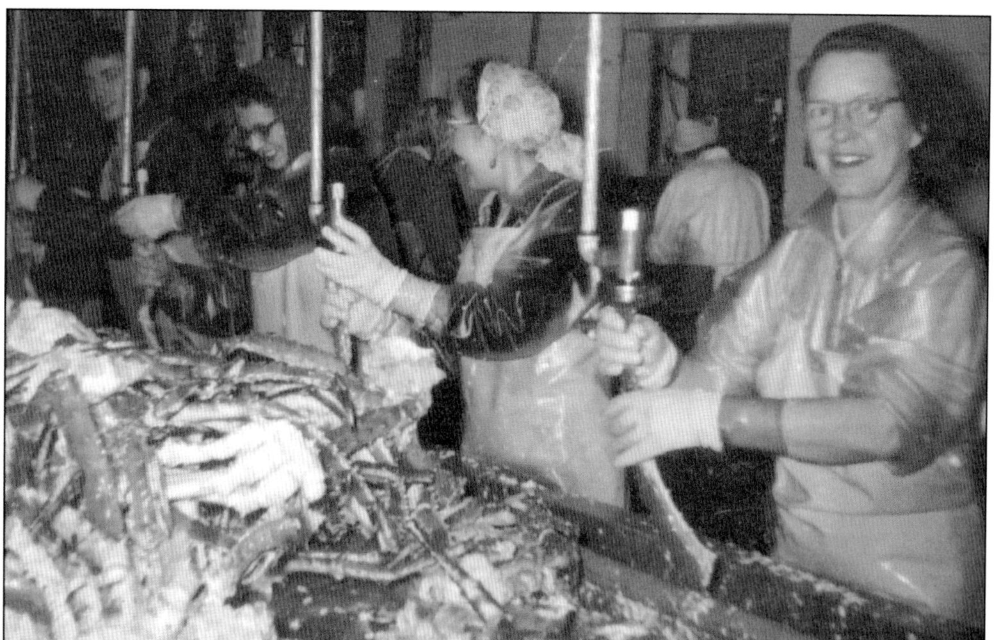

One of the earliest floating canneries in Prince William Sound was brought in for the crab harvest. To prepare the crab for market, the meat was forced from the shell by jets of water. Workers would break the ends of the shell and push the meat against the water jet, shaking it free to create piles and piles of delicious goodness.

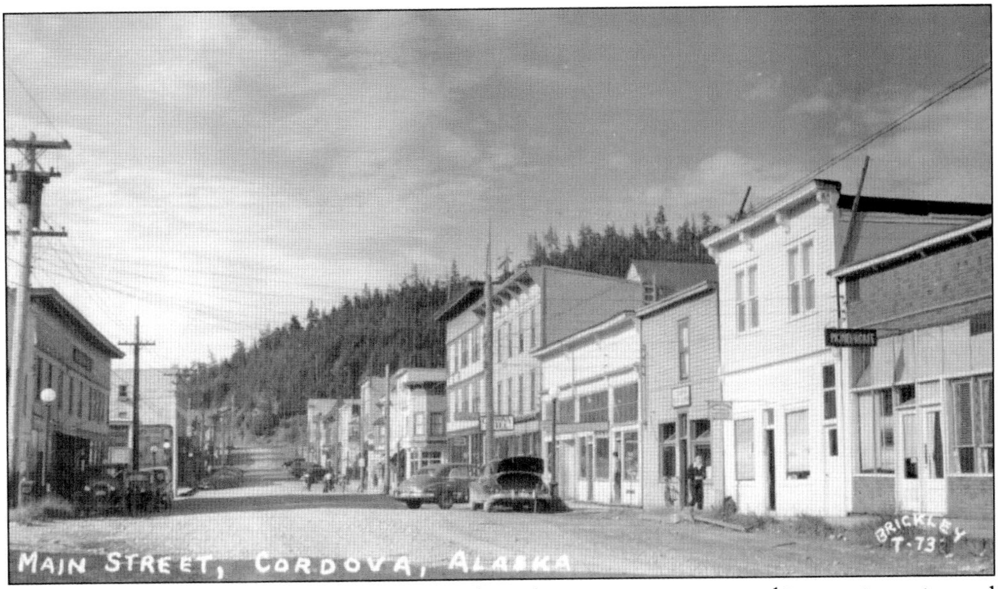

Views of Cordova in the late 1940s and 1950s show the community managed its growing pains and never became the ghost town that was predicted with the closing of the Kennecott Mine and the end of the Copper River & Northwestern Railway run. Regular steamship service and air service provided transportation links; businesses continued to grow and expand despite the steady decline in the fishing industry. Restaurants, car dealerships, a movie theater, and more graced the dirt streets. The population hovered around 1,000, and the community had a new hospital and elementary school. Cordovans were active in territorial politics and discussions about potential statehood.

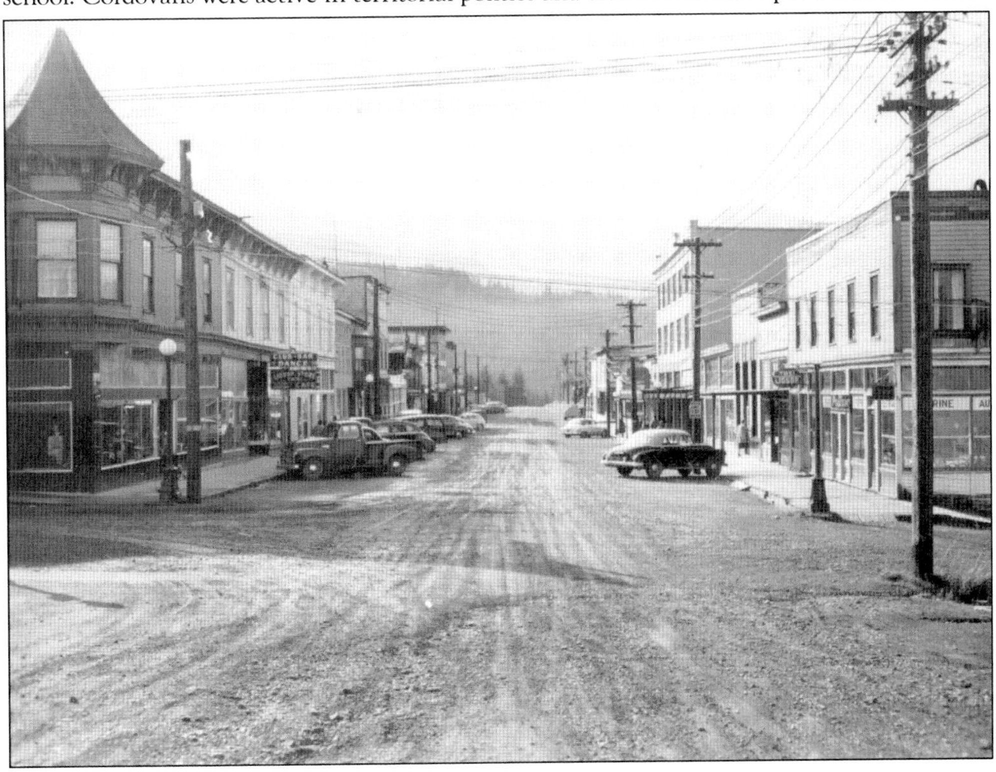

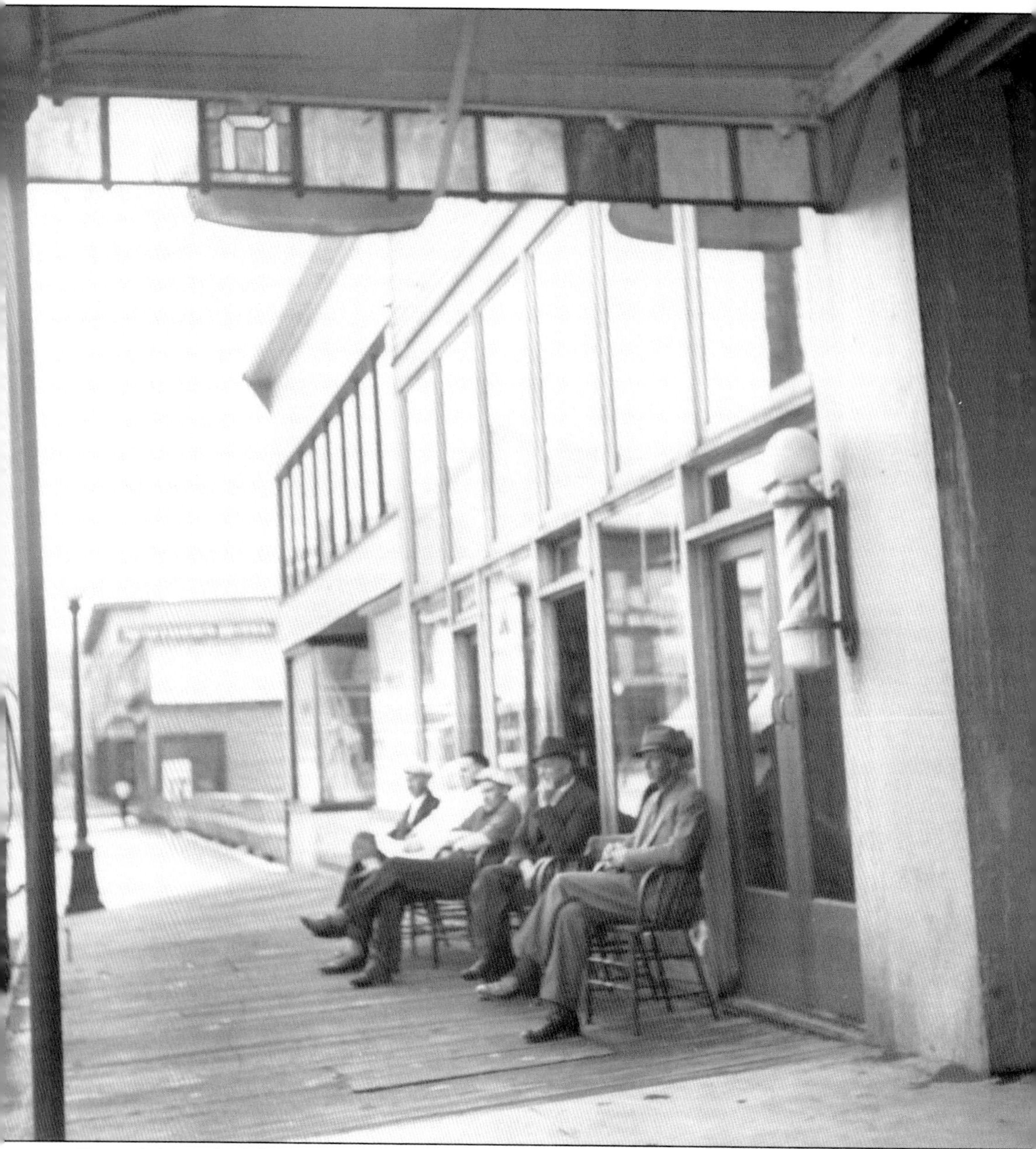

Toward the end of the 1940s, statehood for Alaska loomed large on the horizon and brought an array of mixed emotions to the community of Cordova. Business owners, like Austin E. "Cap" Lathrop, benefited from Alaska's small tax base and did not want themselves or their businesses to be hurt financially by the increase in taxes that would result from statehood. Other Alaskans feared that statehood would result in a flood of more people coming to Alaska, which they did not want. In an advisory vote in the fall of 1946, Alaskans voted 9,630 to 6,822 in favor of joining the union. Once again, Cordova began to face transformation. Statehood would mean changes in the fisheries, changes in business, and changes in lifestyle, and Cordovans were not all on board with change. Moving the community forward while maintaining its way of life was about to become a major topic of street-corner conversations.

Five

Second Growth 1959–1989

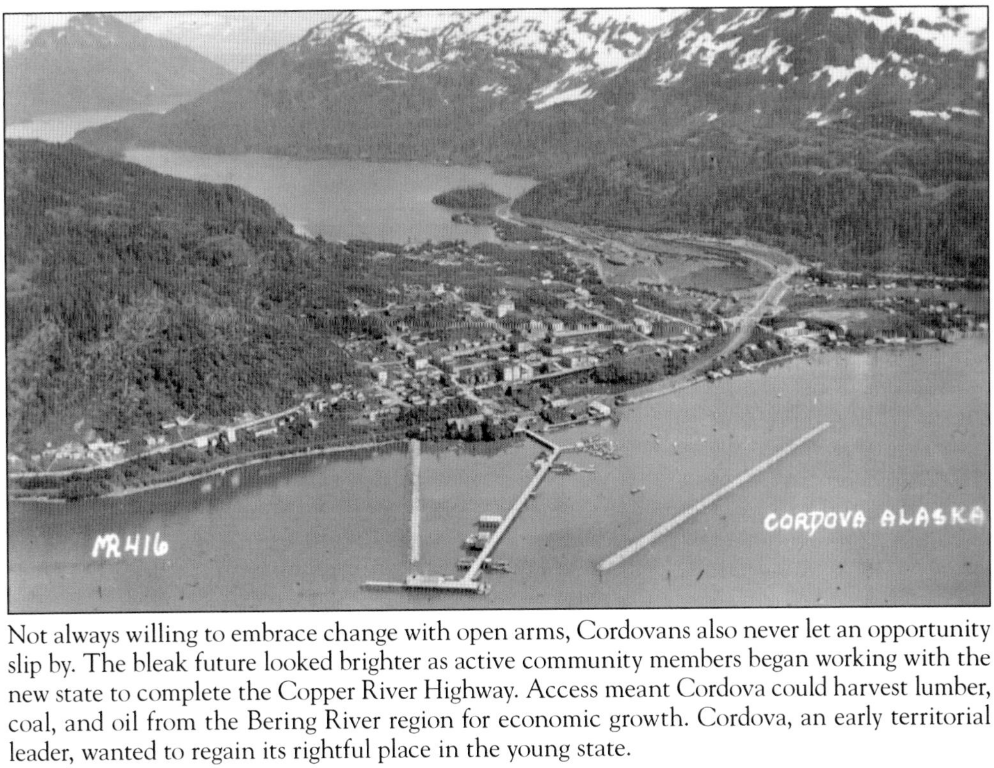

Not always willing to embrace change with open arms, Cordovans also never let an opportunity slip by. The bleak future looked brighter as active community members began working with the new state to complete the Copper River Highway. Access meant Cordova could harvest lumber, coal, and oil from the Bering River region for economic growth. Cordova, an early territorial leader, wanted to regain its rightful place in the young state.

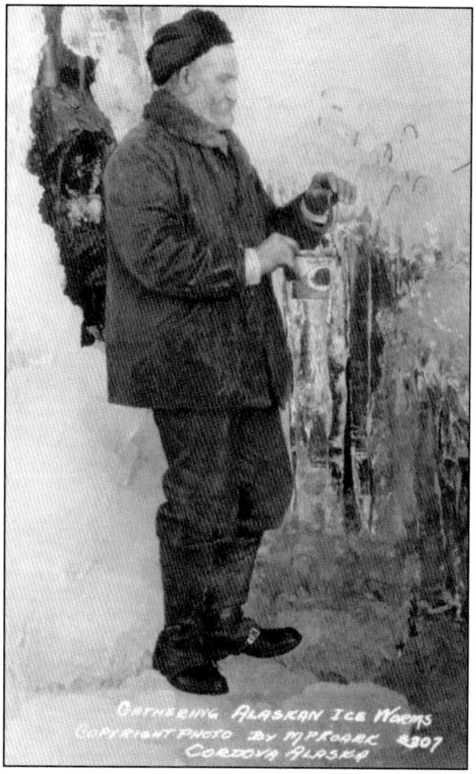

Another effort to revive Cordova was made one cold one night in 1961 when, over glasses of their favorite "antifreeze," Omar Wehr and Merle "Mudhole" Smith discussed that other Alaskan communities had festivals. A unique event was needed, and that evening, the Iceworm Festival was hatched. For the first festival, Cordova Airlines offered a one-day $15 round-trip special ticket, leaving Anchorage at 7:00 a.m. and returning at midnight the same day, including a ticket to the crab-feed dinner. Ever since, the festival has carried on with many of the same events, which still take place—a variety show, the crowning of the iceworm queen, survival-suit race, egg hatch, pet show, arts-and-craft fair, cake bake, and a parade featuring the longest, bluest iceworm known to man powered by the legs of many Cordova kids.

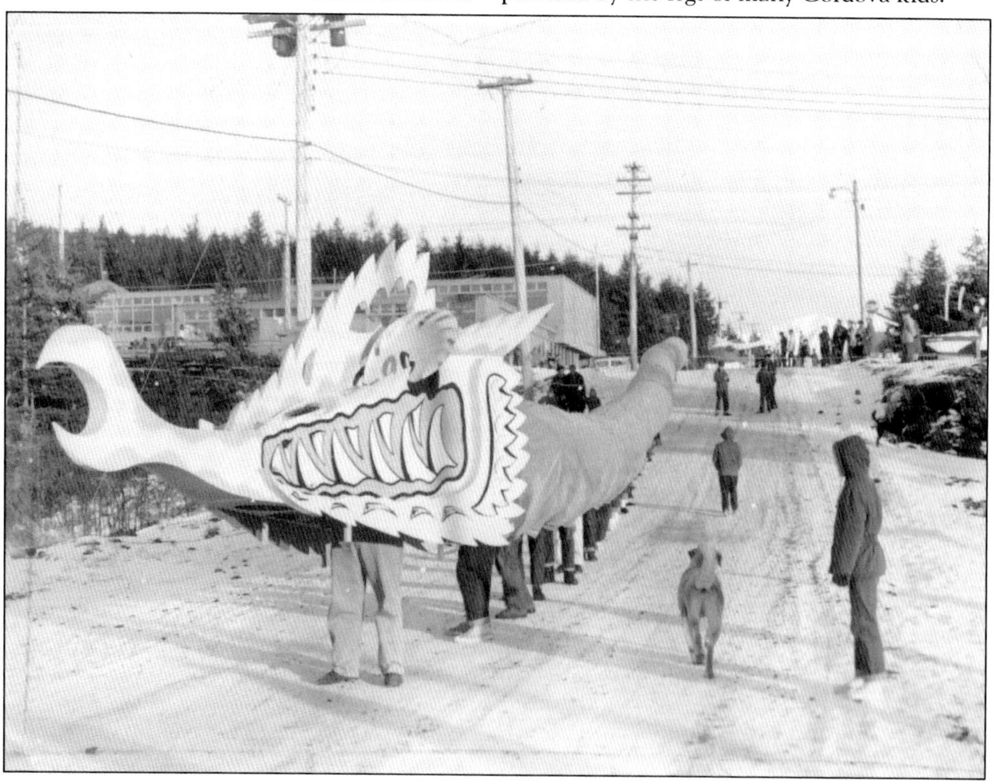

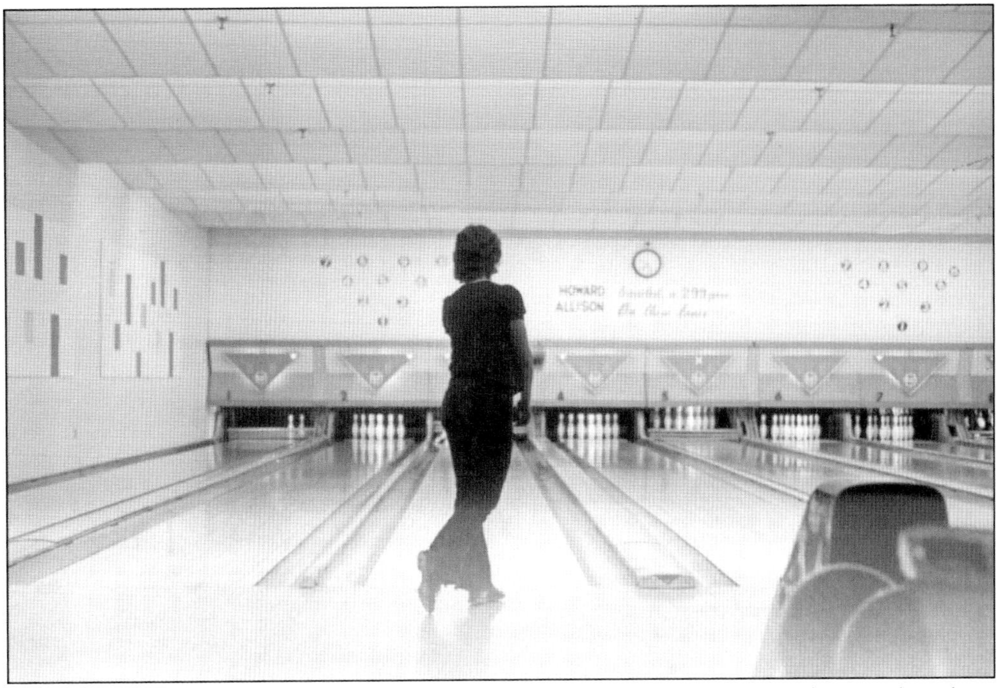

Not only did the Iceworm Festival bring a smile to Cordovans faces in the early 1960s but also a young trio of entrepreneurs, brothers Don and Ken Van Brocklin and friend Bill Sherman. They decided to build a bowling alley for Cordova. The partners drew up plans, and construction began in the summer of 1962. It featured automated equipment and included a modern design of rounded seating arrangements.

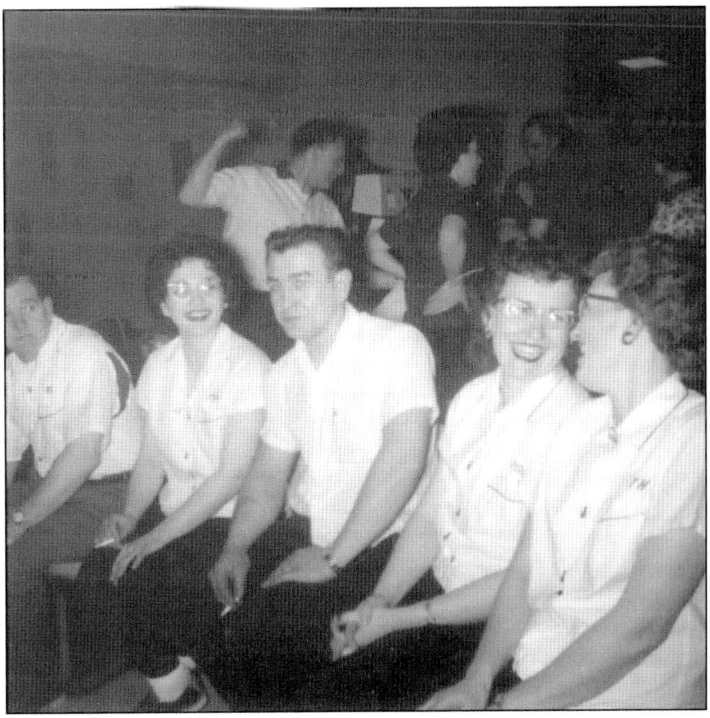

Leagues formed almost immediately, and the Club Bowl would house an average of 100–150 bowlers, who could bowl in four or five leagues. A bowling tournament became a regular sporting event during the Iceworm Festival, and teams would travel to and from Cordova to participate in tournaments across the state. Junior leagues offered instruction for the younger generation, and bowling became a favored indoor activity in rainy Cordova.

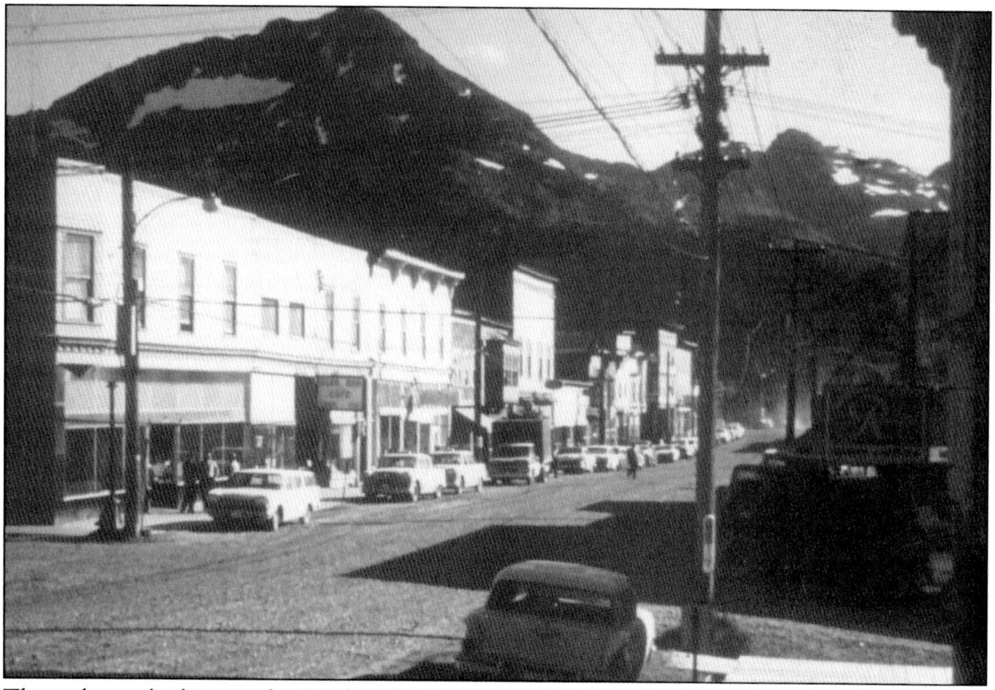

Things began looking up for Cordova by the spring of 1963—the Copper River Highway was on the horizon, fishing was about to start, and spirits were high—when sometime in the very early hours near 4:00 a.m. on the morning of May 2, 1963, the fire started. The conflagration began in the center of the business district on First Street inside the Club Café. The café had received 1,500 gallons of fuel the day before, and now the furnace room fed the flames. By the time the fire was discovered, it had spread the full length of the café and adjacent bar, and within minutes, flames had moved north to wooden, neighboring buildings.

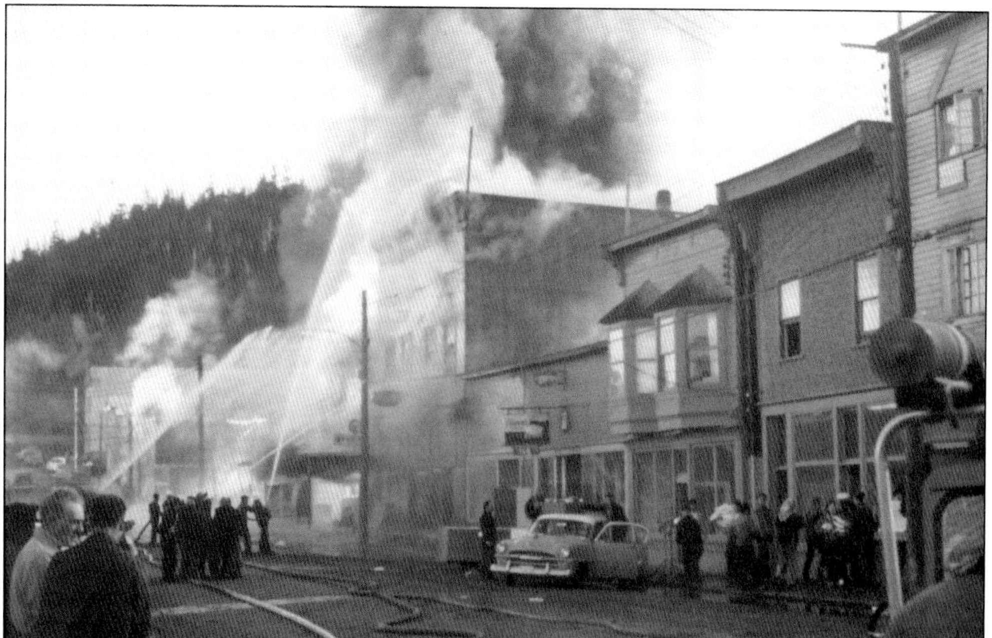

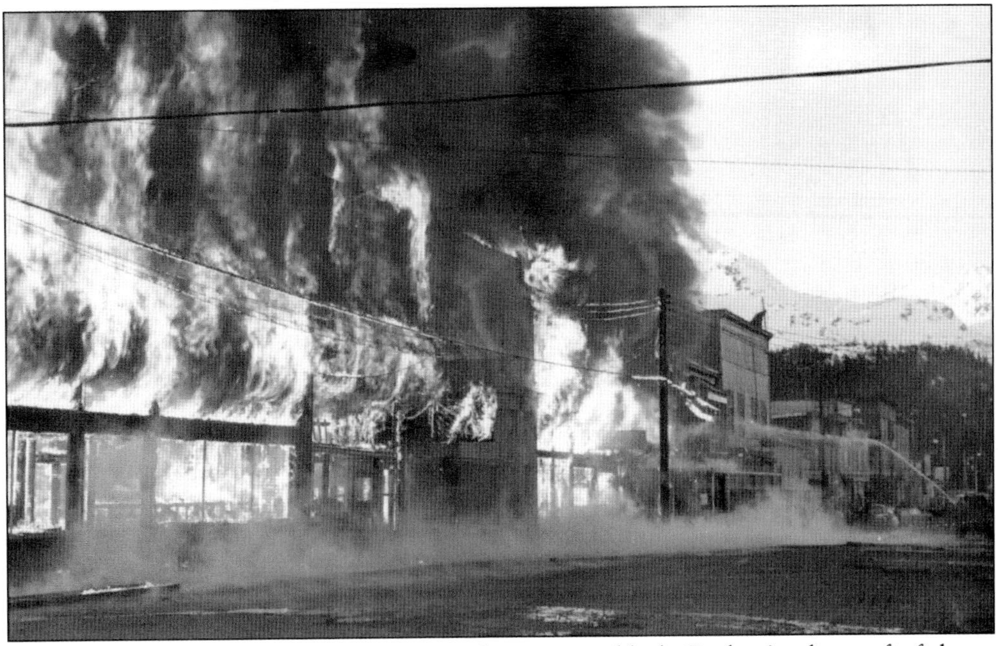

Before anyone knew it, the fire was consuming the entire city block. Cordova's volunteer firefighters, the crew of the Coast Guard cutter *Sedge*, and everyone who could help waged the battle against the devastating blaze. Friends began assisting friends in evacuating stores and apartments of merchandise and personal belongings. Calls for help from other communities went out, and Anchorage began preparing flights with men and equipment. A desperate attempt to dynamite the fire was not enough to stop the well-fueled blaze. It was nearly 2:00 in the afternoon before the fire could be declared actually under control. By the time assistance arrived the following morning, only smoldering remains of what was once a thriving business district were left.

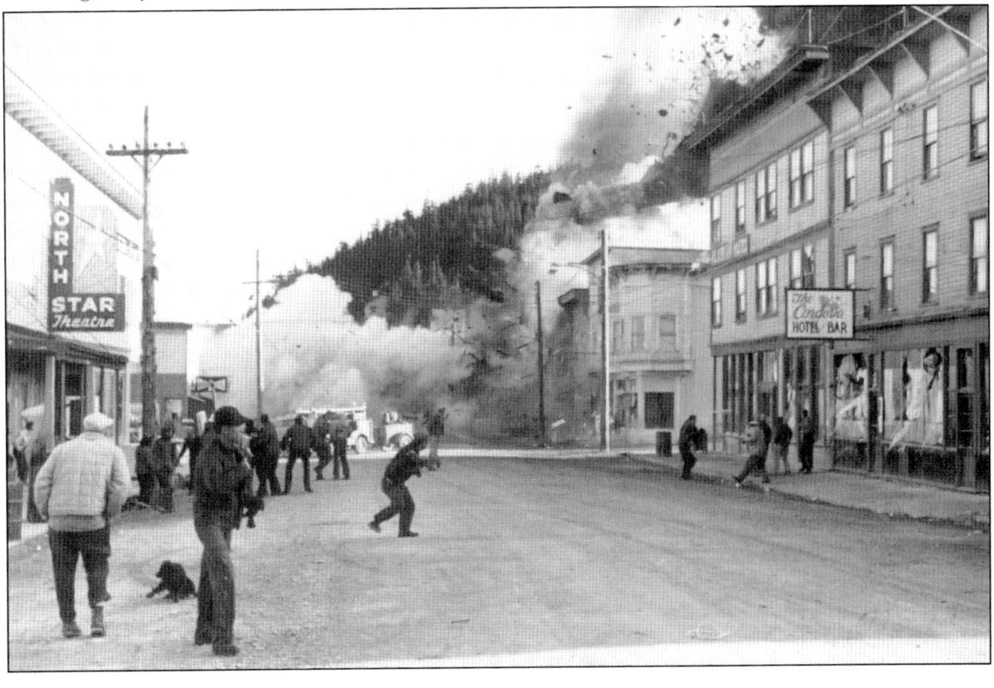

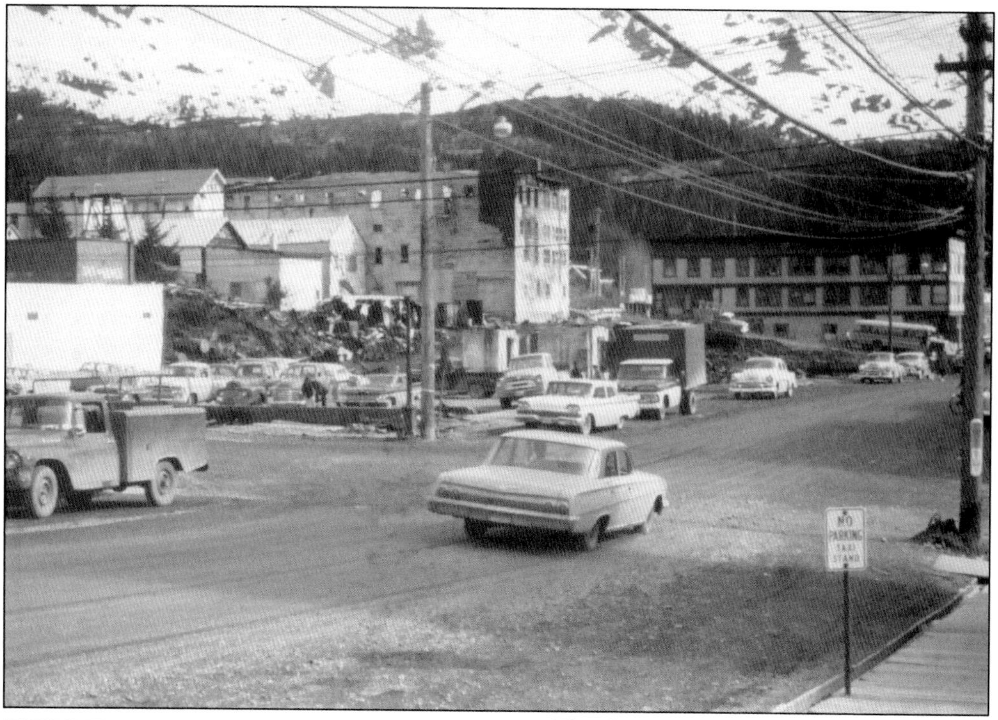

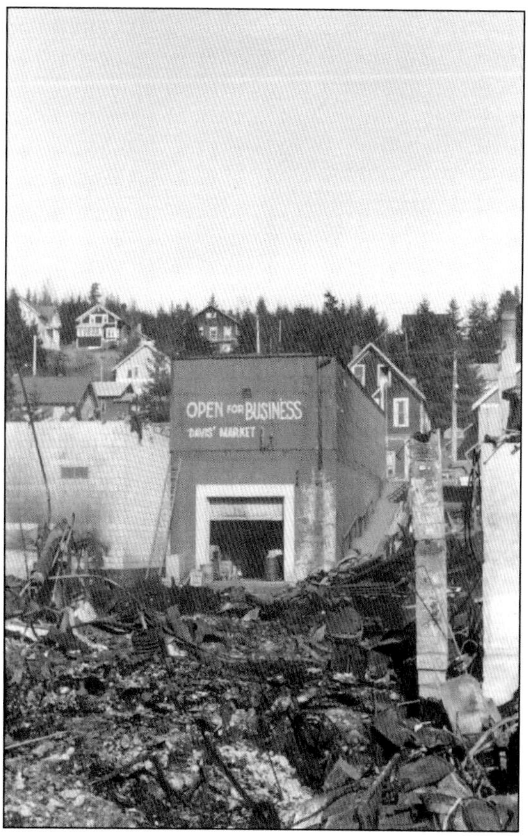

The devastation was great. Fifteen buildings were totally destroyed, and within those buildings, 32 various businesses had been operating. Many more businesses adjacent to the destruction were damaged by either the heat of the fire or the water used to extinguish the flames or the unsuccessful dynamite blast. Roughly 153 people were displaced from their homes. The Small Business Administration declared Cordova a disaster area. Losses totaled nearly $1.8 million, but true to Cordova's "pick yourself up by your rubber boots" attitude, the town began to immediately rebuild. By the following spring, Cordovans were back in business only to find their community about to be tested one more time.

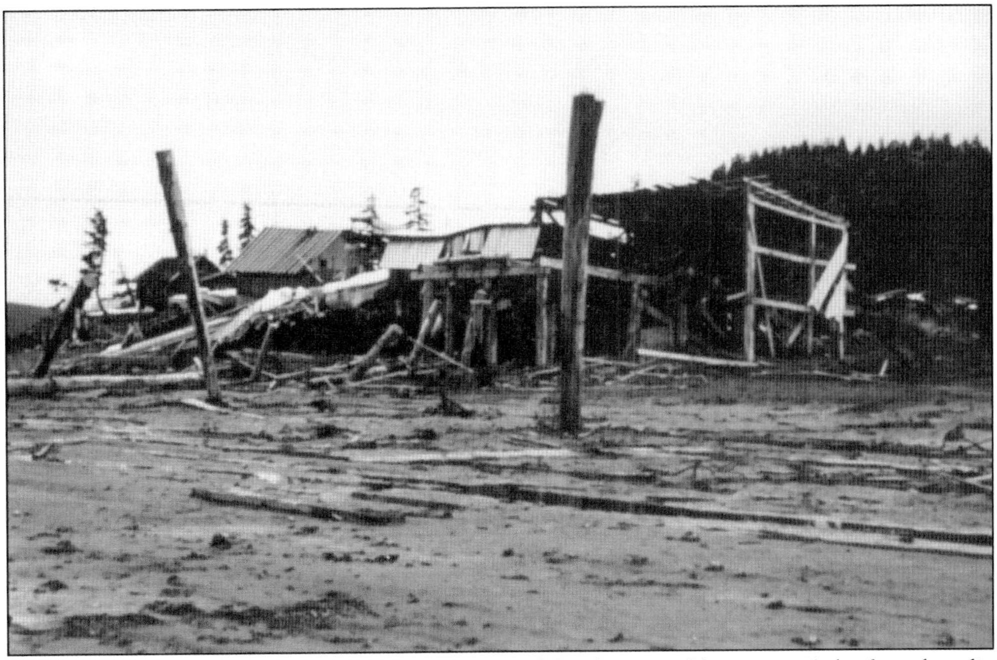

Incredibly, almost one year later, the community of Cordova would once again be forced to dig deep and find the gumption to start over when the 1964 Good Friday Earthquake struck the Prince William Sound Region on March 27. This 9.2-magnitude earthquake wrought major changes in the physical landscape of the Cordova and Prince William Sound area. Some structural damage occurred in town along the waterfront, and there was one fatality at Point Whitshed; however, the tectonic uplift that took place had a much greater impact than was the case in some other Prince William Sound communities, which suffered more structural damage.

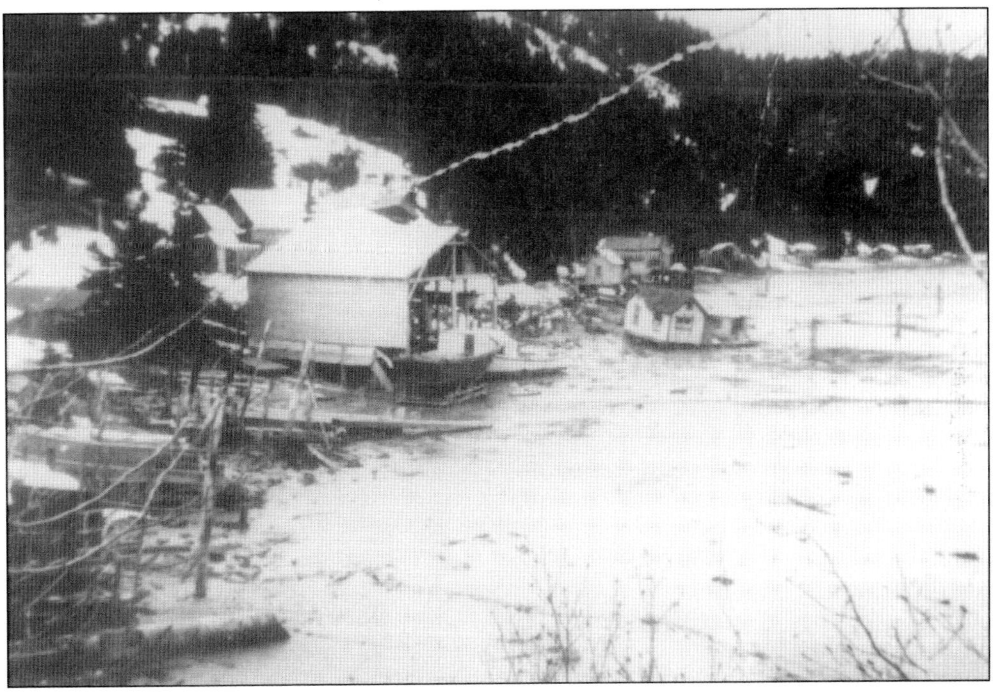

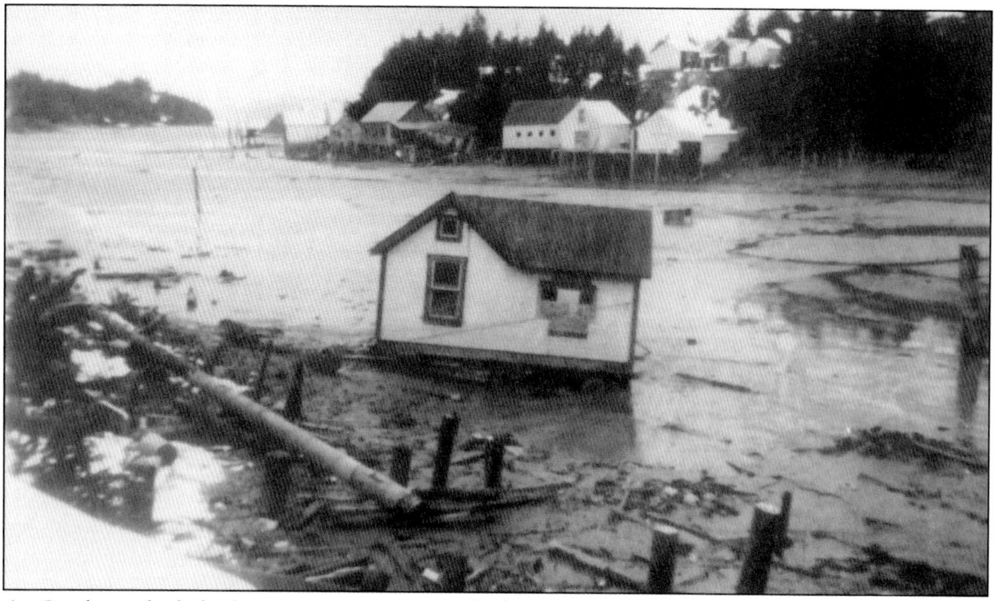

At Cordova, dock facilities were raised so high that they could only be reached by boats at the highest tides. An extensive and difficult dredging project, together with new breakwaters and dock repairs, was necessary to make the facilities usable. In the course of this work, which was done by the Army Corps of Engineers, the boat basin was enlarged, and 20 acres of new land, eventually usable for industrial development, was made from the dredged material. Uplift had an effect on waterfowl habitat on the delta and a drastic impact on the razor clam habitat. Most of the clam beds were left above the reach of normal tides. As a result, razor clam populations are now at a low level, and commercial harvesting has ended.

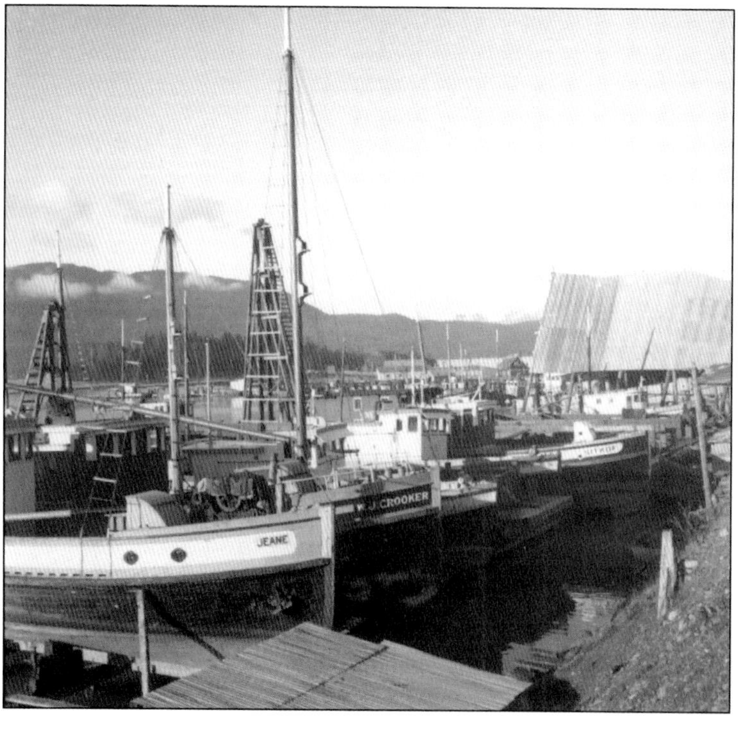

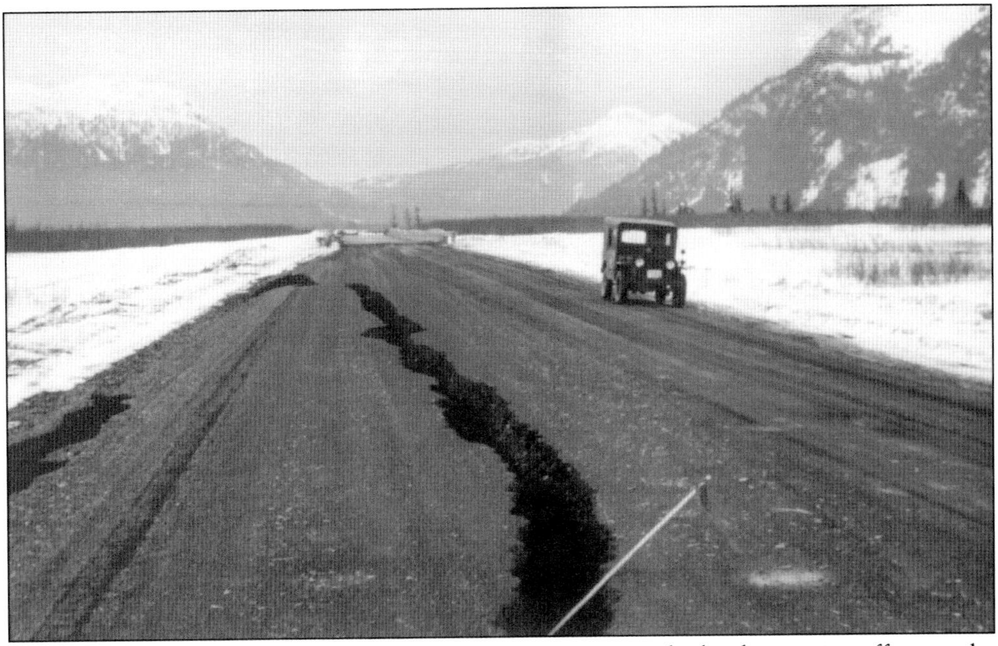

While the earthquake did little structural damage in town, it had a devastating effect on the Copper River Highway. All bridges between town and the airport, which crossed the delta, were either destroyed or badly damaged, while the roadway itself settled differentially and was cut with fissures. At the time of the earthquake, construction on the Copper River Highway route had advanced to the Allen River at mile 59. A survey made just after the quake showed that nearly all of the smaller bridges between miles 27 and 49 along the Copper River Highway had collapsed, and one span of the Million Dollar Bridge was in the river; forcing a reexamination of the entire project.

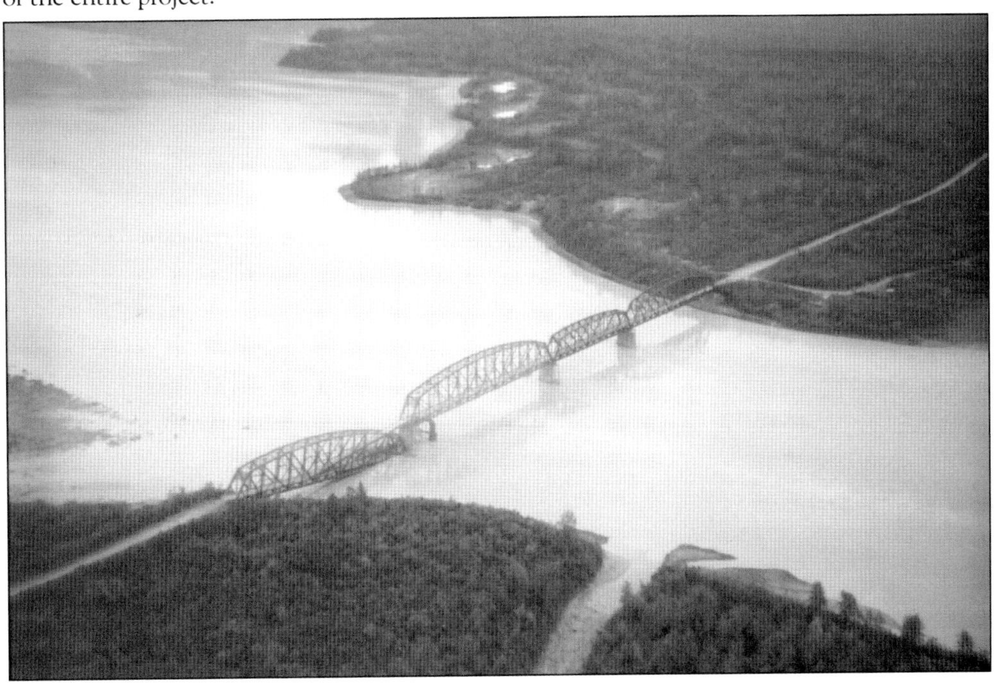

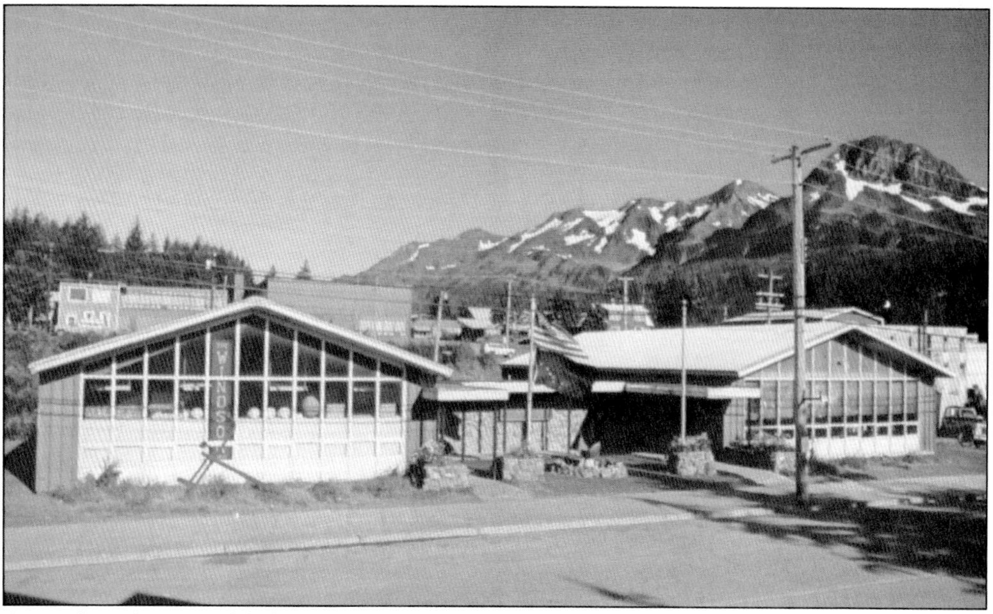

An enthused group of dedicated individuals noted the need to start recording the interesting story of the community. In 1966, these residents founded the Cordova Historical Society and then utilized Alaska State Centennial grant funds to build the Cordova Historical Museum. Located on First Street, it was constructed in 1967. After the Cordova Public Library outgrew its home in the lobby of the Windsor Hotel, it moved into an addition to the museum building in 1971.

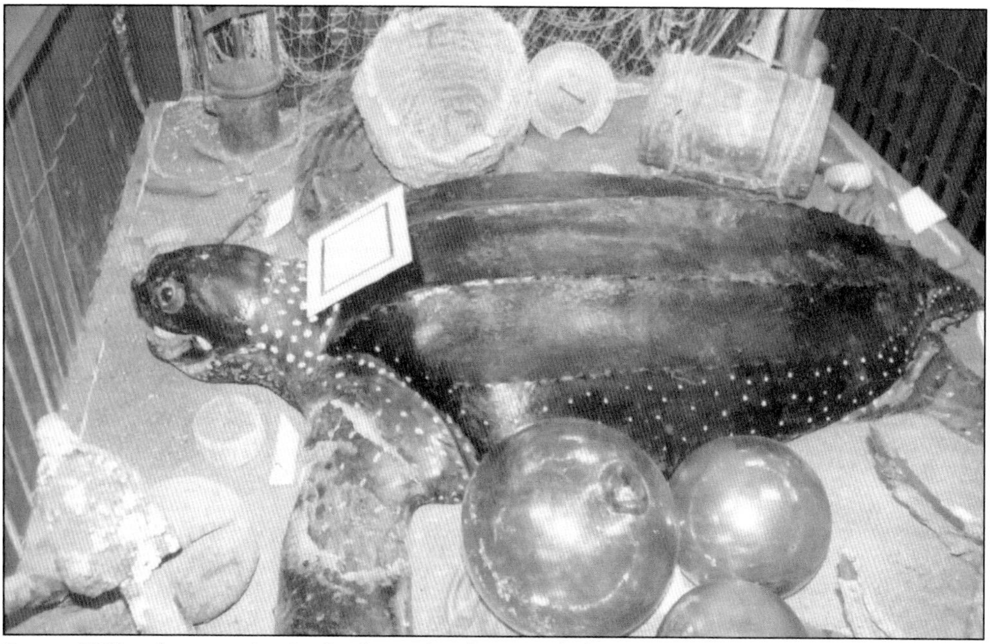

Prince Willy, the great leatherback turtle who traveled too far north following its mealtime jellyfish, ended up in a local fisherman's gillnet in 1964. Both fascinating and terrifying to local school kids, he has become a legend within the Cordova museum and received his name from those same children. Since Prince Willy's demise, numerous other large leatherbacks have been sighted and reached similar fates in Alaskan waters.

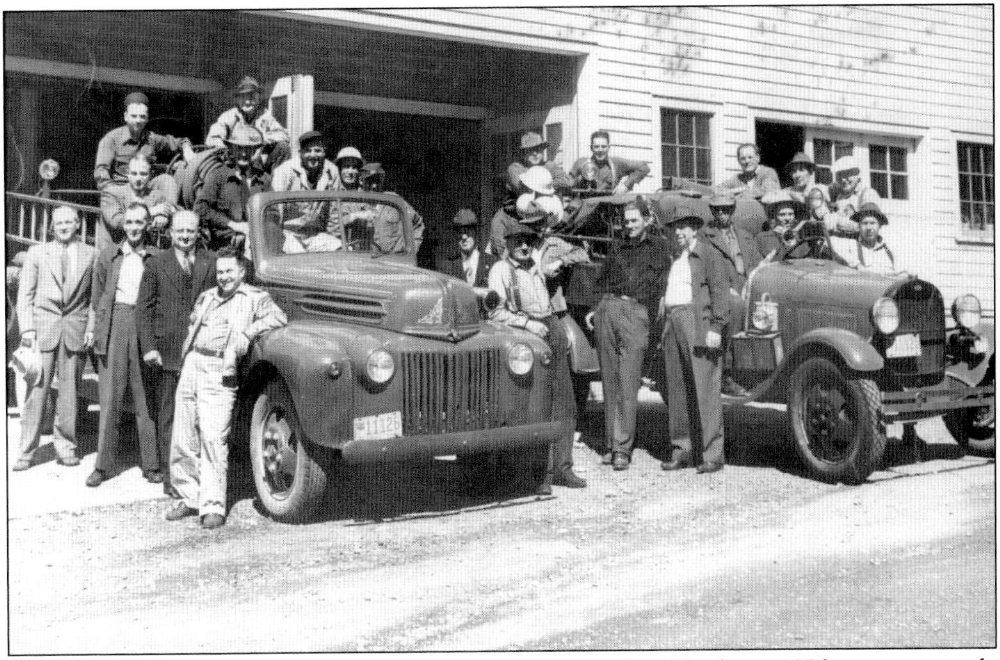

Cordova's first city hall was an old wooden structure that dated back to 1935 but conveniently housed the administration, civil defense, and fire and police departments, as well as the local gymnasium. It was recognized in the late 1960s that improved facilities were needed to house the range of growing city functions in Cordova, along with the fact that basketballs bouncing steadily above office spaces left a little to be desired.

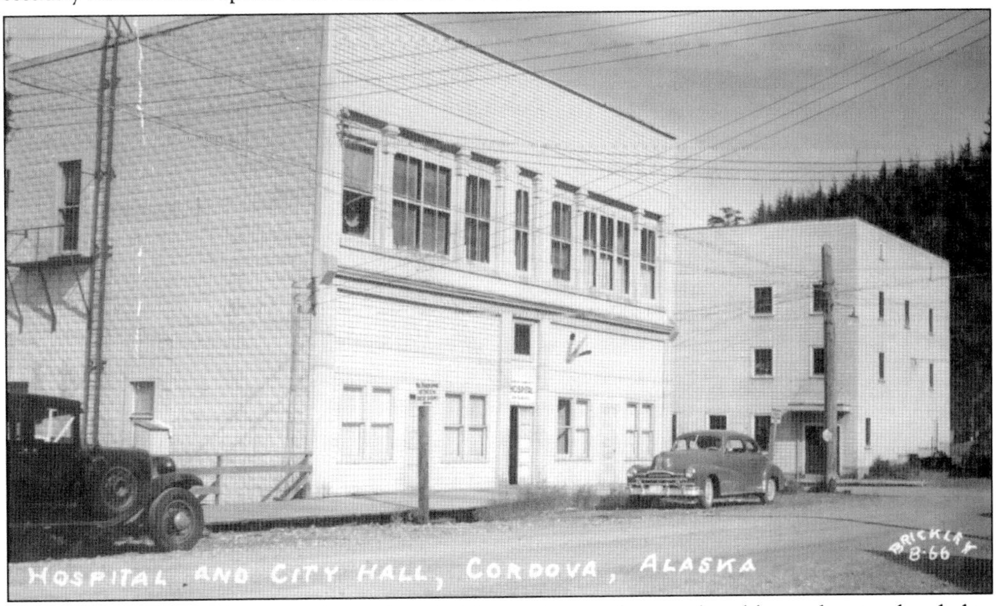

After the war, when the privately run hospital began having financial problems, the city decided to take over the hospital but quickly realized it needed more experienced management. The community canvassed religious organizations, and the North American Baptists agreed to take over the hospital with one stipulation, the construction of a church in Cordova. The Presbyterians agreed in the interest of civic improvement of Cordova to turn their church over to the Baptists.

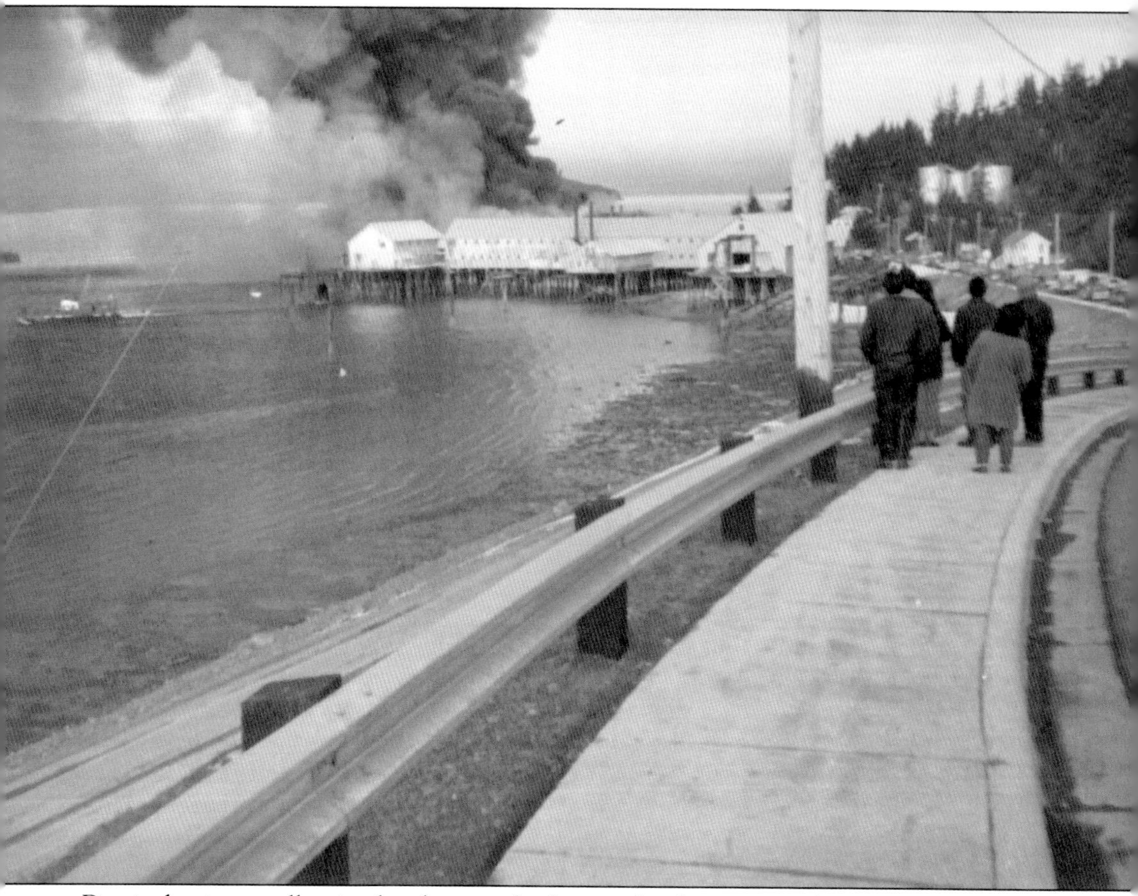

Despite having a well-trained and manned volunteer fire department, fire again hit Cordova in 1968 when a blaze leveled the ocean dock where Standard Oil and Parks Cannery resided. Damage was estimated at a million dollars. One year later, in the spring of 1969, fire struck Cordova again when fast-moving flames roared through First Street, destroying the Northern Hotel and three adjoining buildings and leaving 108 people homeless. Fires have changed the look of Cordova considerably over the years, with the majority of structures now being built of concrete or steel. Today, Cordova still supports a manned volunteer fire department, with a young explorers program to train the next generation of firefighters for the community.

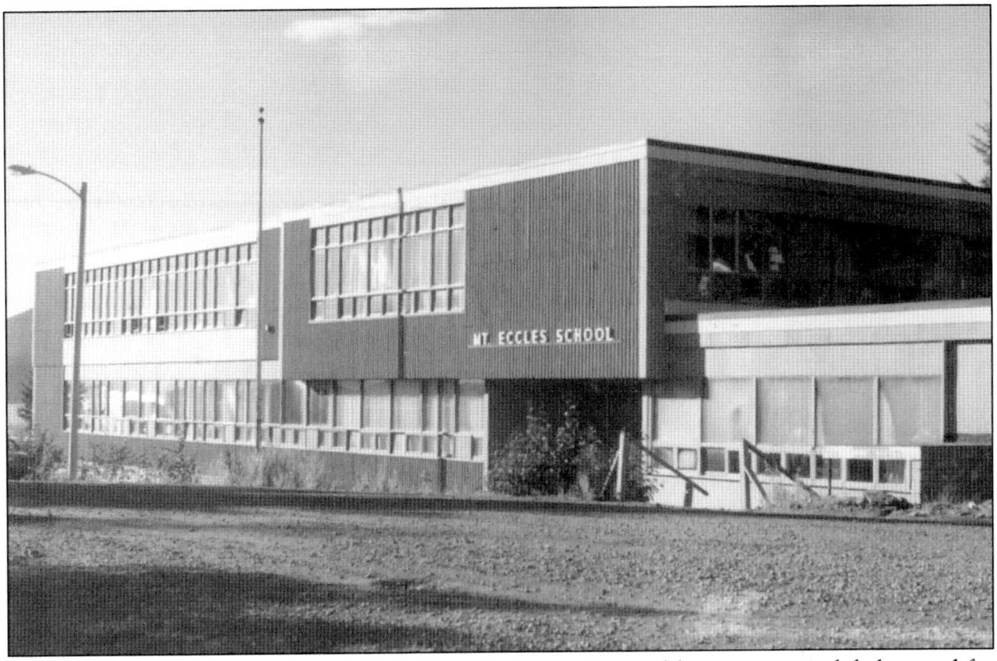

In the mid-1960s, as Cordova's population began to grow steadily stronger, so did the need for improved and enlarged school facilities. Mount Eccles Elementary School, built in the mid-1950s, was built in a central location in the heart of the community and served the town's needs, but the 1925 school was at the end of its useful life as a junior and senior high. A new, modern high school was completed and put to use by the early 1970s. Adjacent to the ball field, the facility featured 12 classrooms, science laboratories, and a full-sized gymnasium. Recently renovated, Mount Eccles Elementary remains one of the oldest operating elementary schools in the state of Alaska, but now features state-of-the-art technology and amenities in a retrofitted facility.

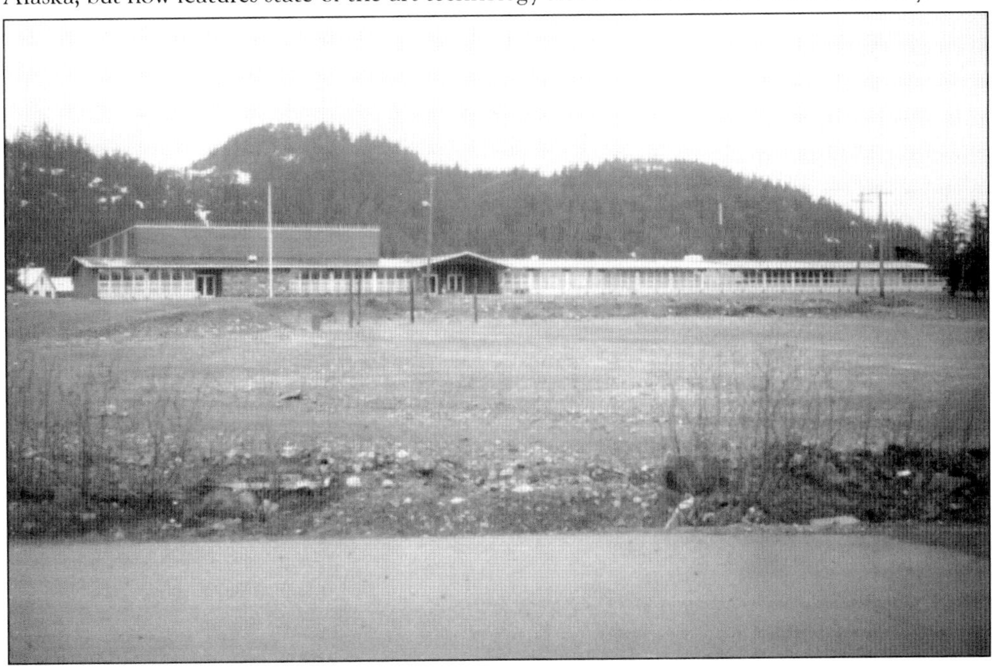

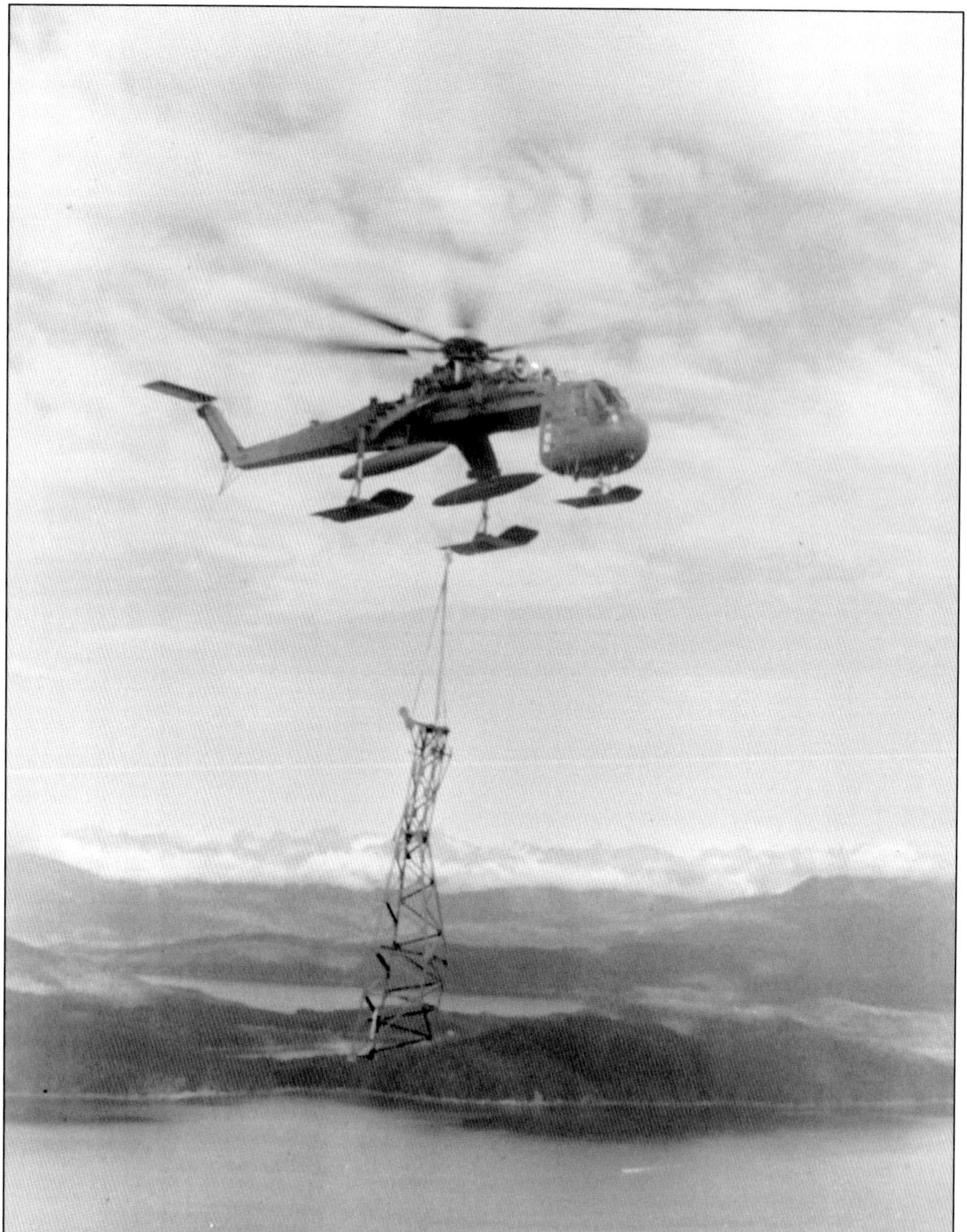

Outdoor recreation has always been important to Cordovans, and skiing is one of the most popular. In 1973, with a commitment from the city and grants, the present ski area facilities were constructed. The Sheridan Ski Club worked with the city to purchase a single-chair ski lift being decommissioned after a 30-year workout in Sun Valley, Idaho. The now rare single-chair lift traveled by train to Seattle and via barge to Cordova. During that summer, volunteers painted the towers and repaired the chairs before helicopters arrived to lift the towers into place. The City of Cordova, with help from the Coast Guard, Army Air National Guard, and US Forest Service, completed the towers, cut several runs through the forested hill above town, and built a road to the ski site for the lift to begin operations in 1974.

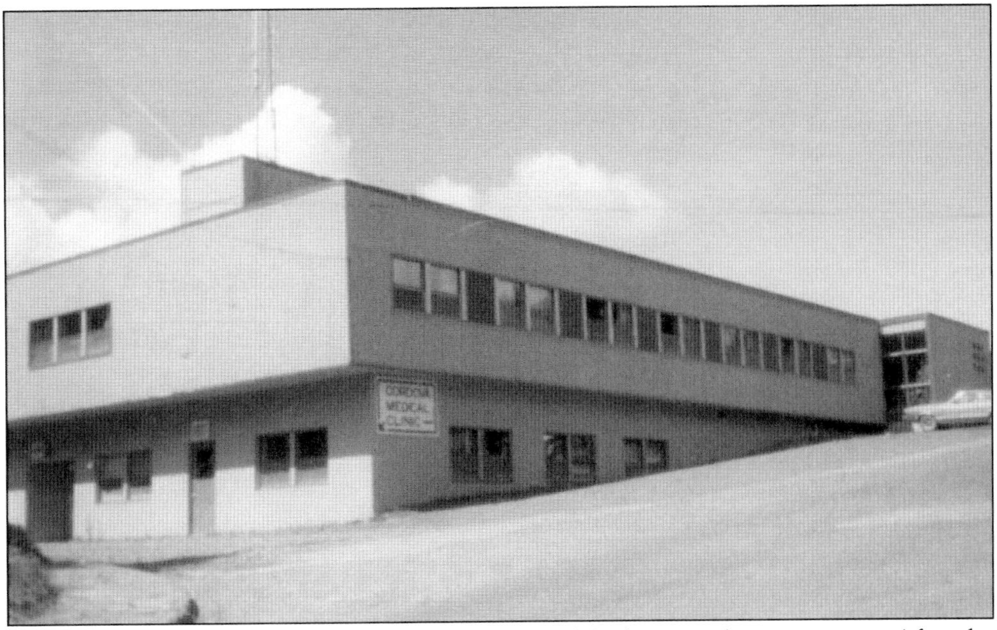

Active residents only increased the need for medical facilities in the community. After the Baptists took over hospital administration for the community, they decided a newer facility would serve the needs of the growing town. The land next to the Baptist church on Second Street was purchased. The total cost of the new hospital was $468,834.28. In 1955, the new hospital was ready to serve the community.

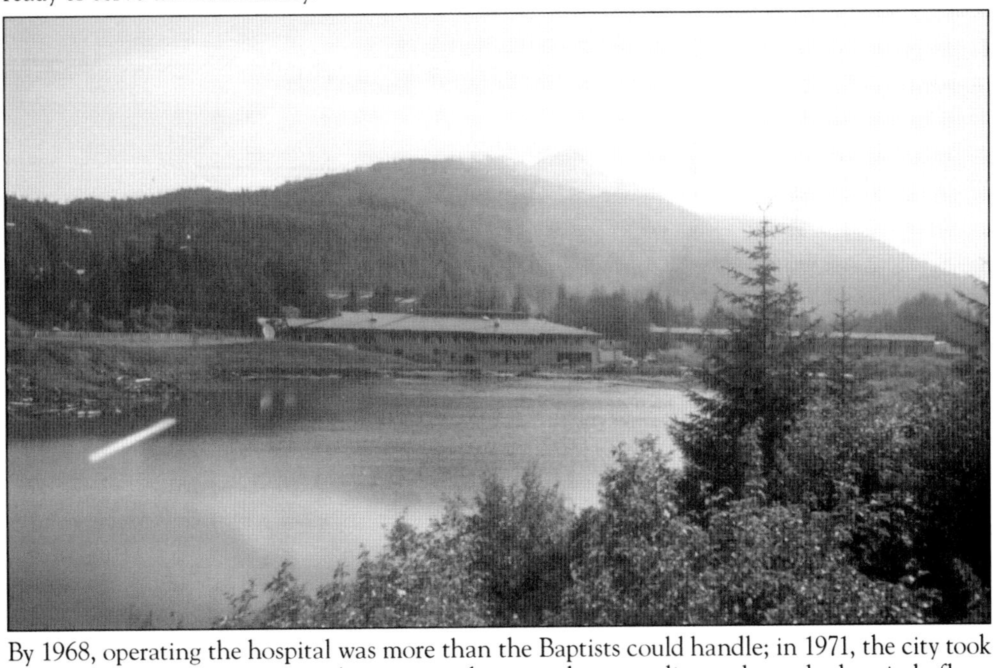

By 1968, operating the hospital was more than the Baptists could handle; in 1971, the city took on management, and by 1976, the municipality was also struggling to keep the hospital afloat. By 1982, a new hospital plan recommended the most cost-effective solution was to build a new facility on a larger, better-located site. With state funding, the city completed construction, and on May 31, 1986, the Cordova Community Hospital opened.

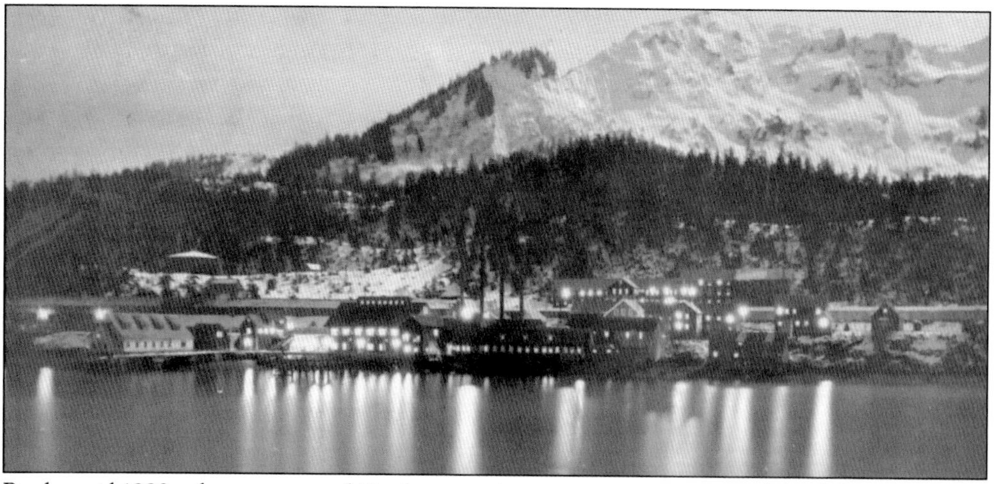

By the mid-1980s, the economy of Cordova was booming again as many of the fisheries took on a new life with improved methods of harvesting, preparation, and transportation. Herring had always been an important harvest to the natives of the area and had also developed commercially in the early 1900s. There were herring reduction and salting plants throughout Prince William Sound at places such as Port Ashton and Latouche (pictured).

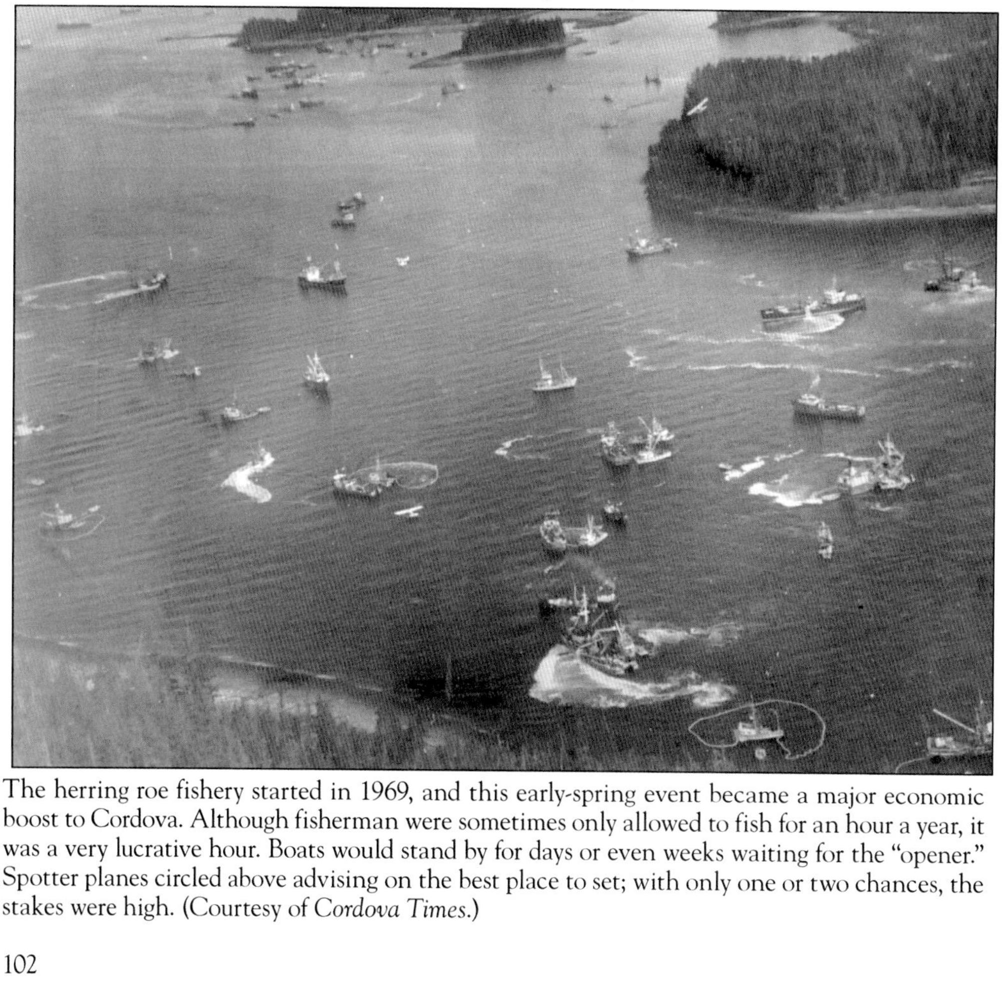

The herring roe fishery started in 1969, and this early-spring event became a major economic boost to Cordova. Although fisherman were sometimes only allowed to fish for an hour a year, it was a very lucrative hour. Boats would stand by for days or even weeks waiting for the "opener." Spotter planes circled above advising on the best place to set; with only one or two chances, the stakes were high. (Courtesy of *Cordova Times*.)

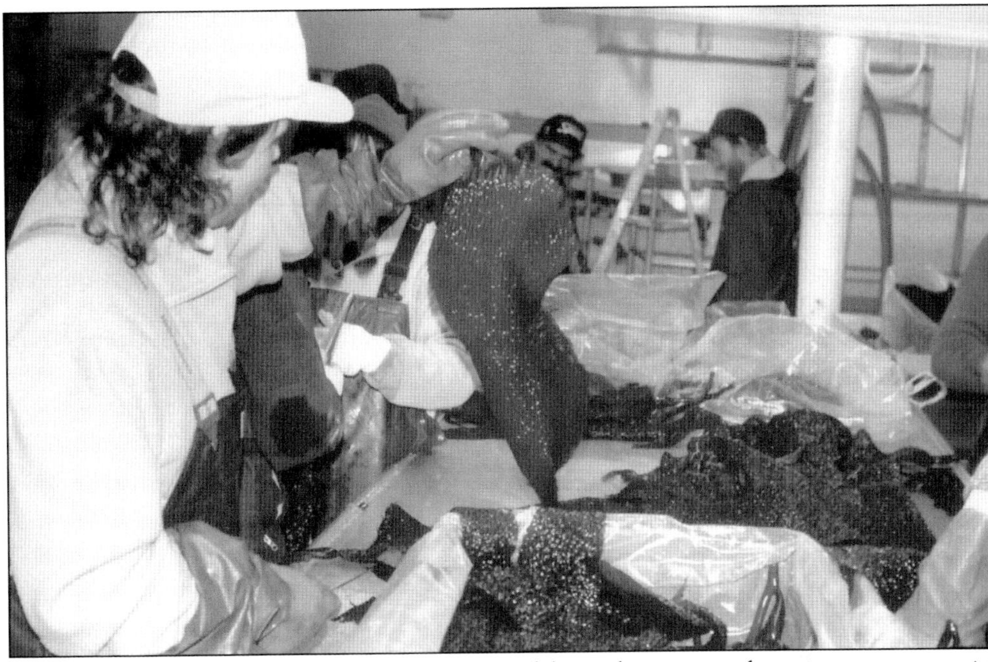

In Asian markets, herring roe on kelp, long a native delicacy, became very lucrative as a commercial harvest. Herring kelp-pounding became a unique undertaking with fishermen building floating "pounds" that would suspend the long pieces of kelp enticingly for the herring to deposit roe on. The kelp was then easily harvested, boxed, and shipped to Asian markets that were willing to pay top dollar for this specialty product. It was a huge boon to Cordova's economy. Fishermen could partake in the early-spring herring harvest and then still have time to ready their boats and nets for the return of the salmon and the commercial harvest in May.

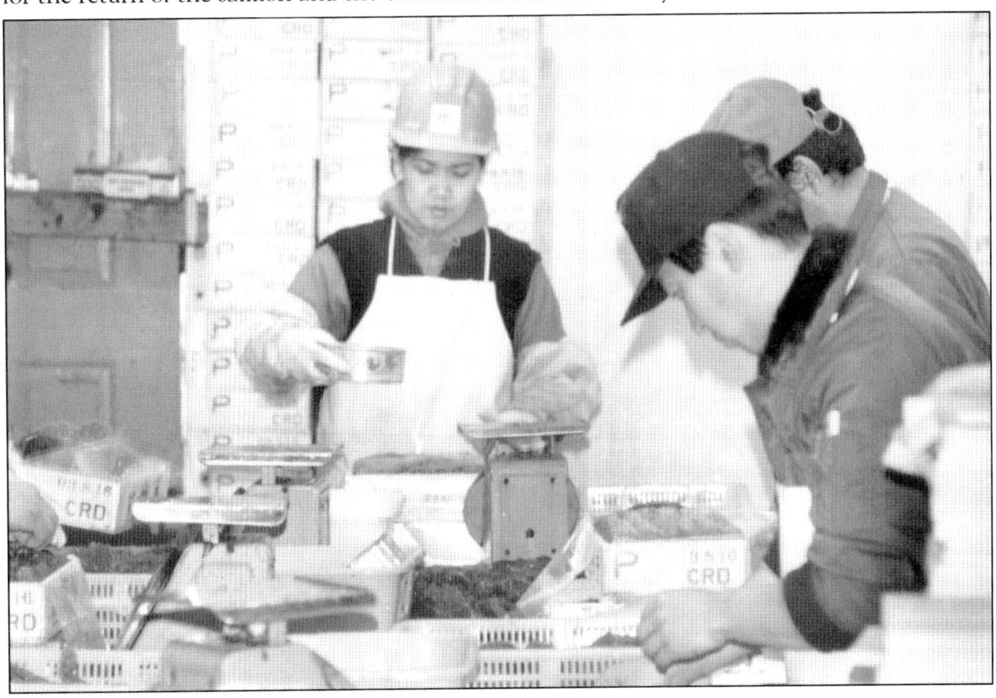

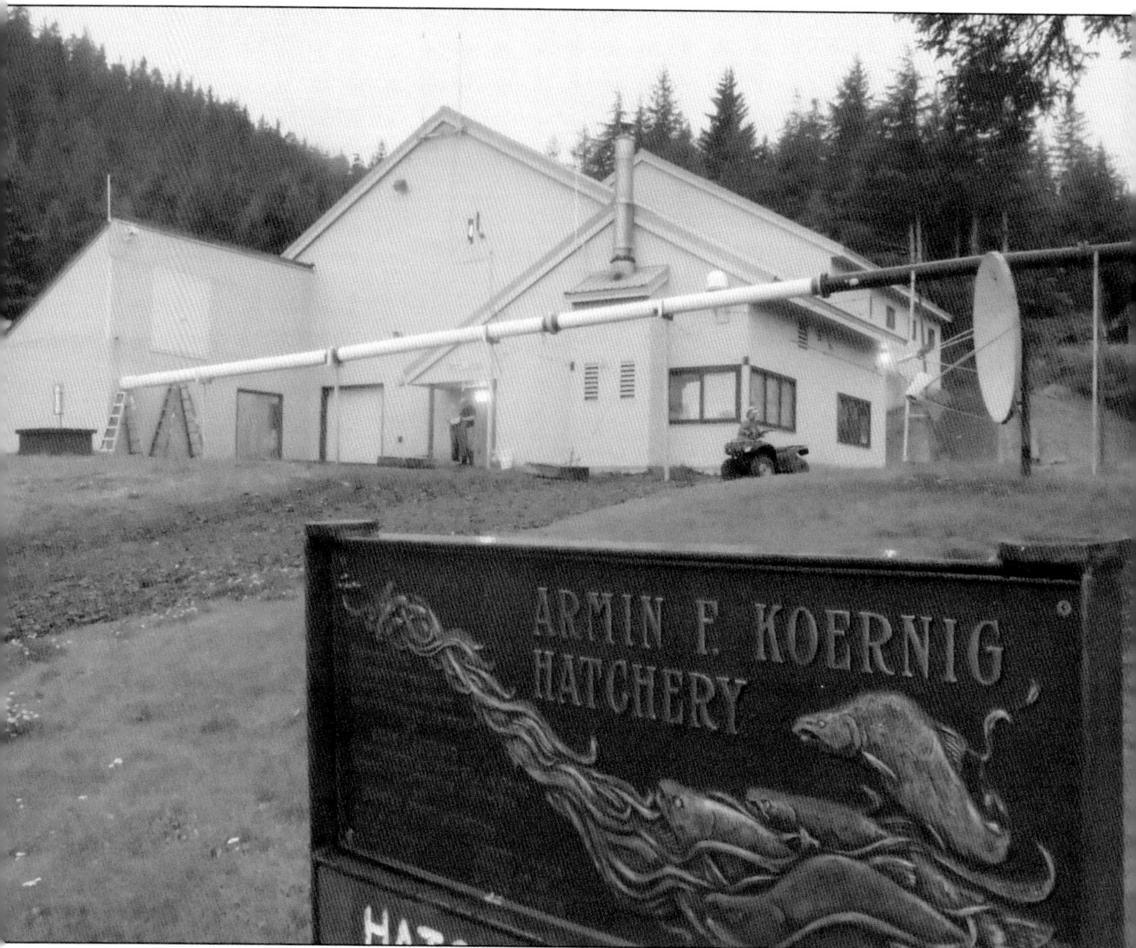

With statehood came the decision to build and operate several state-run fish hatcheries, and by 1983, some 20 such hatcheries operated statewide. Another 15 hatcheries were operated privately or by nonprofit groups, such as Cordova's Prince William Sound Aquaculture Association (PWSAC), formed in 1975. After bleak fishing seasons in the early 1970s, Armin Koernig led a group of Cordova fishermen in the beginning of PWSAC's hatchery program. Marked by tremendous volunteer effort and a strong spirit of cooperation, the group transformed an abandoned cannery at Port San Juan in the southwestern sound into what is now the Armin F. Koernig (AFK) Hatchery. PWSAC has become Alaska's unique, private, not-for-profit regional aquaculture program. Since 1977, the AFK Hatchery has generated $28.5 million in revenues for Area E commercial fishermen. (Courtesy of Dave Janka.)

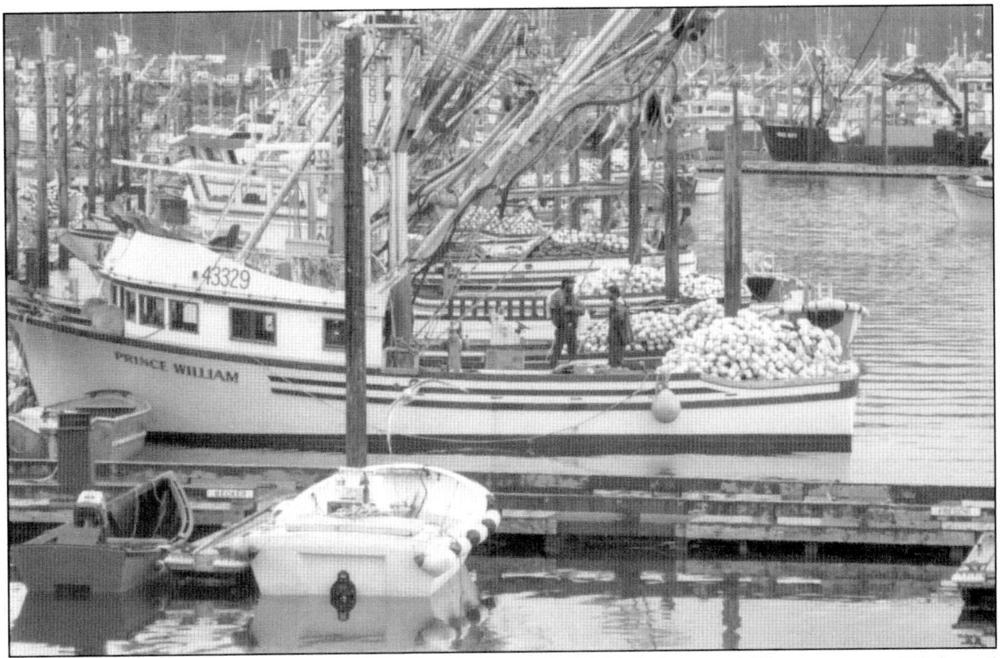

After 1959, Alaska received the authority to manage its own fisheries. A Department of Fish and Game, an outgrowth of the Department of Fisheries created by the territorial legislature in 1949, was charged to set annual catch limits, to determine types of gear that would be permitted, and to define where and when fishing could take place. Cordova's fleet in the early 1980s swelled to fill the newly expanded boat harbor with over 800 slips available to fishermen and other mariners. Industry began building up along Cordova's waterfront at a breakneck pace in an effort to keep up with the growing fisheries and increased demand. (Both, courtesy of *Cordova Times*.)

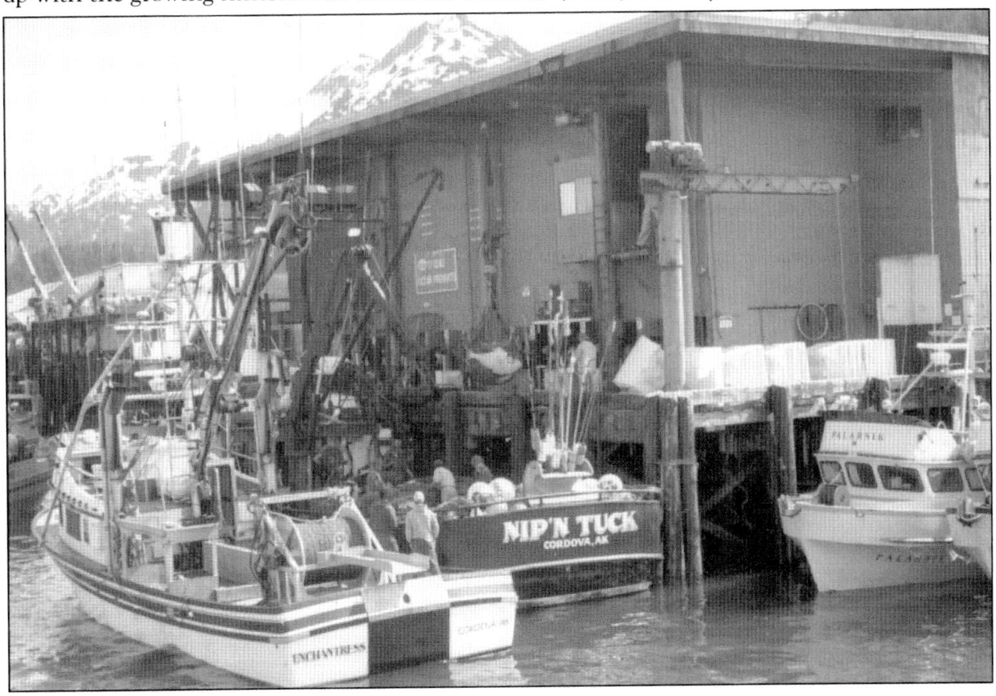

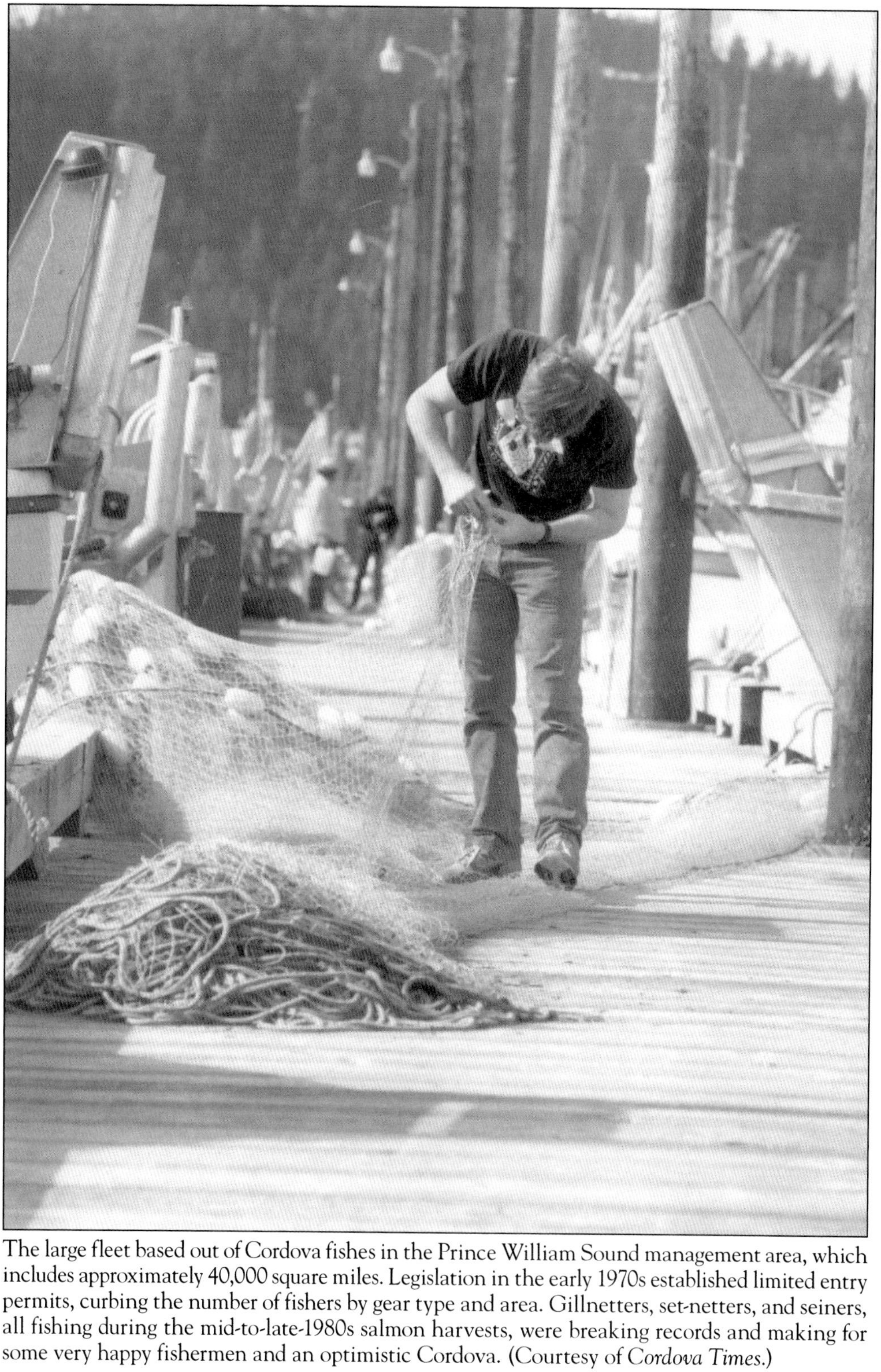

The large fleet based out of Cordova fishes in the Prince William Sound management area, which includes approximately 40,000 square miles. Legislation in the early 1970s established limited entry permits, curbing the number of fishers by gear type and area. Gillnetters, set-netters, and seiners, all fishing during the mid-to-late-1980s salmon harvests, were breaking records and making for some very happy fishermen and an optimistic Cordova. (Courtesy of *Cordova Times*.)

Six

Reality Check

1989 to Present

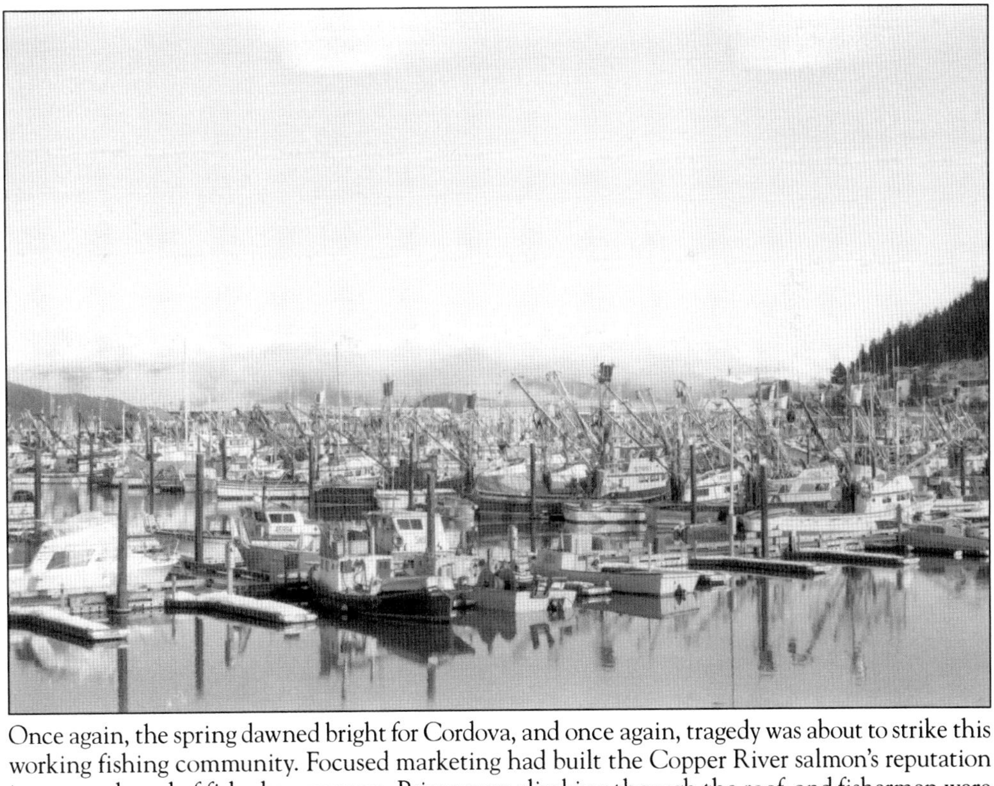

Once again, the spring dawned bright for Cordova, and once again, tragedy was about to strike this working fishing community. Focused marketing had built the Copper River salmon's reputation into an unheard of fish phenomenon. Prices were climbing through the roof, and fishermen were rewarded for proper handling of their cargoes. It could not have been going much better than in the spring of 1989 until the early-morning hours of March 24.

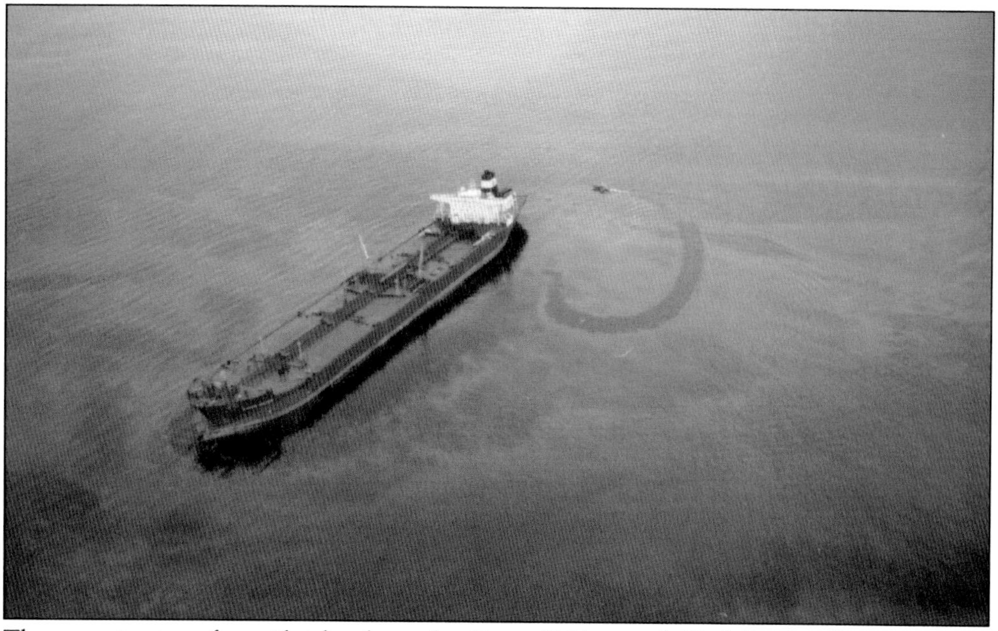

That morning just after midnight, the tanker *Exxon Valdez* struck Bligh Reef, spilling 11 million gallons of North Slope crude oil and creating the largest environmental disaster in North American history at the time. Immediately following the grounding, the response was slow, poorly coordinated, and largely ineffective. Cleanup equipment was limited and not readily available. Then three days later, a storm hit, spreading the oil along 1,400 miles of shoreline.

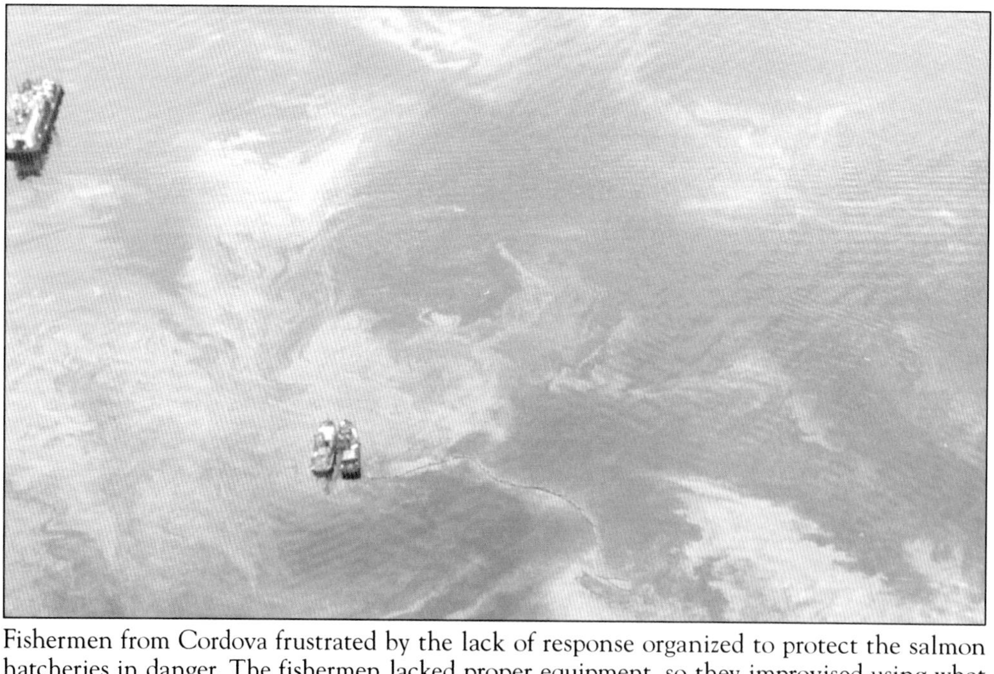

Fishermen from Cordova frustrated by the lack of response organized to protect the salmon hatcheries in danger. The fishermen lacked proper equipment, so they improvised using what they had available, which were five-gallon buckets. The realization of what was happening to their livelihoods was intense for the generations of families who had fished the waters that were now being smothered with crude oil. Emotions ran high in Cordova.

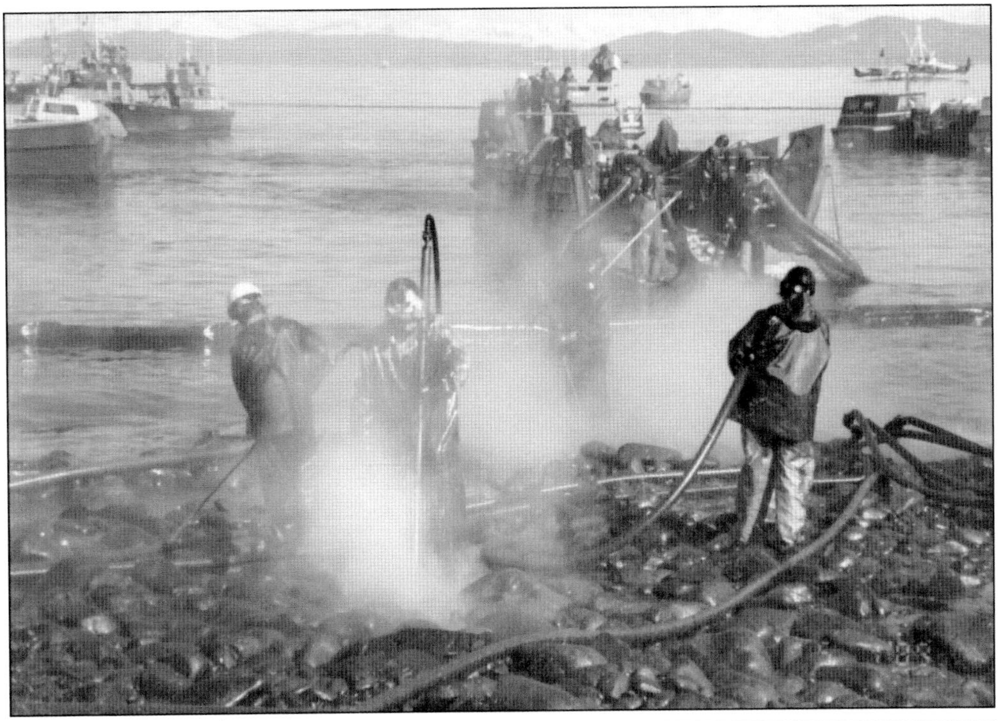

And no one knew what was to come after those first few days. During the next three years, approximately $2.2 billion would be spent on the cleanup; and it involved 11,000 workers, 1,400 vessels, and 85 aircraft. And for that, three to eleven percent of the oil was recovered. The spill stretched 460 miles from Bligh Reef to the village of Chignik on the Alaska Peninsula, which is roughly the volume needed to fill 125 Olympic-sized swimming pools. Salmon seine fishing permits plunged from $240,000 in February 1989 to as low as $12,800 in 2004. Pink salmon runs failed in 1992 and 1993, and herring runs collapsed in 1993, creating an annual loss of $7.8 million to Cordova's economy. The herring stocks have yet to recover. Run failures and lost markets forced fishing families to begin selling boats and permits.

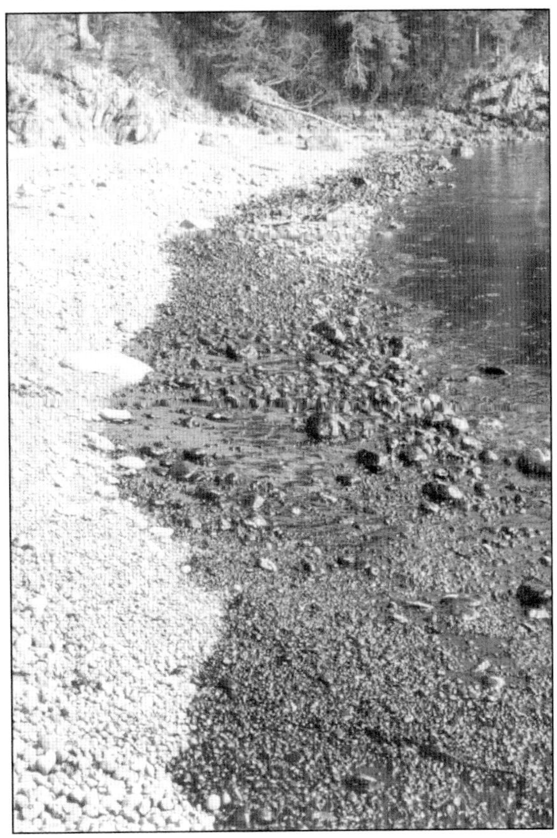

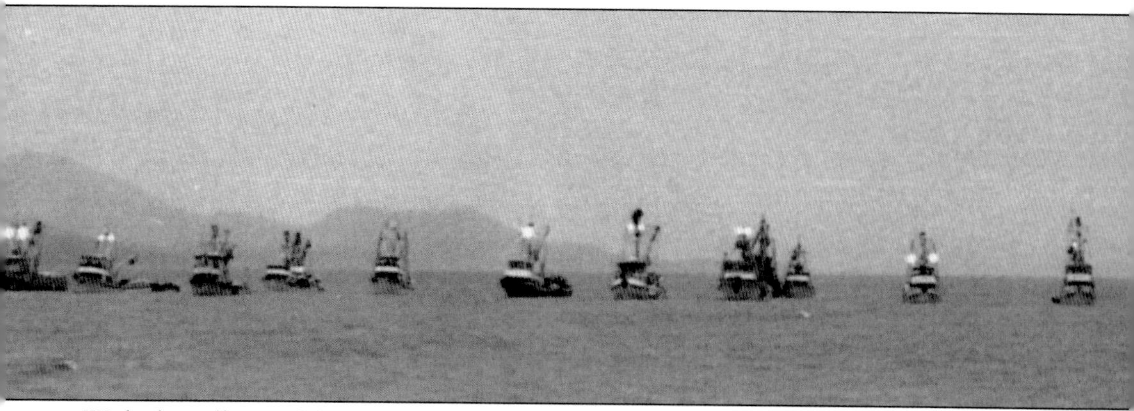

With the collapse of the pink salmon and herring in 1993, fishermen tired of the corporate rhetoric. In an act of civil disobedience, the fleet blockaded Valdez Narrows holding up tanker traffic and 25 percent of the nation's domestic oil supply for three days. Fishermen demanded to know what the long-term implications of oil meant to commercial fishing. By this date, the *Exxon Valdez* Oil Spill (EVOS) Trustee Council had been set up to oversee and distribute funds

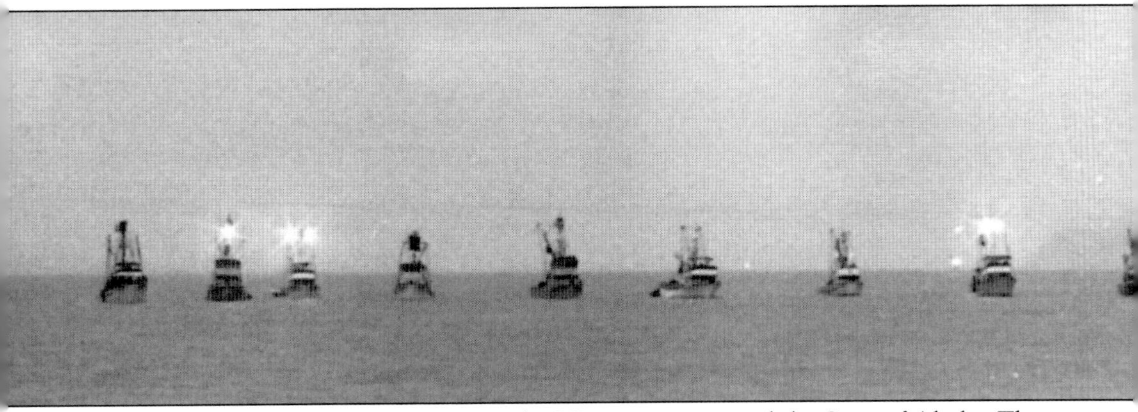

from the civil settlement between Exxon, the US government, and the State of Alaska. These funds were to be used to mitigate losses stemming and to protect critical habitat areas. After the blockade, the EVOS Trustee Council approved the Sound Ecosystem Assessment, a $22.4 million multiproject study of the processes influencing the recovery of damaged pink salmon and herring populations in Prince William Sound.

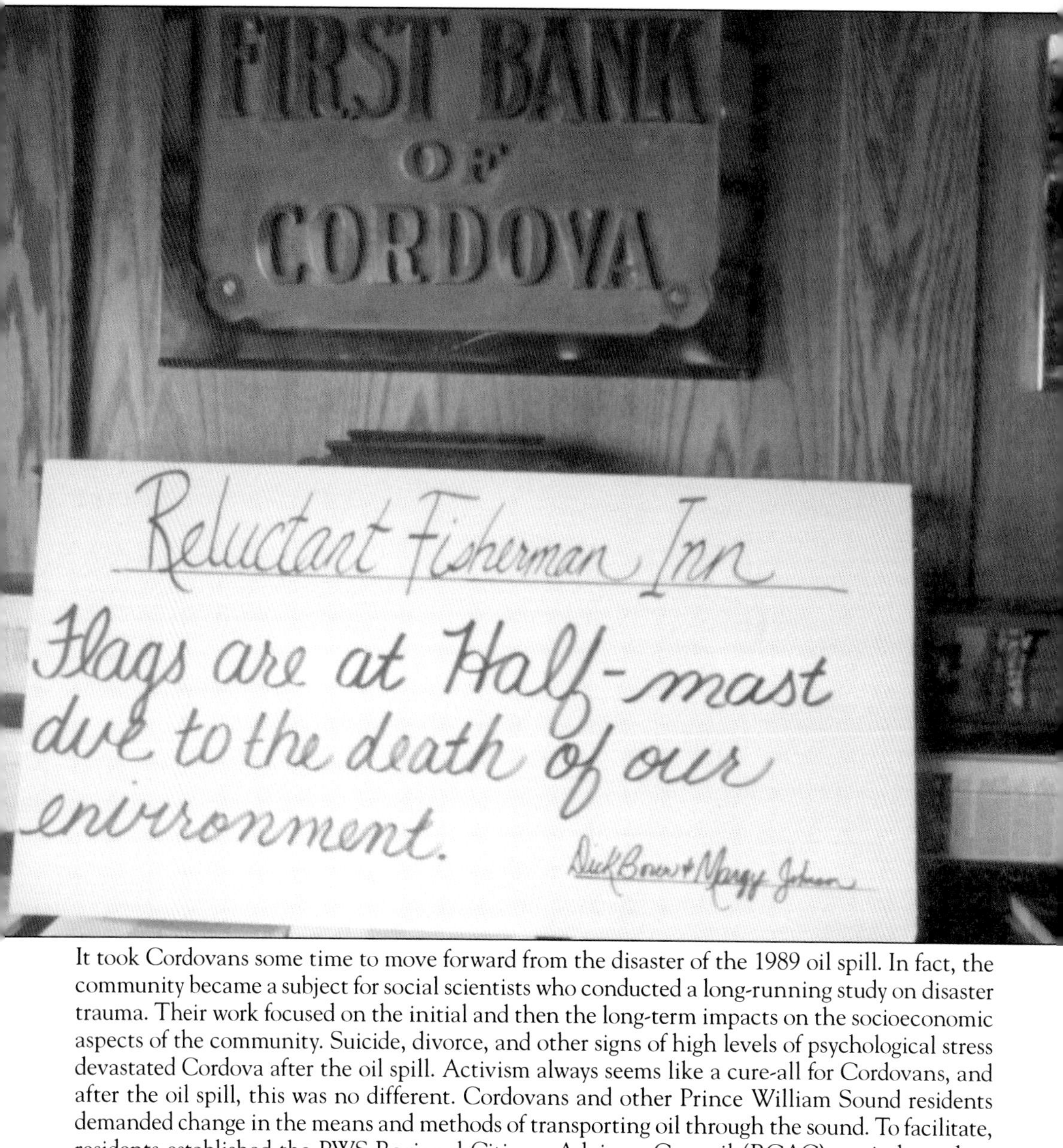

It took Cordovans some time to move forward from the disaster of the 1989 oil spill. In fact, the community became a subject for social scientists who conducted a long-running study on disaster trauma. Their work focused on the initial and then the long-term impacts on the socioeconomic aspects of the community. Suicide, divorce, and other signs of high levels of psychological stress devastated Cordova after the oil spill. Activism always seems like a cure-all for Cordovans, and after the oil spill, this was no different. Cordovans and other Prince William Sound residents demanded change in the means and methods of transporting oil through the sound. To facilitate, residents established the PWS Regional Citizens Advisory Council (RCAC), an independent group of individuals from oiled communities to promote environmentally safe operation of the Alyeska Marine Terminal and the tankers that use it.

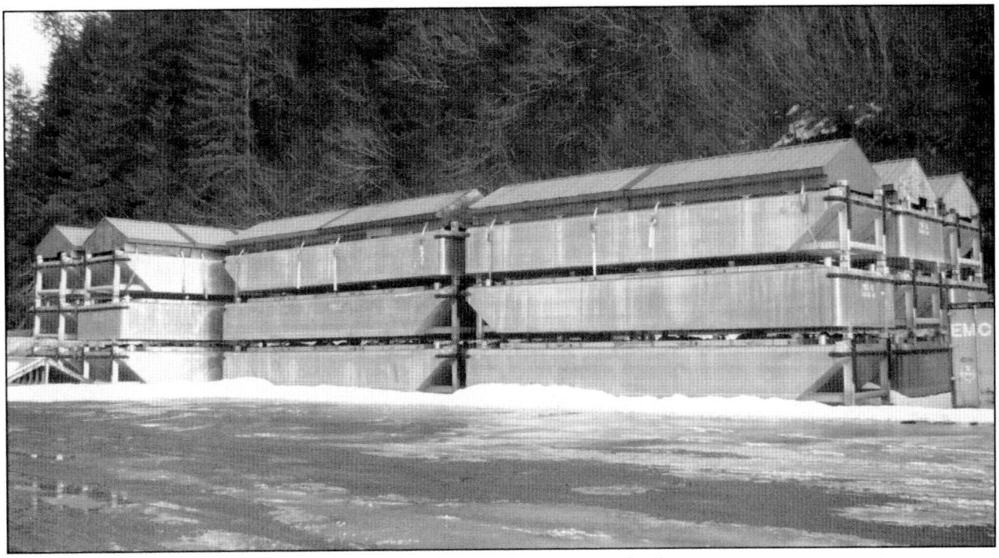

At the time of the *Exxon Valdez* spill, a limited amount of adequate response equipment was stored or located in Prince William Sound. Now, RCAC ensures that state-of-the-art response equipment is located in the PWS communities of Whittier, Valdez, Tatitlek, Chenega, and Cordova. And another positive outcome was to create a small army of rapid responders to any future spills. (Courtesy of Dave Janka.)

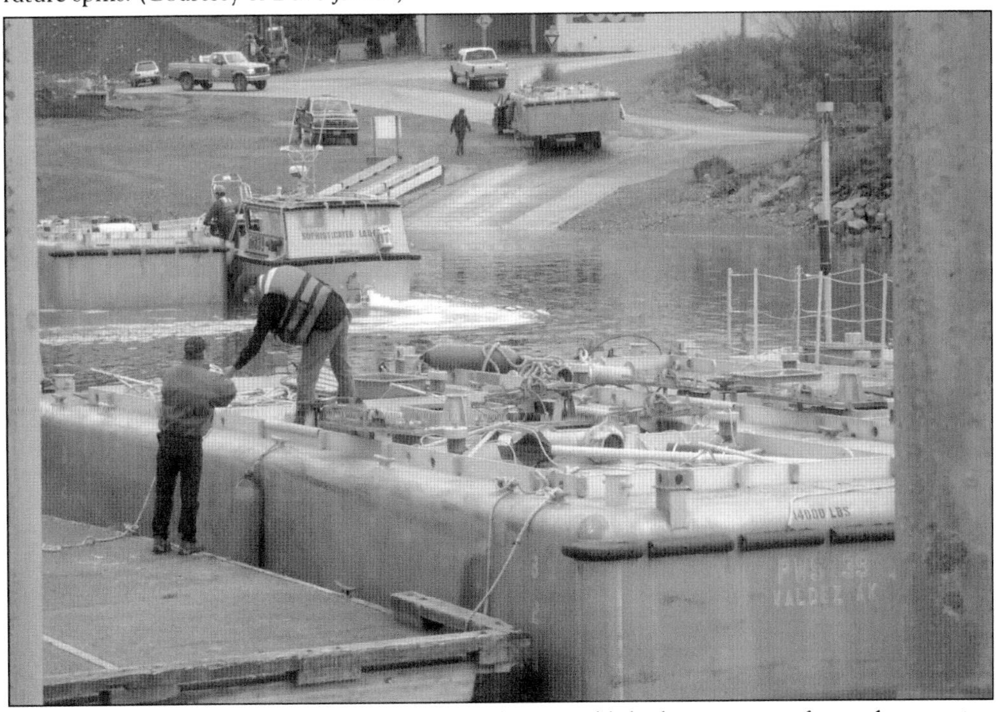

The Ship Escort Response Vessel System (SERVS) was established to improve safety and prevention measures at the Alyeska Terminal and in the sound. Tugs escort the tankers safely out of Prince William Sound and in coordination with the Cordova District Fishermen United contract boats in the local fishing fleet to be prepared for oil spill response. In the event of a spill, local crews can be dispatched effectively. (Courtesy of Dave Janka.)

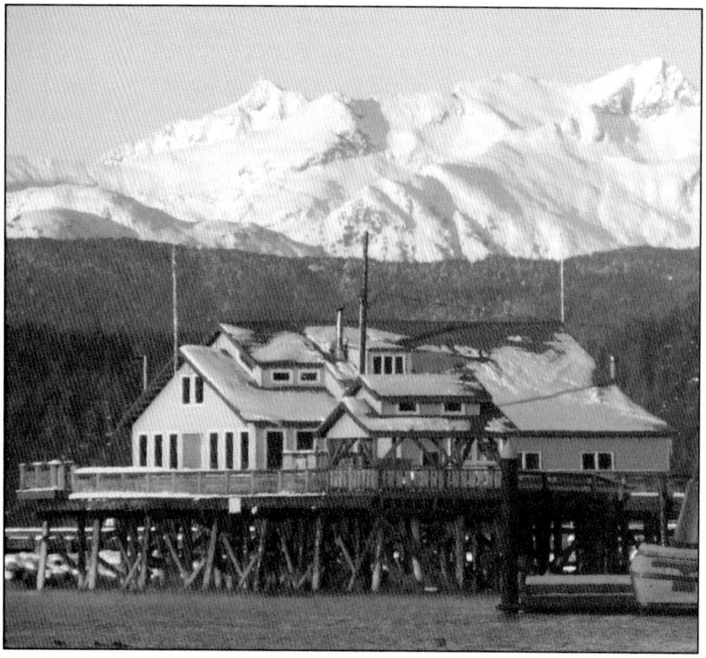

The Prince William Sound Science Center (PWSSC) is also a positive outcome of the 1989 oil spill and serves as a nonprofit research and education entity focusing on Prince William Sound, the Copper River delta, and the north Gulf of Alaska region. PWSSC administers the Oil Spill Recovery Institute (OSRI), which Congress established in 1990 to fund oil pollution research and development projects in the arctic and subarctic marine environments. (Courtesy of Dave Janka.)

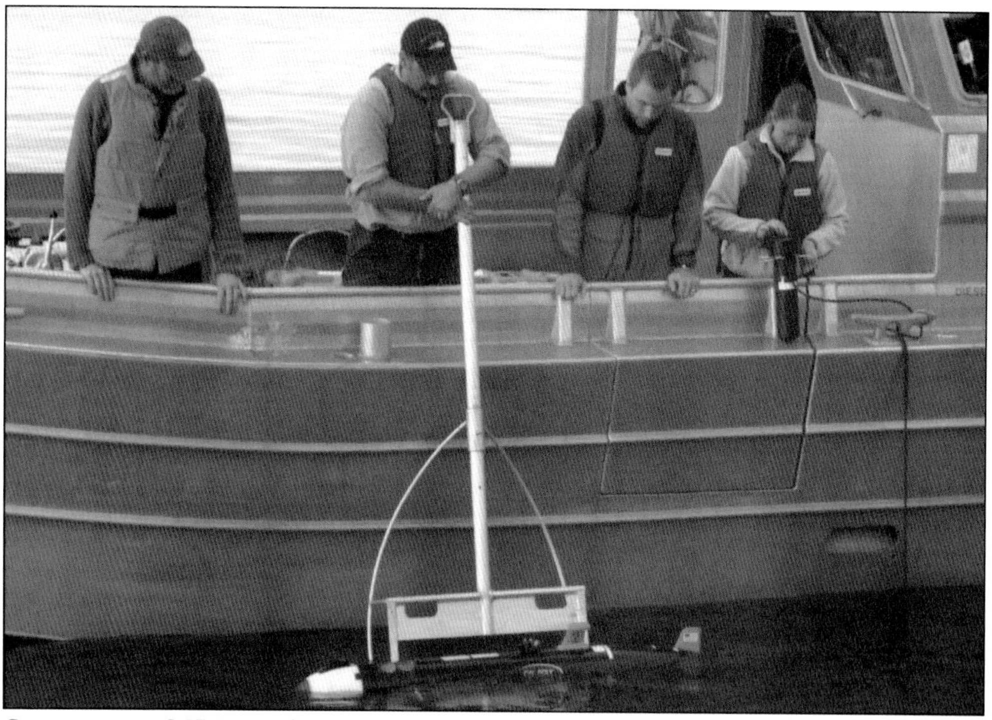

Congress gave OSRI two objectives: one, to identify and develop best available techniques, equipment, and materials to deal with spills in cold water; the other, to assess recovery from spill-induced damage to create a greater understanding of the long-term effects of oil spills on the people and natural resources of Prince William Sound. Legislation passed in 2005 assures OSRI's research program will continue as long as oil exploration and development occurs in Alaska. (Courtesy of Dave Janka.)

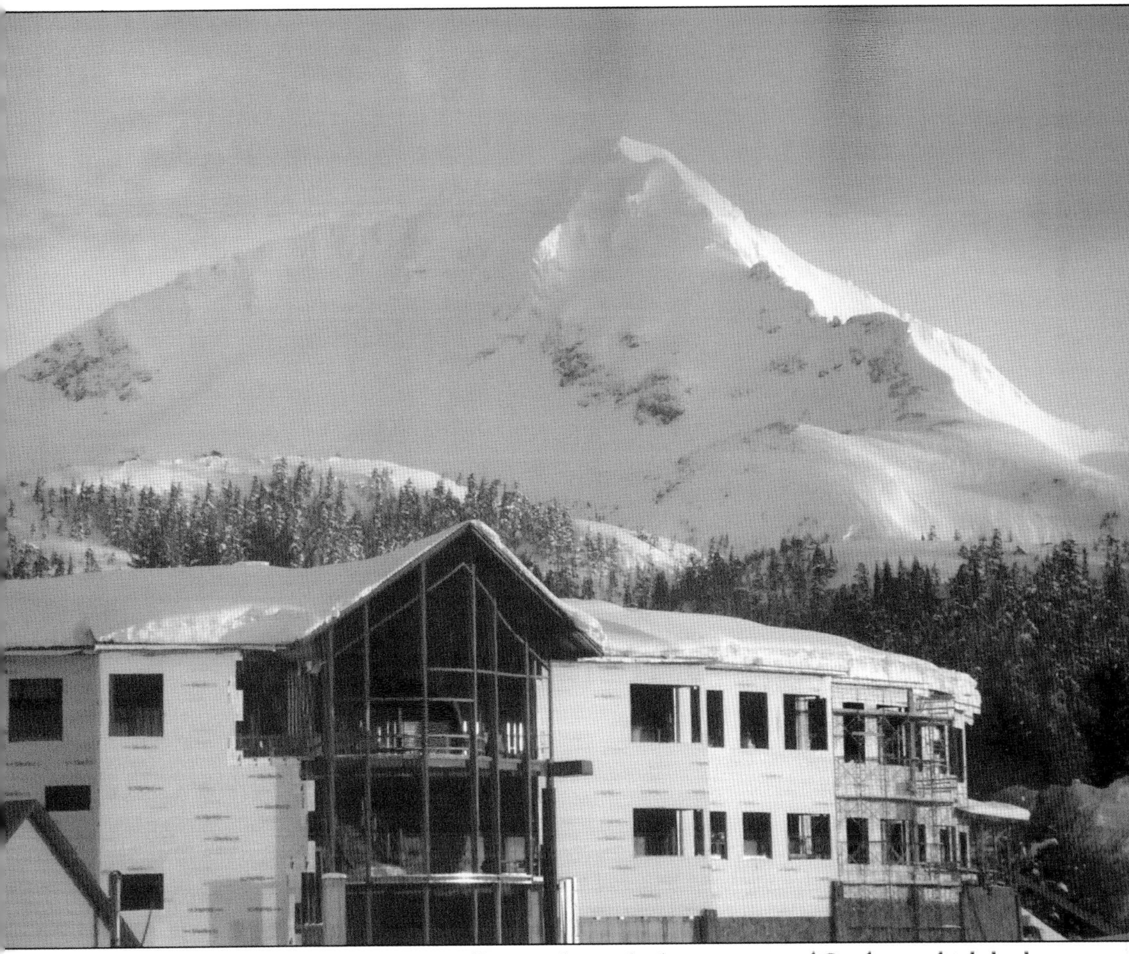

The 1989 oil spill led to community efforts to diversify the economy of Cordova, which had at one time relied on fishing for more than 49 percent of its economic income. Through a series of public meetings, the community decided to develop a more efficient infrastructure to deliver city services as well as provide enticing and convenient conference space to attract the small-meeting market in the state. Scheduled to be complete in 2013, the Cordova Center will provide a home to the Cordova Public Library, Cordova Historical Museum, and administrative offices for the city, as well as a theater and meeting spaces. Another piece to the puzzle of diversifying the economy was improving transportation to and from the community. (Courtesy of Dave Janka.)

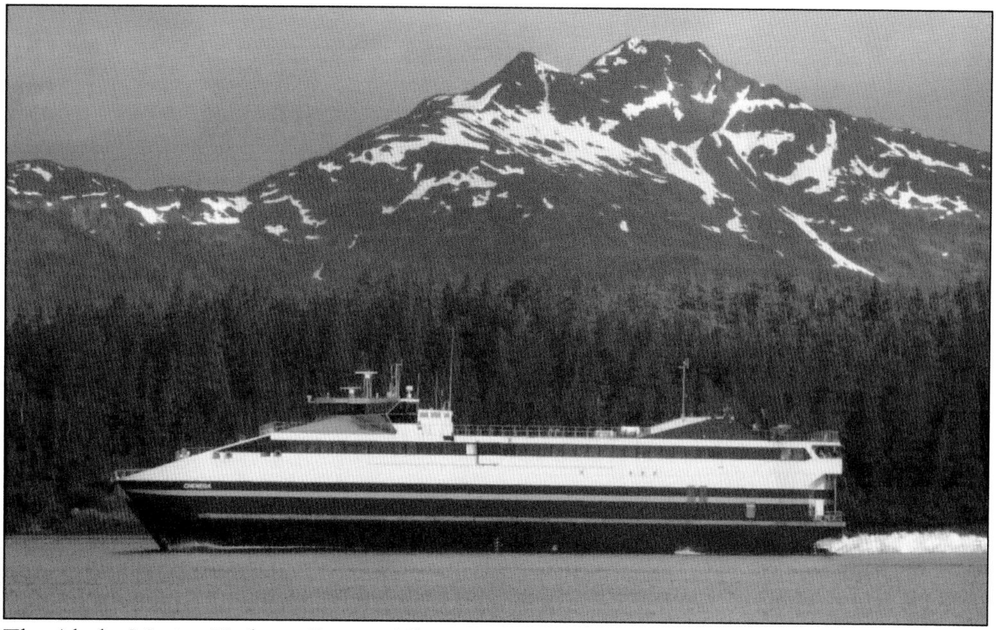

The Alaska Marine Highway System did improve its transportation offerings to Cordova when, in 2009, it unveiled the M/V *Chenega* (above), a catamaran-type vessel that cut the time involved in crossing Prince William Sound in half. The M/V *Chenega* was built by Derecktor Shipyards and is powered by four diesel engines for a service speed of 32 knots rivaled only by its elder sister ship the M/V *Fairweather.* (Courtesy of Dave Janka.)

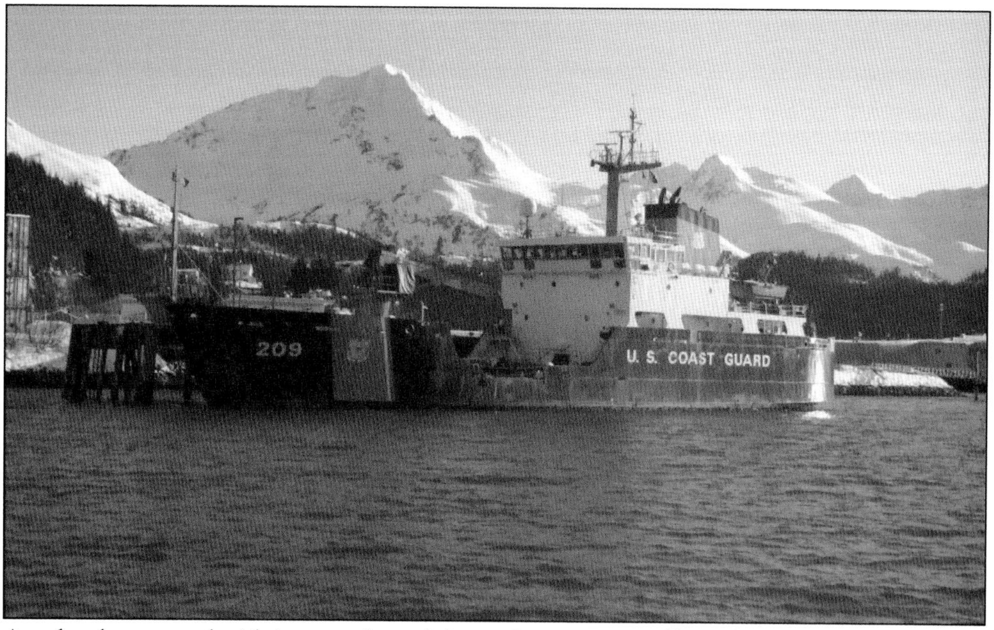

Another large vessel with improved capabilities also came to call Cordova its home port when the 225-foot buoy tender *Sycamore* was commissioned in Cordova in July 2002 to replace the 180-foot *Sweetbrier*, which had served the community since 1976. Equipped with both bow and stern thrusters, which deliver added maneuverability, the *Sycamore* maintains the navigational aids in the Prince William Sound and treacherous north gulf region. (Courtesy of Dave Janka.)

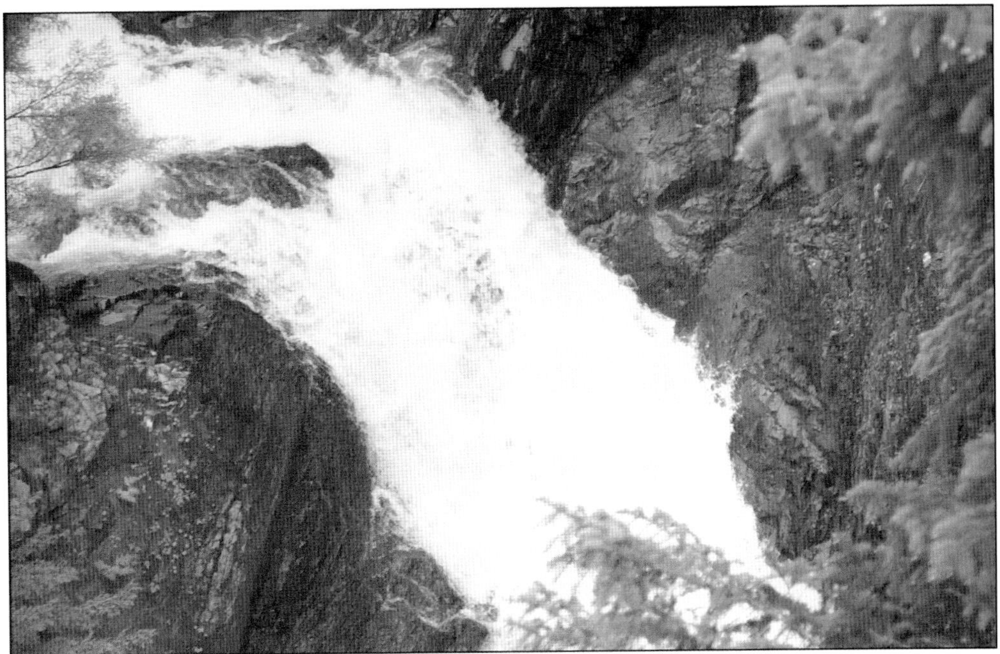

Working to lower the cost of living in a remote locale like Cordova was also a goal of the community in an effort to stabilize the economy. Cordova Electric Cooperative completed two major hydropower projects to provide service to the community. Humpback Creek, seen above and below at its dedication in the spring of 2011, has a total installed generating capacity of 1.5 megawatts. Now online, renewable hydropower energy provides 80 percent of Cordova's needs. Alternative sources of power such as wind generation have also been looked at by the native village of Eyak, and the village has partnered with the community on various innovative recycling programs. (Both, courtesy of Clay Koplin.)

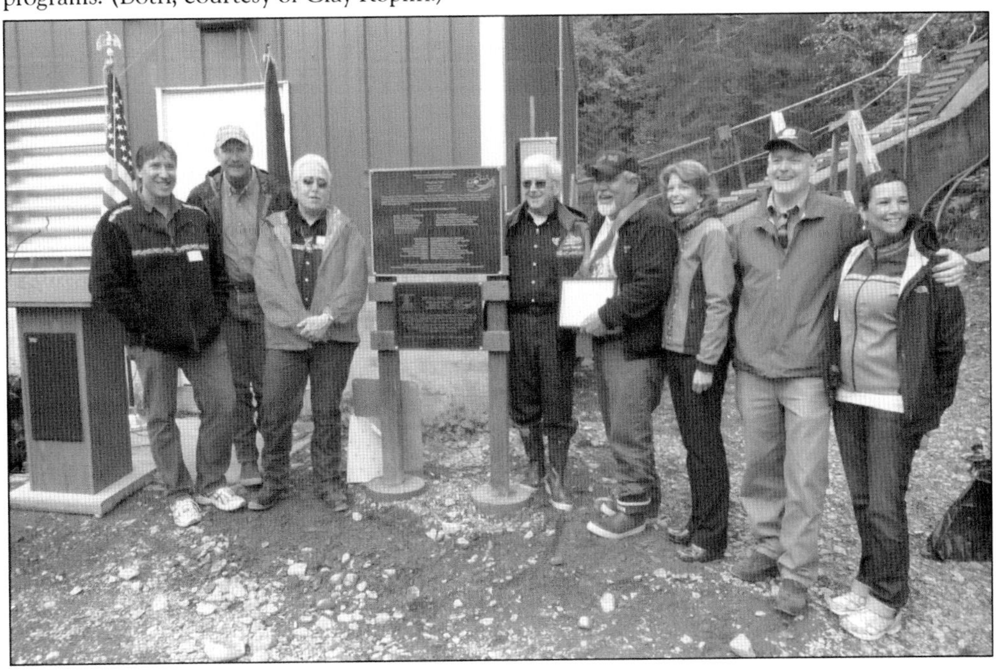

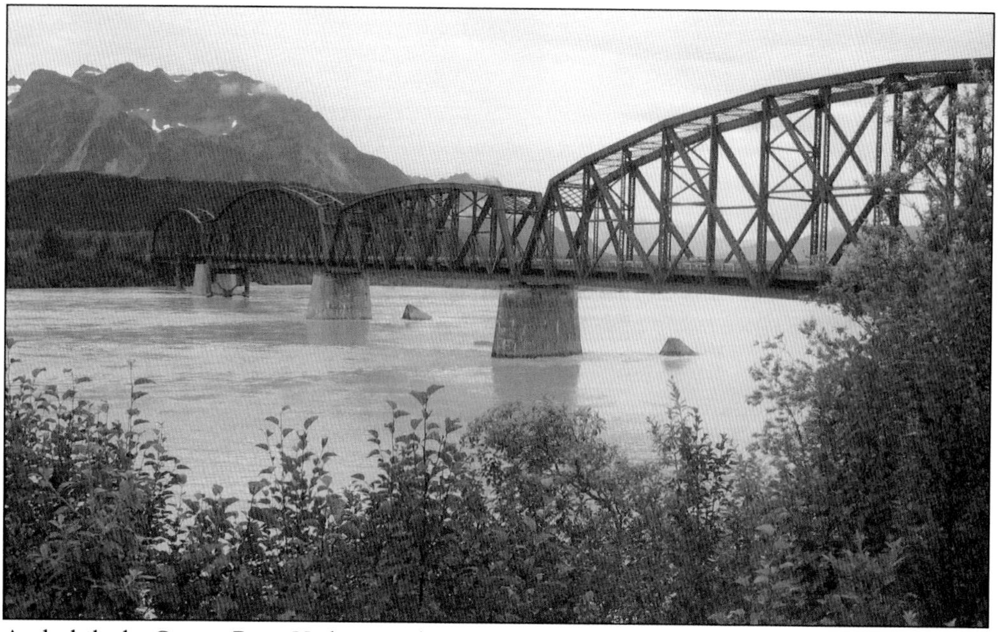

And while the Copper River Highway ends at mile 49, efforts to preserve the Million Dollar Bridge were undertaken by the State of Alaska. Engineers began studying the bridge following floods that caused structural damage in 1995 and determined there was greater value in repairing the bridge then cleaning up debris if it collapsed. $19 million in repairs increased the value of the historic structure, but the name stayed the same. (Courtesy of Dave Janka.)

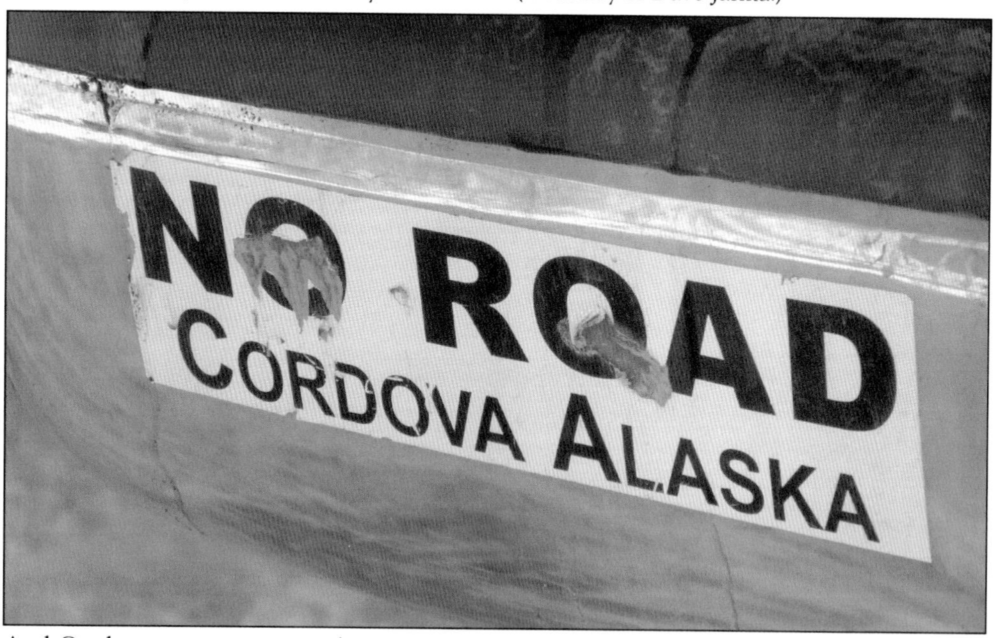

And Cordovans, never ones to let an opportunity pass, brought back the "No Road" debate resulting in the development of a simple bumper sticker to convey the sentiment of "no road—no problem." As locals have a reputation to never agree on anything, feelings continue to be mixed as a variation of the bumper sticker, which only has the word "Road," appears on an equal number of vehicles. (Courtesy of the author.)

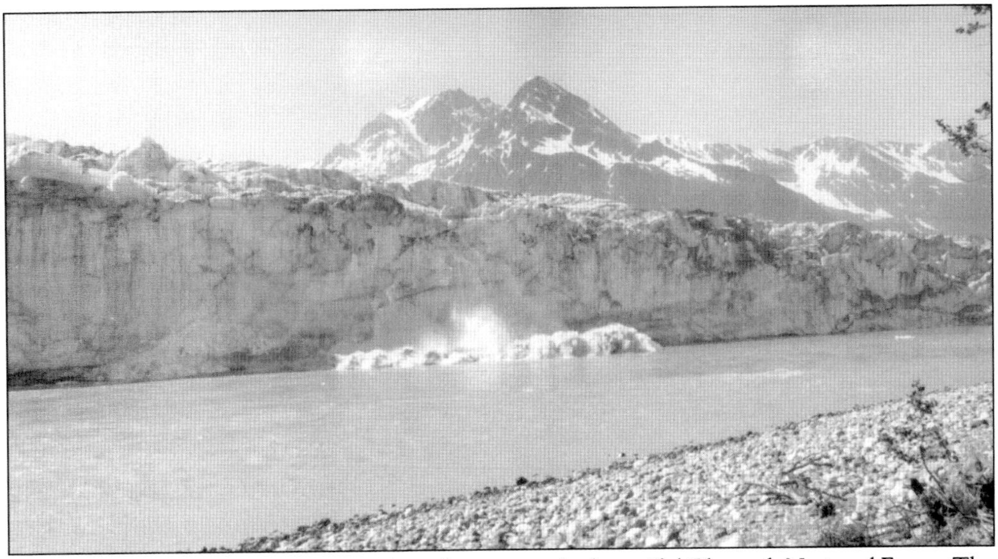

Even 49 miles of road are important when they access the beautiful Chugach National Forest. The Chugach is one of the few places left in the world where glaciers tumble out of the mountains, and the very unique Childs Glacier is one of the few accessible by road where one can sit and watch the glacier calve. Going "out the road" is an important pastime for Cordovans, and while at times in jeopardy when the mighty and unpredictable Copper River overtakes even the smallest amount of road, it remains a mesmerizing experience for all who visit. Icebergs falling from the glacier can sometimes send a 10-foot wave plummeting across to the opposite shore. Even Jet Skis have attempted to ride the crest of the waves. But visitors should pay attention. Sometimes the waves can be strong enough and large enough to roll boulders onto the shore where glacier watchers stand in awe. (Both, courtesy of *Cordova Times*.)

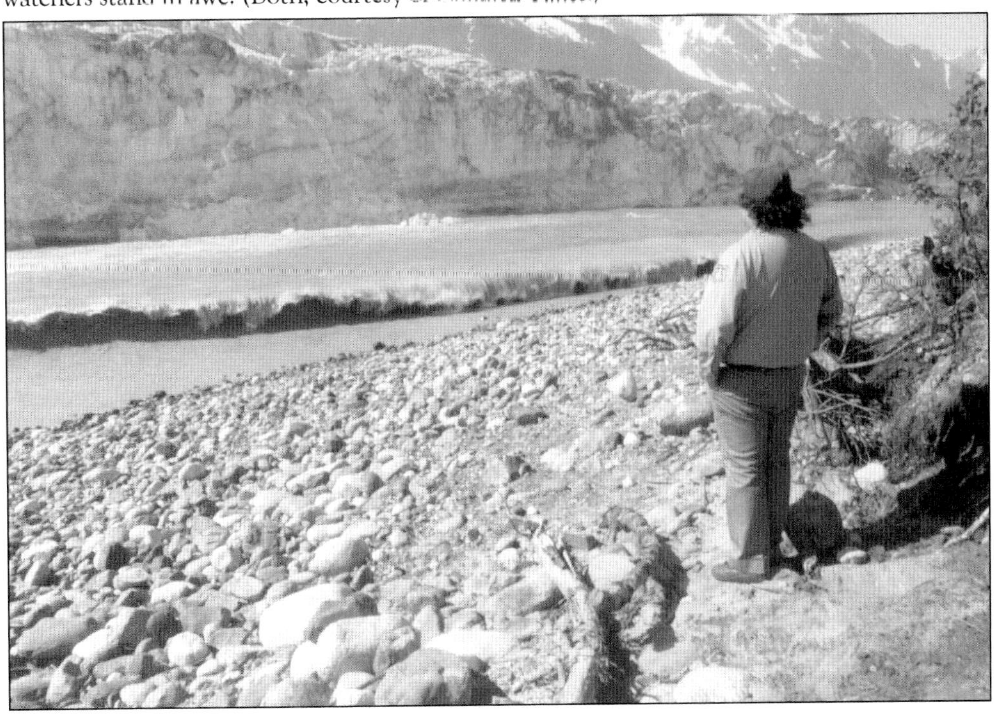

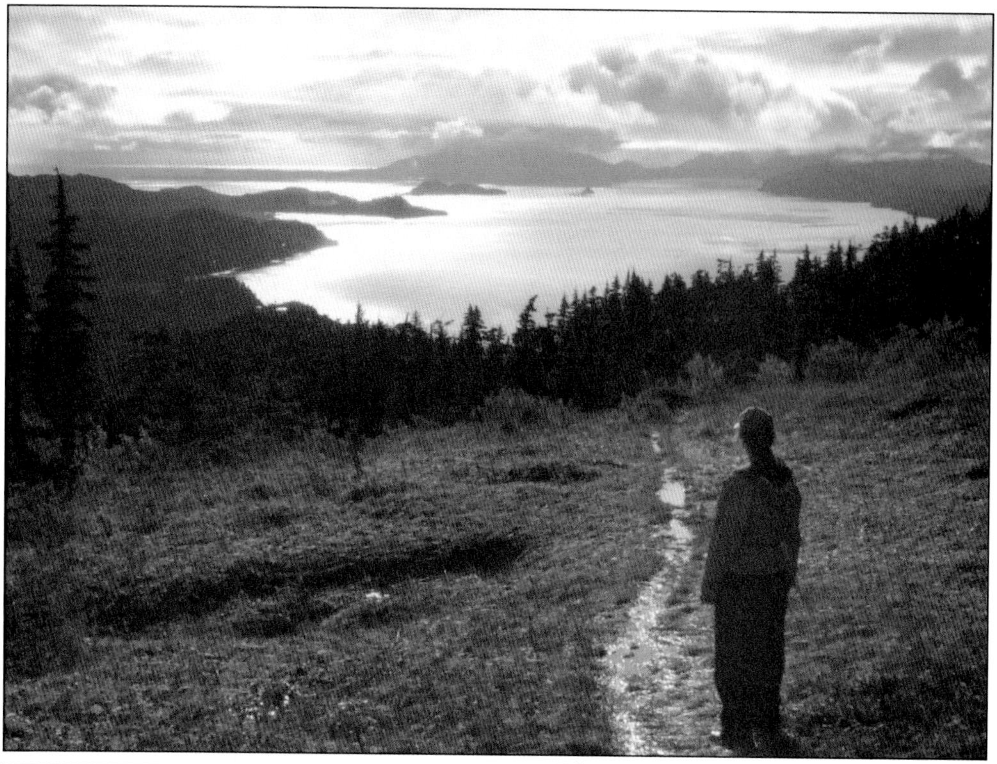

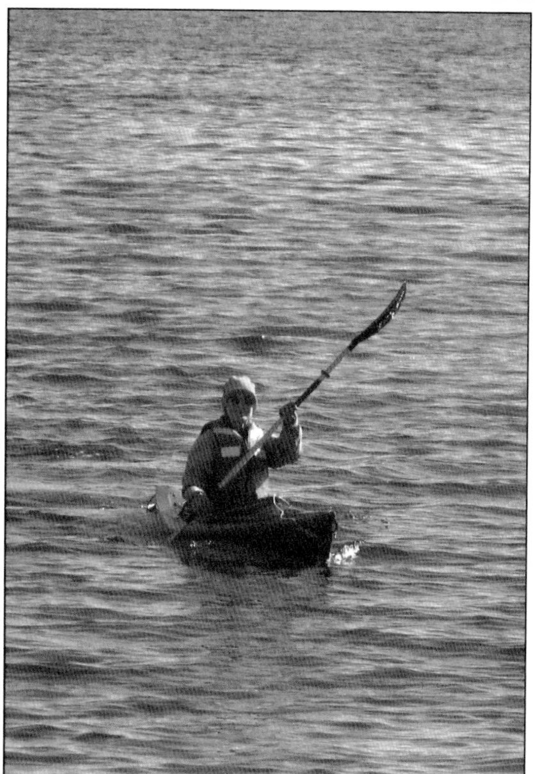

The second-largest national forest, the Chugach serves as a backyard for Cordovans and offers a topographic diversity that is unique among national forests. Wildlife is plentiful, and many Cordovans make the effort to hike away from the roads and into the tranquil rainforest. Wildlife is abundant, and bears may be seen feeding on spawned-out salmon along streams and mountain goats on precarious cliff sides. (Courtesy of Dave Janka.)

A national forest in one's backyard and a marine playground in one's front yard are everyday stuff for Cordovans. Boaters and kayakers in Prince William Sound may see porpoises, harbor seals, sea otters, sea lions, and whales of all species. While many Cordovans earn their livelihoods on the water, spending time and enjoying all that the sound has to offer is a pretty special way to spend downtime too. (Courtesy of Dave Janka.)

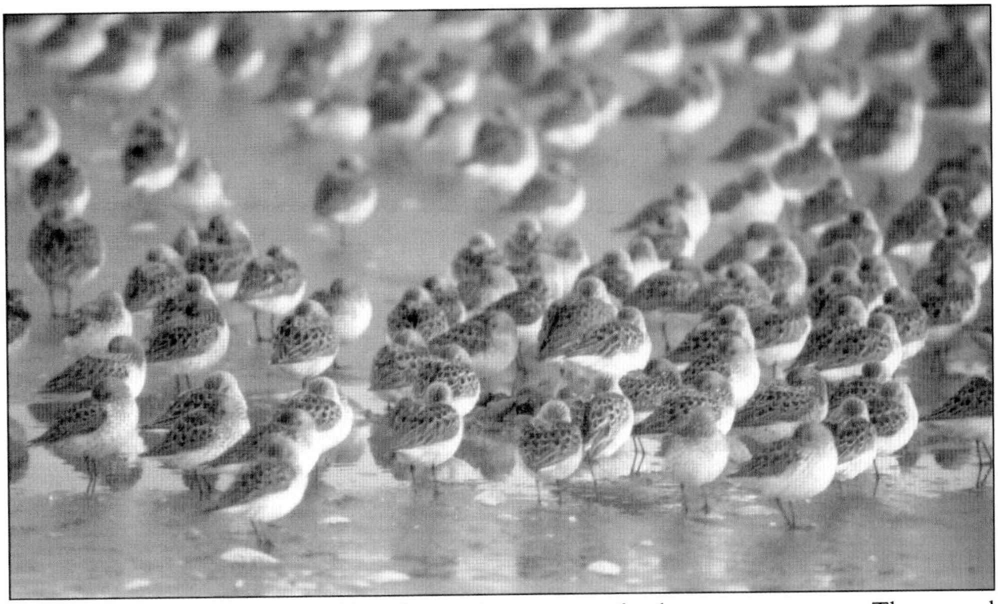

Cordovans strive to carry on old traditions but are not afraid to start new ones. The annual Shorebird Festival, begun in 1991, ushers in spring each year when the more than 214 species of resident and migratory birds return or seem to magically appear as the long-lasting winter snows begin to melt. The Copper River delta protects one of the largest known concentrations of nesting trumpeter swans in North America as well as the total population of dusky Canada geese. Nesting waterfowl are joined in spring and fall by thousands of migrating shorebirds. Recognized as an important stop, the delta is a part of the Western Shorebird Reserve Network, and as many as 1.1 million shorebirds have been observed at one time during the peak of the migration on the mudflats. (Above, courtesy of *Cordova Times*; below, courtesy of Dave Janka.)

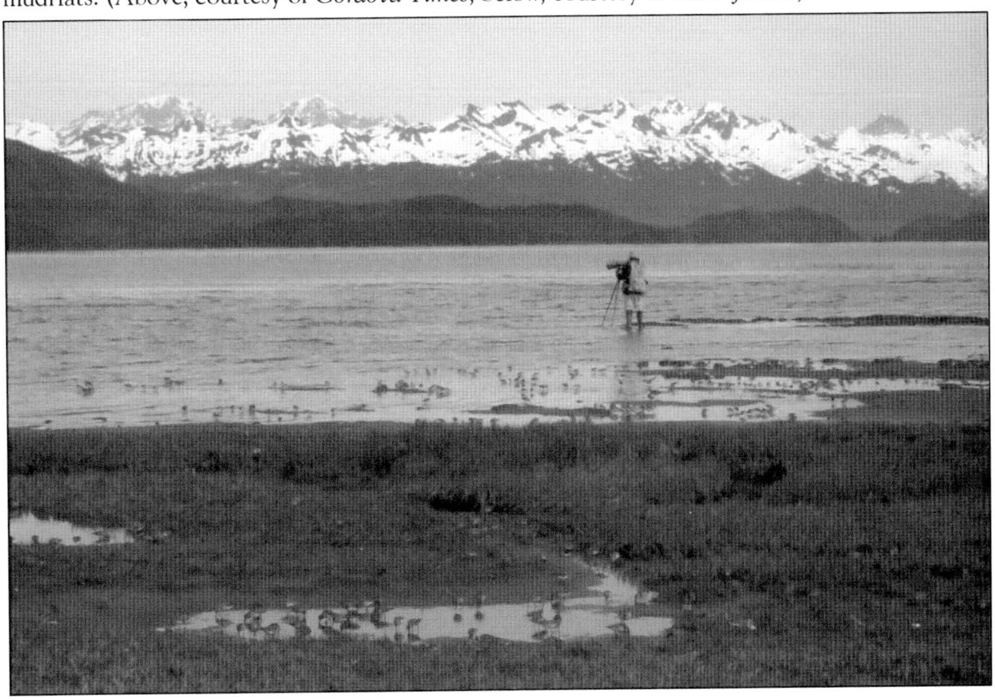

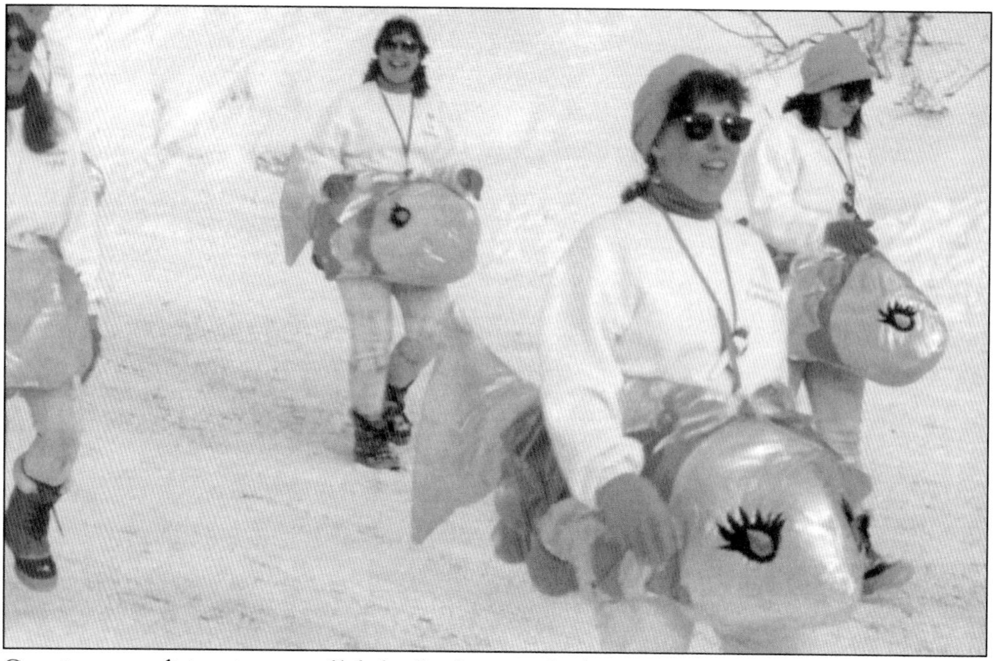

Carrying on traditions is a way of life for Cordovans, whether it is celebrating the annual Iceworm Festival drummed up many years ago over a hot toddy or the return of the fish in the summer. The Copper River Queens made an elegant debut in the Iceworm Parade shortly after the 1989 oil spill, gleefully waving their tails and depositing roe-colored ping-pong balls for the egg takers from the Prince William Sound Aquaculture Corporation. New banners mark the Iceworm Festival, but the queens and the ever-loyal iceworm help Cordovans keep mindful of the fact that while things may change around them, a lot of things stay the same. (Below, courtesy of Dave Janka.)

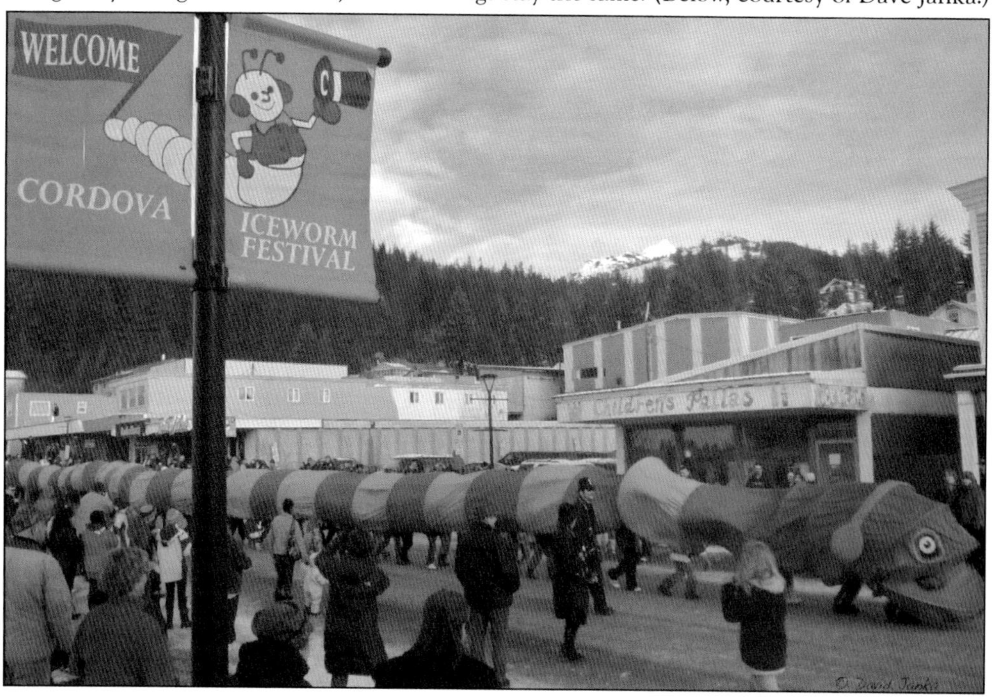

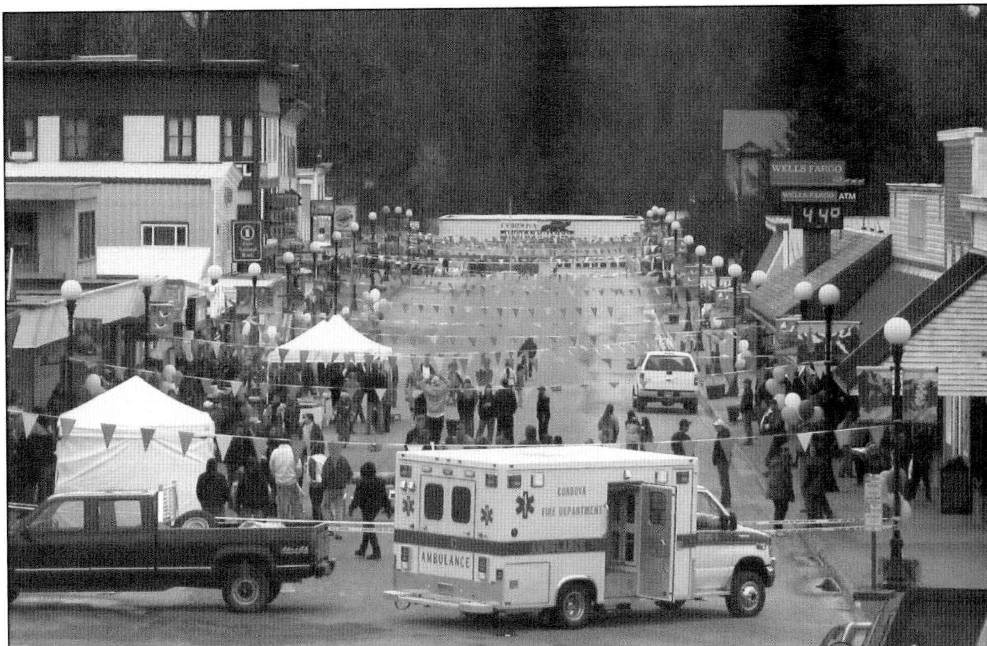

Bringing back old traditions such as the Fourth of July celebration, including the infamous kelp-box derby races, music, pie social, and of course street games, offers an opportunity for Cordovans to kick back, relax, and savor their own little bit of heaven, just as residents of the area have been doing for hundreds of years in the same little place. (Courtesy of Dave Janka.)

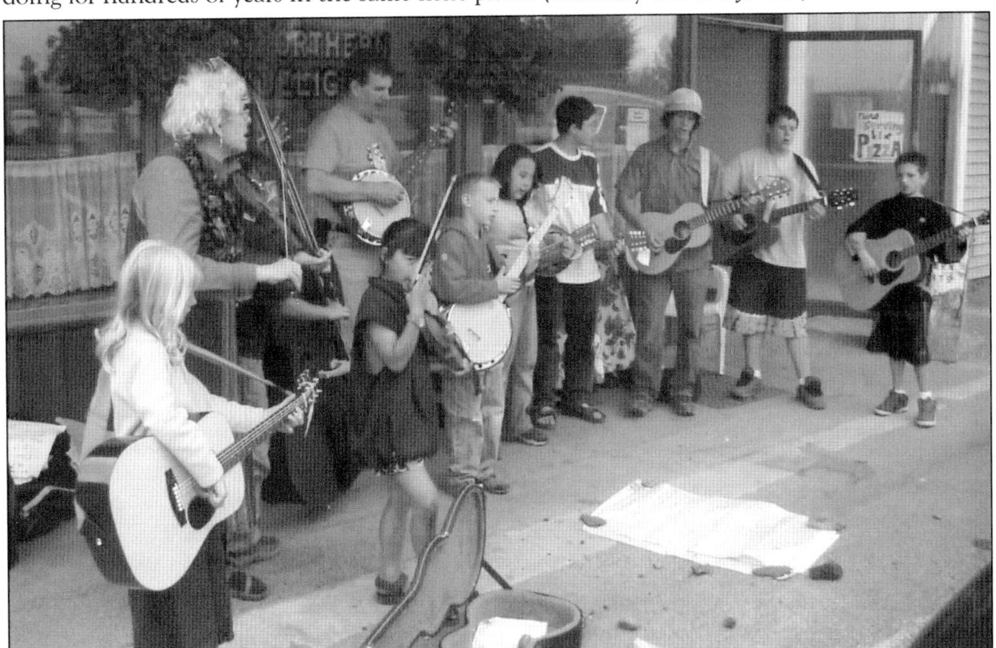

Music continues to be an important part of everyday life in Cordova. The Reverend Belle Mickelson was one of the original founders of the Cordova 4-H Bluegrass Music Camp, which has since spawned hundreds of talented young musicians who play in rain or shine all over town at the finale of the weeklong camp. (Courtesy of Dave Janka.)

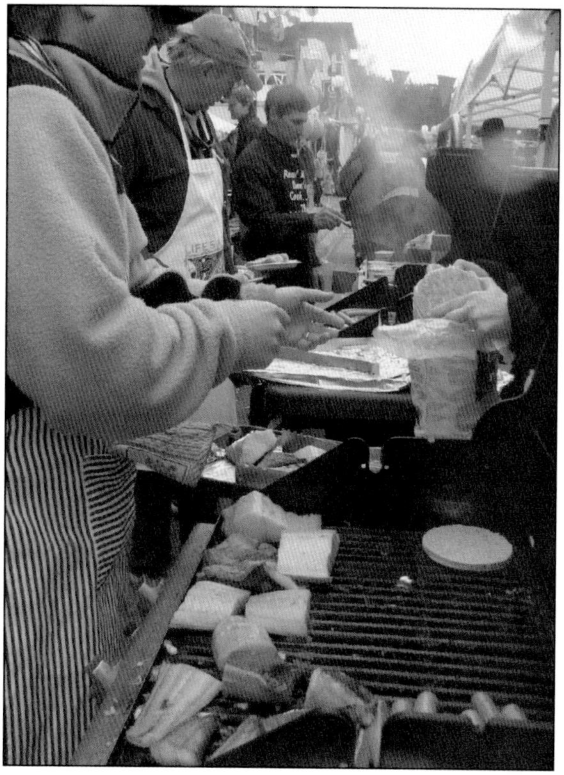

And while Cordovans know how to weather storms on the water and on the land, they also know when all else fails to have a picnic or a potluck as a backup plan. Community events feature a feast fit for kings with every salmon dish possible, berries, venison, birds, and moose from the land. The abundance to live a sustainable life in a beautiful place becomes a healthy, expected event. (Both, courtesy of Dave Janka.)

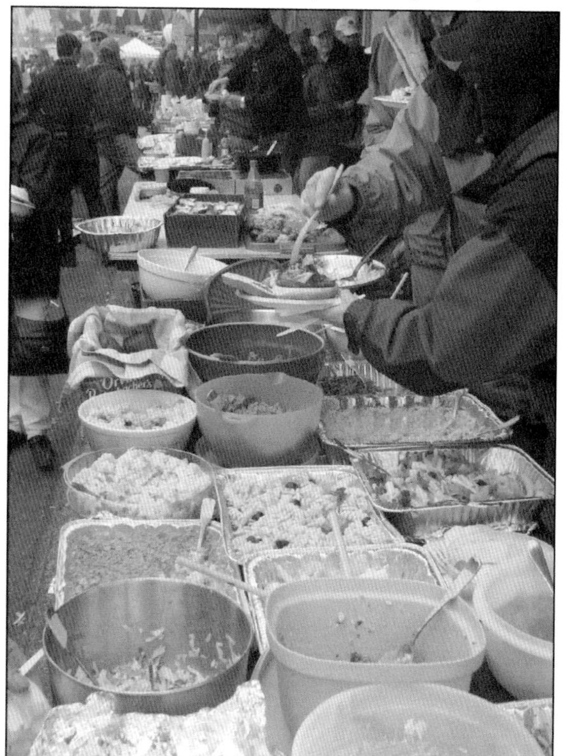

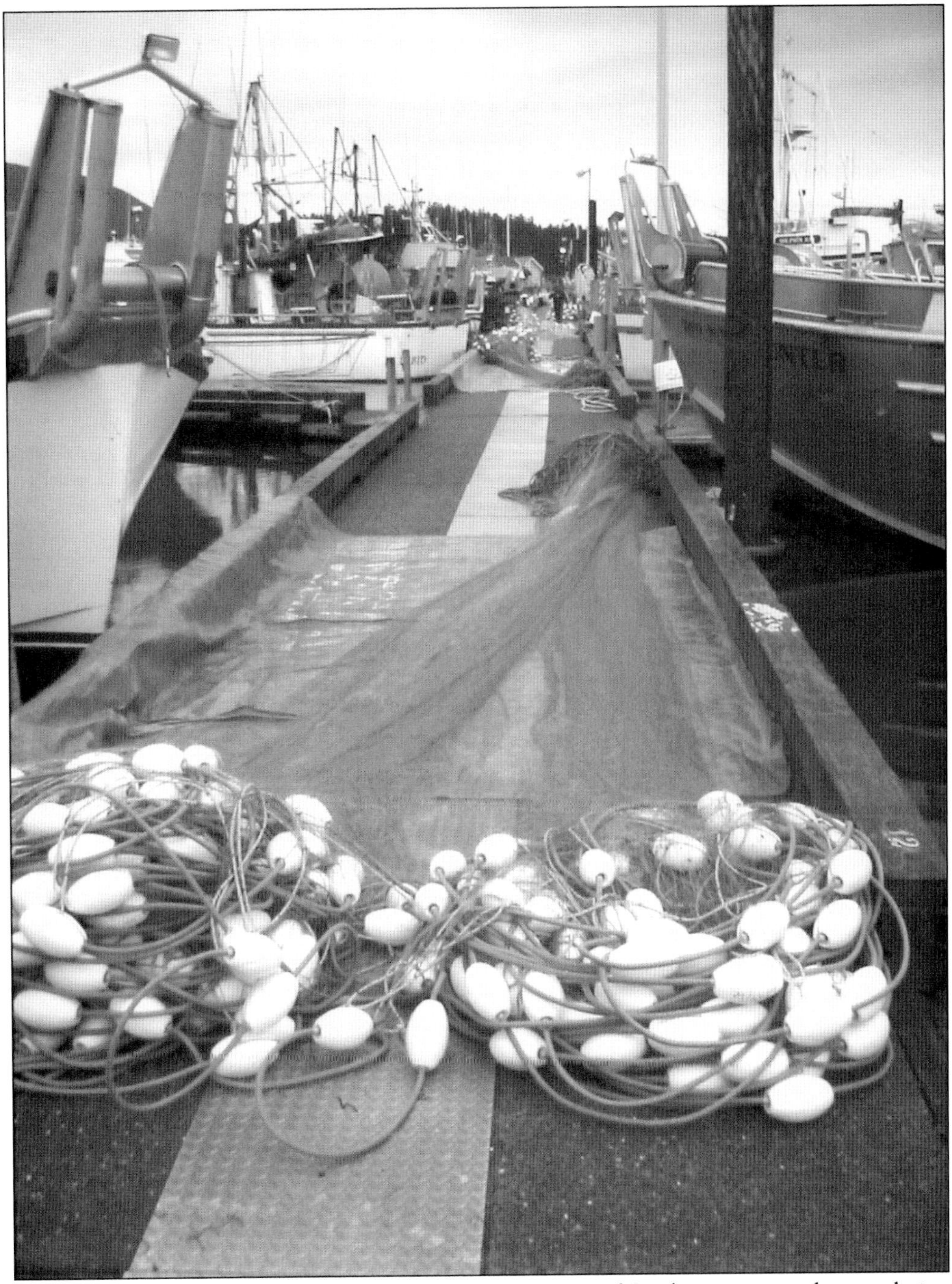

No matter what trials and tribulations face the community of Cordova, it seems the population continues to weather the storms. Cordova has been described as a place one either loves or hates, can live in or cannot stand, but it unquestionably requires a special resilience for an individual. From railroad closures to fishing failures, to fires to man-made oil spills, the cyclic nature of life continually tests the fortitude of each of the individuals who make up this unique community by the sea. And that does not even take into account the feet of rain received each year. (Courtesy of Dave Janka.)

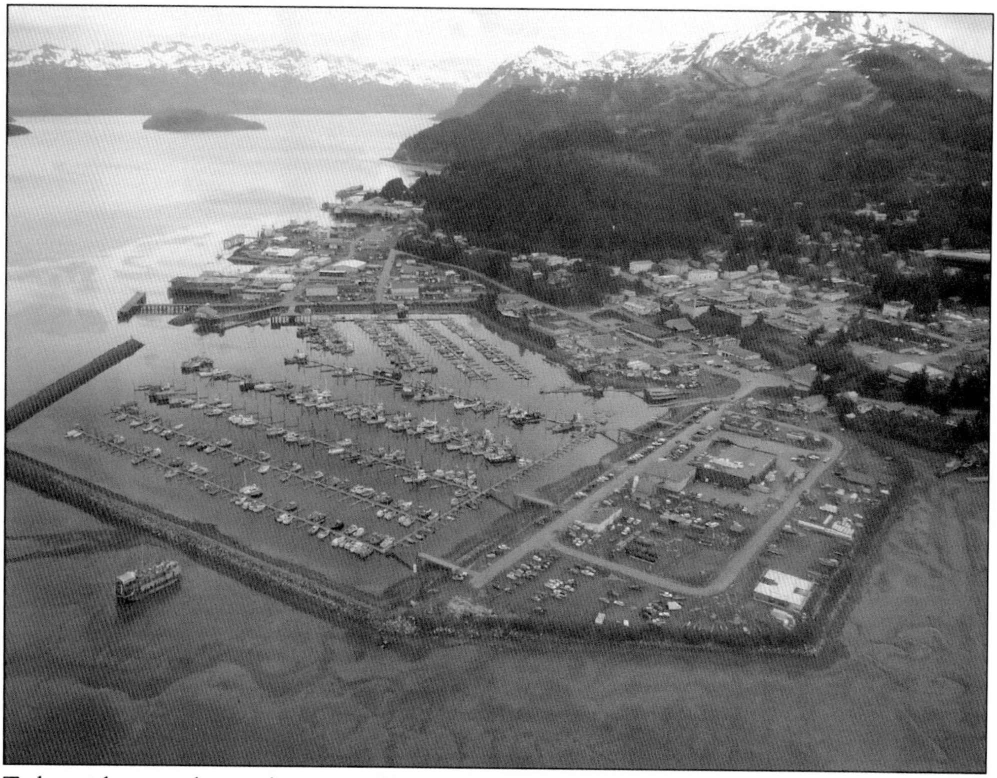

Today with a population that is steadily growing, Cordova looks to the future knowing full well that there will be more ups and more downs ahead. Expansion of the fishing industry, the growing knowledge of the science of the sound, improved avenues of transportation, and continued support of education, the arts, and the importance of quality of life issues will assure Cordova's place in the Alaska history books. (Both, courtesy of Dave Janka.)

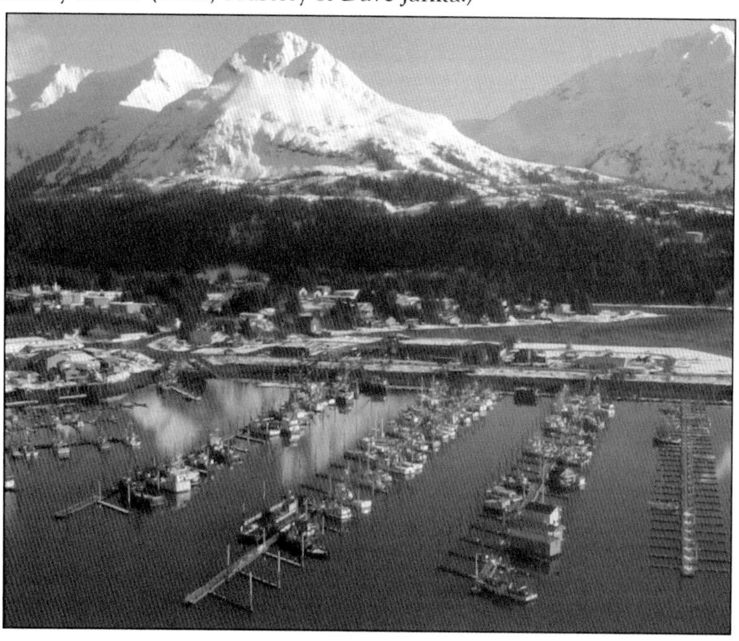

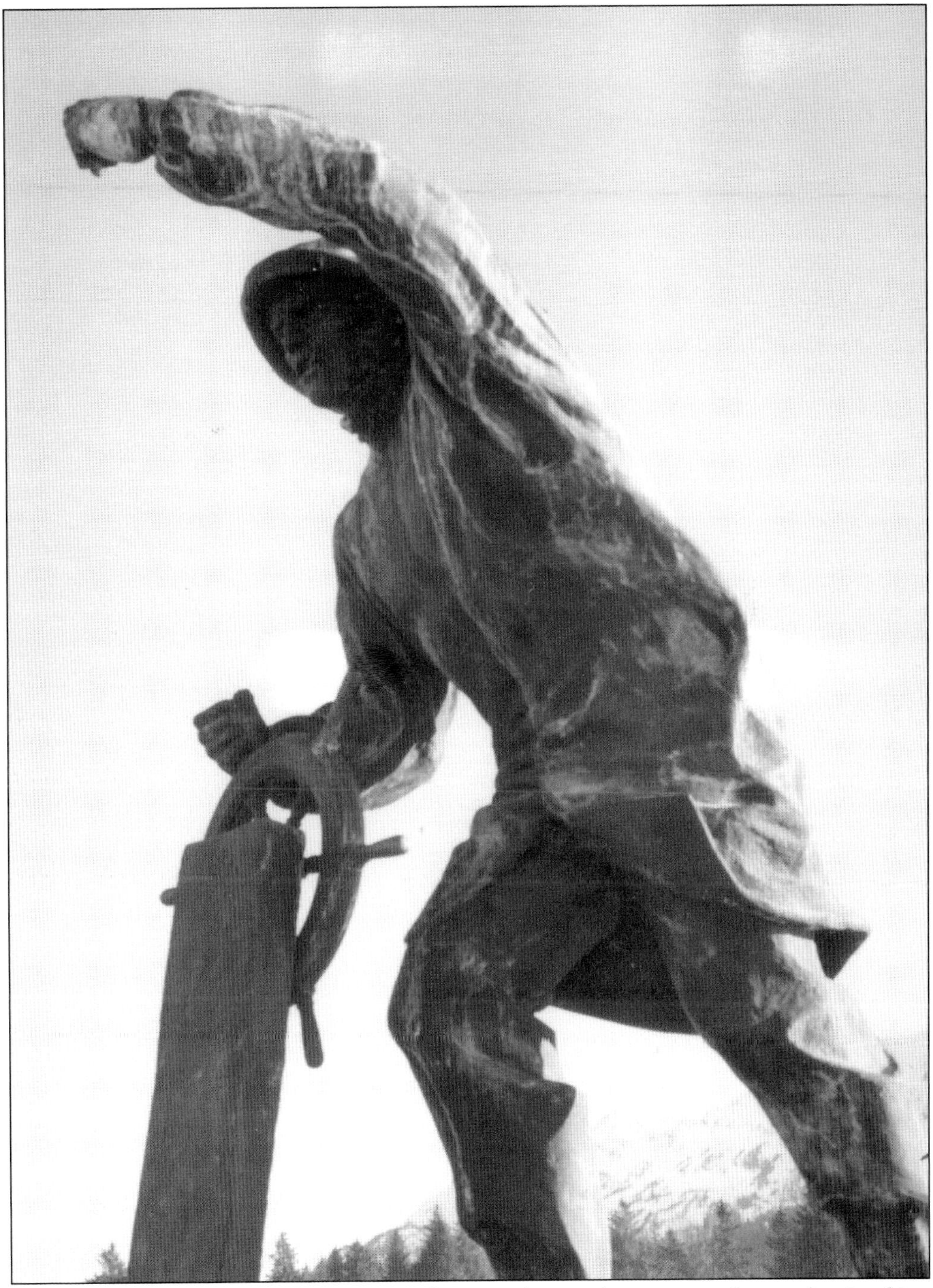

Still, the community of Cordova remains the same despite the constant change that is taking place. While the shape, makeup, and size of the community changes, the constants remain. The fish always return, every year, every spring. And all, once again, seems right with the world. The town remains a community of independent, well-educated thinkers who are as diverse and as generous as can be found anywhere. It is a multicultural community of survivors who have weathered all the storms dealt to it and, with that, continue to thrive.

Discover Thousands of Local History Books Featuring Millions of Vintage Images

Arcadia Publishing, the leading local history publisher in the United States, is committed to making history accessible and meaningful through publishing books that celebrate and preserve the heritage of America's people and places.

Find more books like this at
www.arcadiapublishing.com

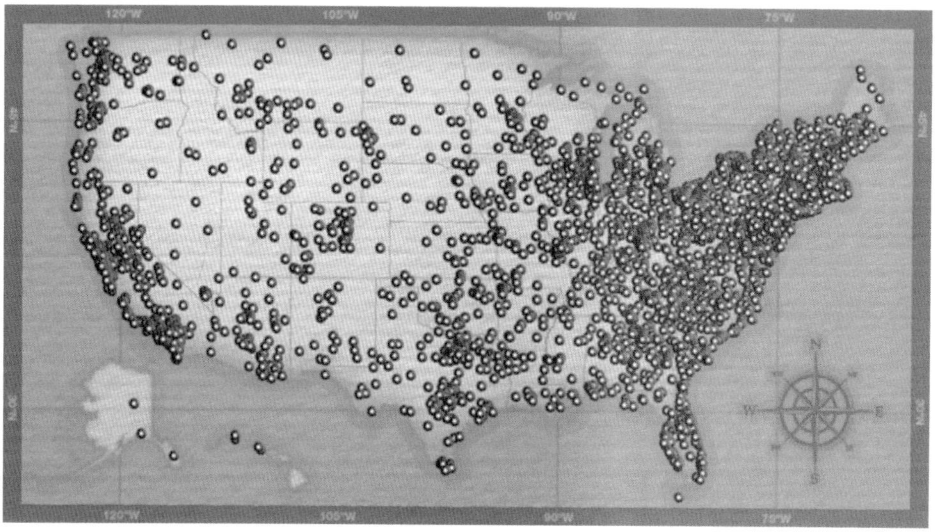

Search for your hometown history, your old stomping grounds, and even your favorite sports team.

Consistent with our mission to preserve history on a local level, this book was printed in South Carolina on American-made paper and manufactured entirely in the United States. Products carrying the accredited Forest Stewardship Council (FSC) label are printed on 100 percent FSC-certified paper.

MADE IN THE USA